UNLIT CORNERS

UNLIT CORNERS
Dirtiness, Miserliness, Shyness, Outrageousness, Shallowness, Indecisiveness, Restlessness, and Cowardliness

Edited by
Salman Akhtar

First published in 2024 by
Karnac Books Limited
62 Bucknell Road
Bicester
Oxfordshire OX26 2DS

Copyright © 2024 to Salman Akhtar for the edited collection, and to the individual authors for their contributions.

The rights of the contributors to be identified as the authors of this work have been asserted in accordance with §§ 77 and 78 of the Copyright Design and Patents Act 1988.

All rights reserved. No part of this publication may be reproduced, stored in a retrieval system, or transmitted, in any form or by any means, electronic, mechanical, photocopying, recording, or otherwise, without the prior written permission of the publisher.

British Library Cataloguing in Publication Data

A C.I.P. for this book is available from the British Library

ISBN: 978-1-80013-257-3 (paperback)
ISBN: 978-1-80013-256-6 (e-book)
ISBN: 978-1-80013-255-9 (PDF)

Typeset by Medlar Publishing Solutions Pvt Ltd, India

www.firingthemind.com

To

JAN WRIGHT

A token of my gratitude for all her help with preparation of numerous manuscripts, maintenance of extensive national and international correspondence, and management of sundry non-clinical aspects of my busy academic life over the last twenty years.

Contents

Acknowledgments ix

About the editor and contributors xi

Introduction xix

**Part I
Mostly public**

CHAPTER ONE
Dirtiness 3
Nina Savelle-Rocklin

CHAPTER TWO
Miserliness 25
Ann Smolen

CHAPTER THREE
Shyness 47
Jerome Blackman

CHAPTER FOUR
Outrageousness 65
Lois W. Choi-Kain

Part II
Mostly private

CHAPTER FIVE
Shallowness 85
Michael Civin

CHAPTER SIX
Indecisiveness 105
M. Sagman Kayatekin and Z. Emel Kayatekin

CHAPTER SEVEN
Restlessness 127
Nilofer Kaul

CHAPTER EIGHT
Cowardliness 151
Salman Akhtar

References 169

Index 189

Acknowledgments

Eight distinguished colleagues devoted much time and effort to writing original works for inclusion in this book. They responded to my editorial suggestions with the utmost grace. My assistant, Jan Wright, to whom this book is dedicated, prepared the manuscript of this book with her characteristic diligence and good humor. Dr. Muge Alkan provided much needed assistance with the task of copy-editing. Kate Pearce, at Karnac Books, provided excellent and patient editorial guidance. To her, and to all the individuals mentioned here, my sincere thanks indeed.

About the editor and contributors

Salman Akhtar, MD, is professor of psychiatry at Jefferson Medical College and a training and supervising analyst at the Psychoanalytic Center of Philadelphia. He has served on the editorial boards of the *International Journal of Psychoanalysis* and the *Journal of the American Psychoanalytic Association*. His more than 450 publications include 110 books, twenty-two of which are solo-authored—*Broken Structures* (1992), *Quest for Answers* (1995), *Inner Torment* (1999), *Immigration and Identity* (1999), *New Clinical Realms* (2003), *Objects of Our Desire* (2005), *Regarding Others* (2007), *Turning Points in Dynamic Psychotherapy* (2009), *The Damaged Core* (2009), *Comprehensive Dictionary of Psychoanalysis* (2009), *Immigration and Acculturation* (2011), *Matters of Life and Death* (2011), *Psychoanalytic Listening* (2013), *Good Stuff* (2013), *Sources of Suffering* (2014), *A Web of Sorrow* (2017), *Mind, Culture and Global Unrest* (2018), *Silent Virtues* (2019), *Tales of Transformation* (2022), *In Leaps and Bounds* (2022), and *In Short* (2024)—edited or coedited volumes in psychiatry and psychoanalysis. Dr. Akhtar has delivered many prestigious addresses and lectures including, most recently, the inaugural address at the first IPA-Asia Congress in Beijing, China (2010). Dr. Akhtar is the recipient of the *Journal of the American*

Psychoanalytic Association's Best Paper of the Year Award (1995), the Margaret Mahler Literature Prize (1996), the American Society of Psychoanalytic Physicians' Sigmund Freud Award (2000), the American College of Psychoanalysts' Laughlin Award (2003), the American Psychoanalytic Association's Edith Sabshin Award (2000), Columbia University's Robert Liebert Award for Distinguished Contributions to Applied Psychoanalysis (2004), the American Psychiatric Association's Kun Po Soo Award (2004), the Irma Bland Award for being the Outstanding Teacher of Psychiatric Residents in the country (2005), and the Nancy Roeske Award (2012). Most recently, he received the Sigourney Award (2013), which is the most prestigious honor in the field of psychoanalysis. Dr. Akhtar is an internationally sought speaker and teacher, and his books have been translated in many languages, including German, Turkish, and Romanian. His interests are wide and he has served as the film review editor for the *International Journal of Psychoanalysis*, and is currently serving as the book review editor for the *International Journal of Applied Psychoanalytic Studies*. He has published eighteen collections of poetry and serves as a scholar-in-residence at the Inter-Act Theatre Company in Philadelphia. His *Selected Papers (Vols I–X)* were recently published and released at a festive event held at the Freud House & Museum in London.

Jerome S. Blackman, MD, DFAPA, FIPA, FACPsa, is a professor of clinical psychiatry at Eastern Virginia Medical School (EVMS) in Norfolk, and a training and supervising analyst with the Contemporary Freudian Society in Washington, DC. From 2018–2021, he was distinguished visiting professor of mental health at Shanxi Medical University in Taiyuan, China, through the collaboration of Harvard Medical School and Shanxi Medical University, and was honored in a special ceremony, in China, as a "High-end Foreign Talent" by Shanxi Province. He is on the board of directors of IRED, the International Psychoanalytical Association's *Inter-Regional Encyclopedic Dictionary of Psychoanalysis* (2023), where he has been a contributing author to several sections. He also sits on the International Scientific Committee of the Association Internationale Interactions de la Psychanalyse, Paris, France, where he has lectured and published articles in its journal, *Topique*. For the past four years, EVMS and the Virginia Psychoanalytic

Society have honored him by naming a conjoint yearly lecture after him, the Jerome S. Blackman MD Lectureship in Psychoanalysis. At the Navy Medical Center—Portsmouth, VA, the yearly teaching award was named after him from 1992–2017. He is the recipient of the American Psychoanalytic Association's Edith Sabshin Award for Teaching (2000) and the Akhtar-Brenner Lectureship in Psychoanalysis at Jefferson Medical College (2017). He is past president of the American College of Psychoanalysts and of the Virginia Psychoanalytic Society. His first book, *101 Defenses: How the Mind Shields Itself* (Routledge, 2004) has been translated into several languages, and is in its second edition in Mandarin (Shanghai: East China Normal University Press, 2021). *Get the Diagnosis Right: Assessment and Treatment Selection for Mental Disorders* (Routledge, 2010; Beijing: Capital Normal University Press, 2018) and *The Therapist's Answer Book: Solutions to 101 Tricky Problems in Psychotherapy* (Routledge, 2013; Beijing: Capital Normal University Press, 2016) have both sold out in China. With Kathleen Dring, JD, PsyD, he has coauthored two books, *Sexual Aggression against Children: Pedophiles' and Abusers' Dynamics, Development, Treatability and the Law* (Routledge, 2016) and *Developmental Evaluation of Children and Adolescents: A Psychodynamic Guide* (Routledge, 2023). He is the author of more than two dozen papers and book chapters in English, French, and Chinese, the most recent being the lead article in the 2020 issue of *American Journal of Psychoanalysis* (80: 119–132), entitled "A psychoanalytic view of reactions to the coronavirus pandemic in China" and in 2023, "Some arguments about free association as a technique" in *American Journal of Psychoanalysis.*

Lois W. Choi-Kain, MD, is currently the director of the Gunderson Personality Disorders Institute (GPDI) at McLean Hospital, an internationally recognized center of training for empirically supported treatments for borderline personality disorder (BPD) and research on outcomes as well as the social cognitive mechanisms targeted in these interventions. Her research training began as a postdoctoral fellow under the supervision of John Gunderson, MD, as PI, coinvestigator, and collaborator on several NIMH and donor-funded grants. In addition, Dr. Choi-Kain developed an intensive residential treatment program, the Gunderson Residence, combining various empirically supported therapies with a milieu setting emphasizing rehabilitation of social and occupational functioning. In her decade-long tenure as founding program and medical director, she implemented or supervised the treatment of approximately 300 suicidal, treatment-resistant individuals with severe personality disorders as well as complex comorbidity as an individual, group, and family therapist, or as a pharmacologist. At the same time, she expanded and diversified McLean Hospital's adult BPD treatment program to include mentalization-based treatment (MBT) and dialectical behavior therapy (DBT) and DBT for PTSD training clinics. She has written books on various applications of Gunderson's good psychiatric management (GPM) adapted to different levels of care, clinical professionals, age groups, and stepped care, and leads the GPM international organization of trainers. Prominent among her publications are the books, *Borderline Personality and Mood Disorders* (2015) and *Good Psychiatric Management for Borderline Personality Disorder* (2019), both coedited with John Gunderson. Dr. Choi-Kain has served on a number of editorial boards for journals publishing research on personality disorders and psychotherapy research, and has been the recipient of the Penn Psychotherapy Professorship, Partners in Excellence Award, NARSAD Young Investigator Award, and the Kenneth Silk M.D. Lectureship for excellence and leadership in personality disorders.

Michael Civin, PhD, is a psychologist/psychoanalyst in New York City. He received his certificate in psychoanalysis and doctoral degree from the Derner Institute of Advanced Psychological Studies at Adelphi University, an MA in English literature from the University of Oregon and an AB from Harvard College. In 2007, Dr. Civin cofounded Rose Hill Psychological Services, a groundbreaking mental health center in the Bronx devoted to providing psychoanalytically informed treatment across the widest possible range of people. Having expanded now to three locations in Manhattan and the Bronx and almost forty therapists, Dr. Civin guides Rose Hill in training and learning from young people who are bucking the anti-Freudian tide to become our psychoanalysts of the future. Currently, he is a cofounder of Pulsion, a revolutionary new psychoanalytic institute, now in the process of seeking approval from the New York State Board of Regents, dedicated to returning to center stage Freud's almost forgotten theories of the drives and their elaboration through Klein, Lacan, and others. Dr. Civin is the author of one of the first psychoanalytic studies of the internet in the form of the book titled *Male, Female, Email* (2000). Translated into numerous languages, this book predicts the enormous impact on and problematics of the development of the digital world. Among his other publications is the award-winning paper, "The sculpture and the dust."

Nilofer Kaul, PhD, is a training and supervising analyst based in New Delhi, India. She taught English literature at Delhi University. Her doctorate work was on "Masks and Mirrors: Configurations of Narcissism in Women's Short Stories" (2012), for which she received the Charles Wallace Grant. She has published many chapters and papers and delivered many papers, including "Parasitism: An autistic island," which received the 2018 Tustin award for best paper. She is a part of a supervision and training group of the Delhi Chapter of the Indian Psychoanalytic Society. Her book, *Plato's Ghost: Minus Links and Liminality in Psychoanalytic Practice* (2021), is highly acclaimed and has received glowing reviews in psychoanalytic journals. Her talk (2023) titled "Mis-understanding, misogyny, and adolescence" at the Freud House & Museum in London was similarly very well received.

M. Sagman Kayatekin, MD, is an adult psychoanalyst and psychiatrist, who worked as a clinician and member of the teaching faculty in diverse cultures—USA, Turkey, and China. He is currently living in Houston, Texas. Throughout his long professional career, Dr. Kayatekin worked in prominent psychotherapeutic hospitals such as The Austen Riggs Center and the Menninger Clinic, in addition to working as a psychoanalyst and family therapist. He is also interested in the liaison of psychoanalysis and social sciences/humanities. He has taught, written papers and chapters to books, presented, and lectured extensively on his areas of interest in English and Turkish. His book about his individual, family, and hospital work was translated to Chinese. He has won numerous teaching awards in several institutions where he worked. At this phase of his professional life Dr. M. S. Kayatekin continues to work as a faculty member at the Menninger Department of Psychiatry, Baylor College of Medicine, undertakes a small private practice, and provides consultations to individuals and families and in psychotherapeutic hospital systems. He continues with individual and group supervisions and teaches nationally and internationally. He has been lecturing on organizational dynamics at the international Business Administration department of Koc University, the most prominent private university in Turkey, located in Istanbul. He is actively writing papers, chapters, and working on a few book projects in psychoanalysis, humanities, and social sciences. Dr. Kayatekin is also in the process of developing psychoanalytic affiliations with Central Asian countries and Vietnam.

Z. Emel Kayatekin, MD, is a psychiatrist, a family therapist, and a psychotherapist, currently living in Houston, Texas. She has worked as a faculty member in USA, Turkey, and China. She has taught, presented, and written extensively in Turkey, China, and USA in addition to treating patients and doing research. She was instrumental in bringing formal family therapy to the Department of Child Psychiatry, Ankara University Medical School in the 1990s and establishing a research department at the Department of Psychiatry, Berkshire Medical Center (affiliate of University of Massachusetts Medical School). Her interest gradually shifted into psychotherapeutic hospital treatment, and she worked at Menninger Clinic leading the team at its Young Adults Program for over a decade. She continues to be a faculty member at the Menninger Department of Psychiatry, Baylor College of Medicine, in addition to working at intense outpatient and psychotherapeutic hospital programs.

Nina Savelle-Rocklin, PsyD, is a Los Angeles-based psychoanalyst specializing in eating disorders. She is the author of *Food for Thought: Perspectives on Eating Disorders* (2016) and *The Binge Cure: Seven Steps to Outsmart Emotional Eating* (2019). She also coedited (with Salman Akhtar) the books titled *Beyond the Primal Addiction* (2019) and *Food Matters* (2023). She has written articles and book chapters on binge eating, bulimia, and mistrust as it pertains to eating disorders, as well as on the origins and fundamentals of psychoanalysis. She is regularly featured in podcasts, radio shows, print media, and online summits throughout the globe. She hosts The Dr. Nina Show radio program on LA Talk Radio. Her TEDx talk is "Why Binge Eating is NOT about Food."

Ann Smolen, PhD, is a supervising and training analyst in child, adolescent, and adult psychoanalysis at the Psychoanalytic Center of Philadelphia. Dr. Smolen graduated summa cum laude from Bryn Mawr College and received her master's degree in social work from Bryn Mawr College School of Social Work and Social Research. She received her doctorate in philosophy from the Clinical Social Work Institute in Washington, DC. Her first profession was as a member of the New York City Ballet. Dr. Smolen has won several national awards for her clinical work, and has presented her clinical work both nationally and internationally. Dr. Smolen has published several articles including "Boys only! No mothers allowed", published in *The International Journal of Psychoanalysis* and translated into three languages. Dr. Smolen is the author of *Mothering Without a Home: Representations of Attachment Behaviors in Homeless Mothers and Children* (Aronson, 2013). She maintains a private practice in child, adolescent, and adult psychotherapy and psychoanalysis in Ardmore, PA.

Introduction

Psychoanalytic investigation of character traits began with "hysterical" charm and seductiveness (Freud, 1905e; Reich, 1933), the triad of orderliness, parsimony, and obstinacy (Abraham, 1923; Freud, 1908b), "oral" dependence (Abraham, 1924), narcissism and grandiosity (Freud, 1914c; Jones, 1913), and self-loathing leading to suicide (Menninger, 1938). A second wave of studies began to address syndromes emanating from schizoid (Fairbairn, 1952; Guntrip, 1969; Khan, 1974), "antisocial" (Winnicott, 1956), and "borderline" (Kernberg, 1967, 1975) tendencies. More recently, psychoanalysis has turned its gaze towards positive character traits such as friendship (Rangell, 1963), dignity (Marcovitz, 1970), tact (Poland, 1975), and forgiveness, generosity, gratitude, and humility (Akhtar, 2002, 2013, 2019). Even though these contributions have greatly enriched our field, the work is far from over.

Many character traits have escaped attention, even though they frequently prove to be a challenge for the clinician. Eight such traits form the focus of this book. Its contents are divided, in accordance with the expressive direction of the subsumed character traits, into two sections. The first part is titled "Mostly public" and contains chapters on dirtiness, miserliness, shyness, and outrageousness. The second part is titled

"Mostly private" and contains chapters on shallowness, indecisiveness, restlessness, and cowardliness. Brief sketches of the first four chapters follows.

- The first chapter of the book is on dirtiness. In it, Nina Savelle-Rocklin explores the complex meaning of dirtiness in the culture and the consulting room, examining the theme of dirtiness both literally and figuratively, from its origins in anality to its intrapsychic, relational, and social implications. The chapter explicates "dirtiness" of the body, mind, and language. A myriad of ways in which conflicts about being dirty or feeling dirty may be expressed and repressed are presented. This discussion includes the disparate but related areas of fantasy, smell, jokes, and money.
- The next chapter deals with miserliness. Written by Ann Smolen, this chapter emphasizes that the trait has little to do with actual monetary status of the subject. It reflects the poverty of internal good objects which are the basic source of generosity. Smolen offers detailed analytic material on a miserly child she treated and also a brief vignette of an adult case. With the help of this expressive clinical material, she elucidates the multilayered nature not only of such psychopathology but of its treatment as well.
- In the next chapter, Jerome Blackman applies his outstanding descriptive skill to the painful experience of shyness. According to him, shyness is a phenomenological result of a variety of underlying pathological constellations. These nuanced potential meanings of shyness are listed and then considered from the standpoint of psychopathology and, when possible, underlying etiology. Blackman highlights his proposals by including many patient and personal vignettes.
- The fourth chapter of this part is about outrageousness. In it, Lois Choi-Kain deftly categorizes outrageousness into a guilt-driven masochistic type, a hope-driven optimistic type, and a hate-driven sadistic type. Taking her cue from Winnicott's (1956) seminal paper on "antisocial tendency," she focuses upon the second type and elucidates its descriptive and dynamic subtleties by presenting a detailed clinical illustration. Fascinatingly, she also includes a subcategory of outrageousness possessed by creative writers and artists who,

almost invariably, resort to the "audacity" (in Auden's phraseology) of imagination in order to arrive at the aesthetic solution to their psychic conundrum and inner pain.

The second part of the book is followed by the grouping of chapters on shallowness, indecisiveness, restlessness, and cowardliness. Here are thumbnail sketches of these chapters.

- The first chapter of this part addresses the trait of shallowness. Written by Michael Civin, it proposes that applied to a human subject, the adjective "shallow" portrays someone with little depth. This chapter rigorously develops "shallow" as a general construct and, from this, studies "shallow" from a psychoanalytic perspective. Through the lens of Freud's tripartite topographical model of conscious, preconscious, and unconscious systems (e.g., Freud, 1915e), the author argues that no human can be described accurately as shallow. Although a person might behave in a superficial manner, all human subjects are endowed with the unfathomable depths of an unconscious, even if representations of those depths may be hindered by impaired preconscious functioning.
- The next chapter is on indecisiveness. In this chapter the Kayatekins note that ego has the capability to mediate between different aspects of the structures and functions of mind and the interpersonal world. It controls, mediates, monitors the infinitely complicated world of human motives both in the ways in which they are represented internally and played out in the real human niche that surrounds us. If we strive towards developing a formulation of the individual ego not mainly as an internal regulator, but equally importantly as the regulator of the relation of the internal with the external, with a capacity to shape and be shaped by internal and external; and with a potential to, consciously or unconsciously, but willfully, choose these "shaping actions," then we will have a more nuanced and realistic understanding of the human mind as the defining aspect of our species as social individuals. The chapter is written with these conjectures in mind.
- Subsequent to this discourse on indecisiveness is the one on restlessness. This chapter, by the New Delhi-based psychoanalyst Nilofer Kaul, looks at "restlessness" and its associations—in psychoanalysis,

but also in literature and culture. What does restlessness look like? Who is restless—the "lover, the lunatic, the poet"? Who else? Is restlessness a symptom of an unresolved psychic conflict (as in *Macbeth*) or is it primary restlessness we are talking of (Bion's "nameless dread")? How do we think with the restless patient? Is restlessness a quest for truth or is it born from an evasion of truth? Is it a plea for change or an appeal against it? Literary and clinical material is provided to highlight such quandaries.
- The final chapter of this section and indeed of this book pertains to the rather distasteful human trait of cowardliness. Carefully deconstructing its phenomenology, the chapter links cowardliness to breeches in the early mother–child bond and the "thin-skinned" nature consequent upon this, as well as arising from deficient identification with the same sex parent. Technical implications of the patient's and analyst's are also addressed. The discourse concludes with the role of cowardice in the professional lives of analysts as well as in the society at large.

This "breathless" summary of the book's contents hardly does justice to them. The fact is that the texture of the chapters contained here is quite variable and their viewpoints hardly homogenous. Some are inclined towards philosophy and literature while others rely more on descriptive psychiatry, social anthropology, and psychoanalysis. Tradition and innovation coexist in the pages of this book and so do meditative meandering and therapeutic pragmatism. The hope I have in offering all this material to you, is to deepen your understanding of the character traits discussed here, improve your capacity to empathize with those struggling with such issues, and enhance your capacity to help them overcome that very struggle.

PART I

Mostly public

CHAPTER ONE

Dirtiness

Nina Savelle-Rocklin

A dubious honor belongs to an Iranian hermit who did not shower for sixty years. Nicknamed "the world's dirtiest man," he explained such behavior on the basis of severe "emotional setbacks" in his youth. The man died at ninety-four, only a few months after bathing for the first time in six decades (Holmes, 2022). The title could have also gone, albeit metaphorically, to the comedian Gilbert Gottfried, whose version of a classic joke was so filthy, referencing incest, rape, pedophilia, animal cruelty, bestiality, and more, it inspired a documentary (*The Aristocrats*, 2005). Another contender is the writer Charles Bukowski, a self-described "dirty old man" whose poems, essays, columns, and books explored the seedy underbelly of Los Angeles, celebrating the bawdy rawness of low-life culture. He is in good company alongside writers as disparate as Chaucer, James Joyce, Nabokov, and Shakespeare, all known for their occasional lewdness.

Clint Eastwood's iconic character "Dirty Harry" in the eponymous film may be a contender. Harry got his nickname because he was handed, "every dirty job that comes along." When Harry's assignment is to deliver ransom money to a serial killer, his partner says, "No wonder they call him Dirty Harry; always gets the shit end of the stick"

(*Dirty Harry*, 1971). In the cult classic movie *Pink Flamingos*, the *raison d'être* of the main character, played by Divine, is to earn the title of the "filthiest person alive." She proves this by scooping up dog feces and putting it in her mouth, a coprophagic act that is one of the more disgusting scenes in cinematic history. Yet that pales compared to the horror of *The Human Centipede*, in which a sadistic doctor sews three people together, mouth to anus, a premise so disgusting and disturbing that the United Kingdom and Australia banned the film. In our cultural vernacular, a "dirty movie" generally refers to a pornographic film in which the only point of the film is to stimulate sexual desire. When the children's television star known as Pee-wee Herman was caught masturbating inside an adult theater in 1991, his arrest for what one journal called "a dirty deed," cost the actor his career.

The concept of "dirtiness" is thus broad, referring to both literal and conceptual. The *Merriam-Webster Dictionary* (1993) defines the word as referring to the state of being 1) unclean, soiled, not pure, 2) morally corrupt, indecent, vulgar, and dishonorable, 3) ill-gotten, abominable, 4) dullish, 5) conveying resentment. For most of us, our natural inclination is to avoid dirt and contamination, or to laugh at dirty jokes, but a broader and deeper understanding of dirtiness serves as an invaluable tool to further psychoanalytic understanding and even to facilitate psychological growth.

I will now explore the symbolism of dirtiness in our culture and in the consulting room, examining the theme of dirtiness both literally and figuratively, and explicating how dirtiness often serves as a means of unconscious intrapsychic and relational communication.

Dirtiness of the environment

Many of us live in a dirty world. Literally. For centuries, inhabitants of towns and cities devised ways to get rid of sewage and other human detritus. In mid-nineteenth-century London, population growth exceeded the means of disposal. As a result, the River Thames, which had long been a dumping ground for waste, emitted a stench so foul and unbearable that Parliament considered moving to a different location. The summer of 1858 was known as The Great Stink, and the excessively dirty conditions facilitated the development of a modern sewage system in the city.

Nearly two centuries later, the residents of Dhaka, Bangladesh, face a similar situation. In this densely populated capital city, all waste is emptied into the river because there are no sewage treatment plants. According to one report (White, 2022), "The garbage rotting in the water exudes a monstrous smell, and the concentration of pathogenic substances is off the scale. In addition, a suffocating smog hangs over the city ... It's hard to breathe in Dhaka, the fetid river and exhaust gases irritate not only the respiratory tract but primarily the eyes."

Although the citizens of places such as Dhaka likely have little choice about where they live and must tolerate these horrible conditions, other societies accept levels of dirtiness as cultural norms. In India, millions of people still cook with animal dung despite the availability of different kinds of cooking fuel. The World Health Organization (*Household Air Pollution*, 2022) estimates that four million people die yearly from illnesses caused by this practice.

Dirtiness of the body

Literal dirtiness is not limited to third world countries. Consider the plethora of upscale spas in the United States, Europe, and other first world countries that offer mud baths. Visitors pay to "cleanse" themselves in mud baths or partake of mud facials that purport to draw out toxins and clean pores, leading to skin renewal. At these spas, dirtiness is essentially the first step to cleanliness.

There is much psychological "dirt" to be mined by considering this practice; purposefully dirtying the body with mud and then washing it off is an act of mastery over dirtiness. First, there is the pleasurable immersion in dirty mud, either by sinking into a vat of mud or having it smeared on the face or body, followed by a literal cleansing of filth. This may represent an enactment of, and regression to, the developmental period Sigmund Freud (1908b) discusses in his explication of the anal stage. This phase occurs between the ages of eighteen and thirty-six months when a child's interest shifts from the mouth to the anus. Initially, children experience pleasure and interest in their bodily functions, becoming preoccupied with their feces. Freud observes (1930a), "The excreta arouse no disgust in children. They seem valuable for them as being a part of their own body, which have come away from it" (p. 99).

The toilet training process creates a conflict between children's pleasure and interest in their excrement and the need to please their parents by controlling bodily functions. Freud (1917c) writes, "Defecation affords the first occasion on which the child must decide between a narcissistic and object-loving attitude. He either parts obediently with his feces, 'sacrifices' them to his love, or else retains them for purposes of autoerotic satisfaction and later to assert his own will" (p. 130). Children either present their stool as a gift to their parents or withhold it in a battle for control. Children thus struggle in the anal stage to find a balance between retaining what is theirs and giving it up.

When all goes well in the anal stage, the outcome is competency, productivity, and an ability to give and receive. Problems in the anal stage can lead to anal retentiveness, referring to people who become stingy, obsessive, or overly rigid, or anal expulsiveness, referring to those who are messy, chaotic, creative, and/or disorganized. According to Freud (1930a) the positive outcome of toilet training renders "the excreta worthless, disgusting, abhorrent and abominable" (p. 99). He also contends that cleanliness is a necessary part of civilized society and that we must give up our pleasure in dirtiness in order to take part in society. Mud baths may recreate this lost pleasure in dirtiness if only for a brief period.

Some individual and societal practices represent an unconscious return to the conflicts of this stage. One rare but perverse outcome of the anal stage is coprophagia, the eating of feces. Another perversity is the smearing of feces on the skin. Akhtar (2009) notes that we may view this latter act a "cutaneous re-introjection" (p. 14). Both eating and smearing are mechanisms of taking back into the body that which was previously given up. Conversely, consider the popularity of colon cleanses, in which gallons of water are flushed through the colon via a tube placed into the anus. Ostensibly, these colonic treatments "cleanse" the body of anything considered toxic. Given that there is no scientific evidence for this and that the purpose of our excretory system is to eliminate waste, colonics function as a way of consciously ridding the body and unconsciously ridding the self of real and figurative dirtiness. By cleansing our messy, dirty insides, we hope to cleanse ourselves of mental impurities or perceived dirty qualities.

The way to get rid of literal dirt is to wash it off. Symbolic dirt is a more complicated matter. Recently, there's been a movement toward "clean eating" which refers to eating only fresh, healthy food. Consuming "clean" and pure food can become an unhealthy preoccupation, resulting in what Steven Bratman (1997) calls "orthorexia." The term derives from the Greek *orthos*, which means "right," or "correct." Bratman states, "While an anorexic primarily wants to lose weight, an orthorexic primarily wants to feel pure" (personal communication, July 2015). Orthorexics appear to find moral virtue in their insistence on purity and cleanliness.

The obsession with eating "clean" is a way to disavow any unwanted (or dirty) thoughts, wishes, conflicts, emotions, or impulses perceived as messy or impure, such as aggression and sexual desire. In orthorexia, clean food entering the body is a way of warding off any internal dirtiness of thought or behavior. As I have previously (Savelle-Rocklin, 2016) observed, "Orthorexics are intent on purifying their bodies. They do not hate their bodies; they fear their bodies. They wish to render their messy, bloody, intestinal tracts into clean and perfect structures, shining with metaphorical light in an attempt to attain spirituality through pure food" (p. 42).

People who struggle with obsessive compulsive disorder (OCD) often compulsively wash their hands because they feel dirty or are afraid of contamination. The psychoanalytic perspective is that sexuality is often associated with filth and impurity, so these obsessions and compulsions result from conflict about sexual and aggressive fantasies. Patients unconsciously repress these fantasies, yet these disavowed fantasies create feelings of dirtiness that cause a compulsion to wash. In researching the neurological components of OCD, Thiel et al. (2014) confirmed this perspective, finding that "it is not fear which is the trigger in OCD patients while confronted with aggressive stimuli, but probably rather self-reference and guilt, because of their (repressed) aggressive phantasies and potential. These results strongly support the psychodynamic theory of OCD patients" (p. 92). As Karpman (1948) notes, "This fear of, and feeling of being contaminated by, dirt is a symbolic expression of the consciousness of guilt which has to be washed away" (p. 268).

Thus, methods of cleansing the body and keeping the body "pure" such as colonics and orthorexia function as a way of denying any dirty thoughts, impulses, wishes, fantasies, or anything perceived as unclean.

Just as our eyes perceive dirtiness, so do our olfactory senses. Many people avoid the dirty, unwashed homeless on the streets, hurrying past and averting their gaze as they do so. The sight of such dirty, ragged, bedraggled figures facilitates a variety of reactions. We may feel pity for them or be angry that they can't get their act together and find a job, or overcome addiction, or we may feel powerless to help. Yet a whiff of their smell usually elicits only one reaction: disgust. In the analytic situation, body odors can function as a means of unconscious and meaningful communication.

Freud (1923b) states, "ego is first and foremost a bodily ego" (p. 26) meaning that bodily sensations and motor tendencies influence our earliest sense of self. The interplay between body and mind influences our perception of ourselves and the world. Winnicott also (1949) proposes that the mind and body are interrelated and influence each other. When all goes well in the mother–infant relationship, children develop a healthy sense of self and feel at ease with their body and mind. When there is erratic or unpredictable parenting, children do not develop a connection between mind and body, leading to a mind–body split. Anzieu (1987, 1995) developed a theory of what he calls a "skin-ego" in which the skin serves as the body's protective envelope. The skin-ego is like a wrapper around the body, a container that protects the psyche. When there are ruptures in development, the body communicates what cannot be mentalized or processed by the mind. As McDougall (1989) asserts, the body speaks what the mind cannot.

Brown (2015) conceives of unpleasant bodily smells as "a meaningful communication which is within the scope of psychoanalytic thought to understand" (p. 30). Other theorists (Hilty, 2020; Sidoli, 1996) propose that failures in early object relationships cause deficits in the ability to care for one's body in the most basic ways. Our first communication is somatic and preverbal. Babies "speak" through gestures, noises, and gazes. Failures in this early period, when caregivers do not respond, do not understand, or are neglectful, facilitate an inability to create self-response and self-care later in life. These circumstances may create a developmental arrest in which communication remains preverbal. Body odor can therefore be understood as a form of unconscious communication. As Hilty (2020) puts it, bodily odors may illuminate "unsymbolized experiences of early physical and emotional neglect, as well as evacuating the toxicity of those experiences" (p. 200). She reports her reaction to meeting a patient whose hair was greasy, his socks mismatched, and his clothes were obviously dirty. Yet it was his smell that impacted her with the most force. She writes, "I suddenly noticed the room was beginning to fill with a very strong smell that caused me to feel disgusted, claustrophobic and unable to think" (p. 203).

She came to understand that her patient's smell was an unconscious way of communicating early physical and emotional neglect, and also served to keep a distance between them. She recognized that her patient's body odor served both as a bridge to his unprocessed experience and also as a drawbridge, keeping her and other people at a distance. Interestingly, the more this patient expressed his anger and worked through past trauma, the less odiferous he became.

Gorender (2005) writes of treating many patients with halitosis, all referred to him by a local dentist. Many of them stopped having bad breath after they spoke about what was bothering them. "It is almost as if those people had something literally at the tip of their tongue, or ready to be vomited out. The unsaid words smelt bad, the unexpressed desires stank" (p. 204).

Early in my career as a psychotherapist, before I began analytic training, I briefly treated a confident, stylish, extremely well-dressed, and perfectly coiffed patient who smelled awful. A Black woman at the top of her profession, she exuded a rancid smell that I found almost unbearable. I always scheduled her as my last patient of the day since her smell lingered long after she left the room and nothing could alleviate the stench. I was frankly relieved when she left treatment. Now, I wonder what I overlooked. From a psychoanalytic perspective, her body odor might have communicated the aspects of herself that she could not show, perhaps an imperfect, dirty, messy internal world. Her odor may also have given expression to the aggression hidden behind the facade of perfection.

She had often spoken of the challenge of being a Black woman in a profession of primarily white men. She had to "force her way into the old boys' network." Perhaps she also had to force her way into my mind by leaving her smell behind. We can shut our eyes and our mouths, but we cannot shut our noses. By forcing me to experience her long after she had left the room, she stayed with me, taking up space in my office, my nose, and my mind.

Fear of dirtiness

While some individuals convey their conflicts and deficits in nurturing through being dirty, others fear physical dirtiness and delusionally believe they emit a foul smell when they do not. In Japan, the condition of *taijin kyofusho* refers to a syndrome in which individuals fear that their bodies or bodily functions displease, embarrass, or are offensive to others. It's estimated that 17 percent of individuals with *taijin kyofusho* experience a variant known as *jiko-shu-kyofu*, which is a specific fear that their bodies are emitting a bad odor (Matsunaga et al., 2001). This is considered a culturally bound syndrome that differs from social anxiety because individuals with *taijin kyofusho* are preoccupied with fears of embarrassing or displeasing others. In contrast, individuals with social anxiety are afraid of embarrassing themselves.

The *Diagnostic and Statistical Manual of Mental Disorders: DSM-5-TR* (2022) notes that olfactory reference syndrome is related to the *jiko-shu-kyofu* variant (p. 879) and categorizes it as a type of other specified obsessive-compulsive and related disorder in which individuals believe they give off an unpleasant odor when they do not. The fears of individuals with olfactory reference syndrome pertain solely to bodily odors, including fears of having bad breath or smelling bad. Thomas et al. (2017) note that this syndrome is "often accompanied by repetitive behaviour such as frequent showering in an attempt to camouflage the perceived odour. The body odour concerns may have a delusional quality and do not respond to simple reassurance or counterexample" (p. 1).

This is in line with what Meltzer (1964) terms a "somatic delusion … the physical and psychic expression of (*a*) a wide and deep split in the self, whereby (*b*) an expelled portion becomes represented by, and takes possession of, the function of a particular body part; (*c*) this part is then felt to take up a life completely of its own, totally ego-alien in orientation, and powerfully effective in its interference with all good internal and external relationships" (p. 246).

Fears about smelling bad can be understood in several different ways. This fear may be a reaction formation, disguising an unconscious wish to make a stink, leave an impression, or express aggression and hostility. It may also represent relational anxiety, since fears about smelling bad inherently suggest that someone is close enough to perceive the smell.

Robertiello (1974) proposes that olfactory-based anxieties are a way of managing fears about rejection. If we don't allow ourselves to get in close physical proximity to others due to a fear of offending them, we will never create emotional closeness and therefore forestall any potential rejection. Rizzuto (1991) suggests that fears about bodily odors are associated with shame and relational trauma. Olfactory fears may be thus understood as a defensive attitude that keeps people at a safe distance both physically and relationally.

The sense of smell is essential to the development of object relations. As most parents can likely attest, one of the first pleasures of parenthood is the smell of a newborn's head. Recent scientific research (Bowen, 2018) suggests that the scent of a newborn triggers a dopamine surge in mothers. Babies also respond to their mother's scent, so smell is part of the science of bonding. Interestingly, one term of endearment for a playfully mischievous child is "little stinker."

Lemma (2014) points out, "An object that cannot receive the baby's bodily smells is an object that cannot function as a receptive olfactory container" (p. 54) and therefore does not feel safe or welcoming. This may lead to splitting off of aspects of self "that are felt to be smelly or dirty in order to preserve a more idealized relationship with an object who is presented only the clean parts of the self" (p. 53). This was the case with Vivian, a woman in her fifties who entered treatment after a lifetime of struggling with bulimia. She was the oldest of three girls and vividly recalled being left in her father's care, along with her sisters, when her mother went to weekly mahjong games. She cringed as she recounted her father's revulsion on those occasions when he "babysat" the girls and had to change her youngest sister's diaper. His face would contort into a look of repugnance as he shoved the soiled diaper into a container, exclaiming loudly, "Jesus, that's disgusting. Jesus Christ!"

She imagined he had a similar reaction to changing her diapers when she was a baby. Vivian had spent most of her life pursuing perfection: the perfect body, the perfect job, the perfect family, the perfect life. Bulimia served as a way of symbolically purging any dirty, disgusting, gross parts of herself, including thoughts and emotions. She always "felt clean" after she purged, whether she used laxatives or made herself throw up.

Conflicts about dirty, unwanted, frightening aspects of the self are often consciously denied, yet unconsciously expressed. Lemma (2014) describes an experience with a compliant, clean, grateful, and reliable woman who had been a model patient for two years. This patient felt that her mother could not tolerate her smelly, less "nice" parts and related only to her when she was pleasantly accommodating. When the patient uses Dr. Lemma's toilet for the first time, she leaves the bathroom in a dirty and messy state. Dr. Lemma discovers "the toilet seat was covered in urine, the floor around the toilet was wet, and the tap in the sink had not been turned off properly" (p. 48). The patient was revealing the messy, angry, split off parts that had been hidden until then. The patient made use of the toilet as a symbolic container for the aspects of herself she felt to be unacceptable. Exploring this analytically led to integration of all parts and a more solid self.

Such use of the toilet is not confined to the analytic situation. A book about Donald Trump (Haberman, 2022) describes the scene aboard one of the former president's planes regarding an interaction between Trump and Rudy Giuliani. Trump made it a point to "loudly complain" about "the odor after Giuliani had used one of the plane's bathrooms so that other aides could hear." "Rudy! That's fucking disgusting!" Trump yelled (p. 254).

Throughout Trump's presidency, Giuliani had publicly and obsequiously supported his client. Trump responded to this fealty by publicly mocking Giuliani, saying he "sucked" and calling him "weak." It is possible that the stink Giuliani left in the toilet was an unconscious communication about his true feelings toward Trump, consciously disavowed but unconsciously expressed.

Whether bodily dirtiness is real or imagined, it is a means by which unprocessed experiences and conflicts are unconsciously communicated. By experiencing a new relational paradigm with an analyst, in which one's thoughts, needs, emotions, wishes, and most private self is cared for and understood in a new way, patients can communicate with words instead of the somatic expression or the conscious anxieties of dirtiness and smell to express their internal worlds.

Dirtiness of the mind

Dirtiness is a multidimensional concept, referring both to a sense of internal dirtiness and an actual physical dirtiness. In *Macbeth*, Lady Macbeth's guilt and remorse for her part in the murders of King

Duncan and Macduff's family cause her to hallucinate blood on her hands. Believing her hands are stained with the blood of the dead, she frantically tries to scrub them clean. Yet she will never be able to clean her hands, for it is her conscience that is dirty.

Lady Macbeth's situation is extreme, yet the experience of guilt and shame is ubiquitous, and in some individuals facilitates a sense of inner dirtiness, defectiveness, or corruption. Early analytic theorists saw shame as connected to morality, a state that arose out of conflict about forbidden impulses. Freud (1908b) notes that between the ages of five and eleven, "reaction formations, or counter-forces, such as shame, disgust, and morality, are created in the mind" (p. 171). Anna Freud (1965a) amplifies this idea when she writes, "The qualities of shame, disgust, pity, are known not to be acquired by any child except as the result of internal struggles with exhibitionism, messing, cruelty" (p. 16). Fenichel (1945) observes that disgust, shame, guilt, and anxiety are the primary motives for defense.

Others theorists view shame as an affect that is not due to conflicts about morality, but instead the result of a blow to the ego. Lewis (1971) sees shame as a feeling that arises out of failing to achieve some personal goal or as a response to a situation that is experienced as a personal failure. Miller (1985, 1986) points out that shame and disgust may be used defensively, but they function as far more than a defense mechanism. She makes the analogy that a book can be used to prop open a window, but should not be defined as a window prop, for that is just one of its possible functions (p. 11). Akhtar (2009) breaks down shame into five components: "1) collapse of self-esteem, 2) feeling of humiliation, 3) rupture of self-continuity, 4) sense of isolation and standing apart from the group, and 5) feeling of being watched by critical others" (p. 264). Benau (2017) also explicates different types of shame, including "a recurring and recursive traumatic state" (p. 5).

Those who are shame ridden often have a pervasive sense of inner dirtiness. In contrast to shame experienced as a short-term, transitory reaction to a specific situation, individuals who feel a sense of shame about themselves think that there is something inherently wrong with them. They believe themselves to be inferior, bad, disgusting, defective, and gross and often think they don't deserve to be happy. This notion that there is something very wrong and bad about the basic self is sometimes described as dirtiness. One patient who was the victim of sexual abuse from a young age told me, with characteristic understatement, that what happened to her was "a dirty shame." She described her abuser, a grandfather who lived with the family, as "a dirty old man." She felt there was also something dirty about her, as if the abuse perpetrated on her had infected her in some way, leaving her forever tainted.

The term "a dirty shame" references an unfortunate circumstance; the experience of self-shame refers to the sense that something is deeply wrong with the self. Such beliefs are related to experiences that facilitate disgust, guilt, and shame. These may be as egregious as sexual, emotional, or physical abuse, or they may be experiences of repeated misattunement. John Bowlby (1965) studied how certain kinds of family dynamics impact child development. He examined how early interactions with caregivers influence a child's sense of self, which has implications for self-esteem and also shapes expectations about relationships. Ainsworth and Bell (1970) expanded on this idea and identified specific types of attachment styles. Contemporary neuroscientific research (Schore, 2000, 2002, 2010) confirms that early experiences with caregivers affect brain development. In an exploration of the neuroscience of self-disgust, Cozolino (2014) explicates the role of the part of the brain known as the insula in the development of the self. He notes, "In the context of secure attachment, the insula may associate feelings of love with the organization of self-awareness. These early neural connections may establish a sense of self-love, well-being, and an expectation of positive outcomes" (p. 334). Conversely, if infants feel neglected, abused, or see disgust in the eyes of caregivers, they develop negative self-concepts. Specifically, in cases of abuse, neglect, or exploitation, victimized individuals often experience themselves as dirty.

Rachman (1993) terms the belief that there is something dirty and disgusting about one's inner self as "mental pollution" (p. 311). Whereas physical dirtiness is due to a lack of hygiene or contact with actual dirt, inner dirtiness is caused by painful experiences with people. Mental contamination, as defined by Ishikawa (2015) is "an internal, emotional feeling of dirtiness that may be evoked by unwanted thoughts and images, as well as by memories of negative events, such as sexual assaults" (p. 21). Those who struggle with a sense of mental contamination have a pervasive and persistent sense of inner dirtiness, often accompanied by disgust and shame. Some studies (Berman et al., 2012; Fairbrother & Rachman, 2004) indicate that childhood trauma, emotional abuse, and sexual assault contribute to the formation of mental contamination. As Miller (1993) observes, "Contact with the disgusting makes one disgusting" (p. 713). The following clinical examples highlight this latter point:

Clinical vignette: 1

Emma, a married woman in her forties and the mother of three children, had battled bulimia since she was an adolescent. She recalled visiting Harrods department store in London as a young child and waiting in a long line for the opportunity to sit on Santa's lap. While perched on his lap, she felt what she thought was "another leg" pressing into her. A vaguely bad feeling enveloped her, a sense of dread that something was amiss. She instantly felt an aversion to Santa and tried to squirm off his lap, but he held her in a tight grip, all the while smiling at the photographer.

Emma remembered seeing her mother holding up her baby brother to watch, as her father pointed toward her on Santa's lap. The family was watching but did not see what was happening. Nobody realized how trapped and frightened Emma felt at that moment. As an adult, she avoided shopping malls over the holidays, viewing each mall Santa as a potential "dirty old man." She could not bear to revive the memories of that day as she "didn't want to think about what was in Santa's mind." The idea of his "dirty thoughts" made her "want to throw up." Thus, her bulimia was an attempt to symbolically purge the thoughts that others had about her, which she felt were located inside her body.

Clinical vignette: 2

Mina, a single woman in her early thirties, reported a disturbing interaction with her father when she was in high school. She entered the kitchen wearing a new pair of black jeans that fit her well and showed off her figure. When her father asked if the pants were new, she told him that she'd recently bought them with her babysitting money, thinking he might say something complimentary about her hard work. Instead, his next words were, "You probably masturbate all the time."

She recalled her body tensing and flooding with shock, horror, and embarrassment. She could only say, "Oh my God, Dad" and flee to her room.

They never spoke of this incident, but she started gaining weight shortly afterward. She never correlated the weight gain to his comment until we explored this incident. She vividly remembered how his "dirty mind" had made her feel not only "grossed out" but "gross."

Clinical vignette: 3

Lila, a married woman in her mid-sixties, recalled how, as a young woman, her grandfather gave her books by Harold Robbins, a writer known for his salacious sex scenes. Her grandfather had leaned in and whispered that he "marked the dirty parts" for her. Decades later, the memory made her shudder. She said that just thinking about that exchange made her "feel dirty."

For all these women, the experience of being sexualized, objectified, or inappropriately touched in a "dirty" way had given them the sense that there was something inherently dirty about them or within them. Their attempts to manage this dirtiness included symbolically purging that which disgusted them, feeling themselves to be gross, or trying to hold back the inner dirtiness. These patients were dealing with the shame and disgust they felt about themselves because of other people's inappropriate actions or thoughts.

Other individuals experience themselves as containers of inner dirtiness. William, a single man in his thirties, reported being molested by his babysitter as a child, and later by a friend's older brother. He frequently had what he called "share regret" after he talked about anything that bothered him. In most sessions, he spoke very little. I sensed he parsed his words as if they were finite and he didn't want to use them all up. On the occasions when he shared his internal world, he immediately followed up with harsh self-recrimination. He thought he had "said too much" and "revealed too much." He feared that my view of him would change if he said the wrong thing, and that I'd reject him.

William labeled his spoken thoughts as "word vomit" and feared "puking" out a volume of disgusting thoughts and emotions. He didn't want to "make a stink" and feared that I would be "grossed out" by his words.

For William, the term "word vomit" had an almost literal connotation. The meaning of the vernacular expression "word vomit" is to release a torrent of thoughts, but William felt his words to be inherently disgusting, as if he were "puking up all the hate and gross stuff inside."

Many of us have "dirty thoughts" that we do not act upon and remain in the realm of fantasy. According to *Merriam-Webster* the definition of "dirty mind" is "a mind often occupied with thinking about sex in an indecent or offensive way." Those with "a dirty mind" have obscene, lewd, and vulgar thoughts about others. The definition of what is "indecent" or "offensive" may be questionable, but there are certain fantasies that pertain to literal dirtiness, such as fantasies or thoughts about urinating or defecating on others. Social psychologist Justin Lehmiller (2020), a leading researcher in the field of human sexuality, found that fantasies about bodily fluids (not limited to urination) are the third most common sexual fantasy.

In an early paper on psychoanalytic technique, Jelliffe (1915) makes the point that any area of the body is capable of experiencing the gratification of erotic satisfaction, suggesting "there can be respiratory, lip, stomach, urethral, anal, skin, retinal, cochlear, vestibular, muscular, gustatory, and olfactory eroticism" (p. 198). Urinary eroticism refers to the pleasure of urinating. This solo experience of urination is later directed toward objects, and may involve fantasies about urination. Sexual interest, fantasies, and satisfaction involving urine and urination is known as urolagnia, which is a kind of paraphilia, a persistent and recurrent fantasy or behavior involving atypical activities, objects, or situations. Urolagniac fantasies and behavior includes watching others while they urinate, being urinated upon during sexual activity, or vice versa, and even consuming one's own urine. Fenichel (1945) explicates the various types of fantasies involving urination, including "urinating at objects, being urinated on by objects ..." (p. 69). McDougall (2000) suggests a connection between the primal scene and the development of paraphilias such as urolagnia. She writes, "... prior to the phallic-oedipal psychic phase this scene is imagined in every form of *pregenital* excitement: fantasies of mutual devoration or of urinary, fecal, and anal-erotic exchanges. When these fundamental elements have failed to be integrated into adult genital eroticism, they in turn will require deviant solutions in order to achieve sexual and love relations in adulthood" (p. 157).

Other sexual fantasies involving "dirtiness" are coprophilic, referring to the state of arousal from defecation and feces. Coprophilia is a type of paraphilia involving fascination with feces and uncleanliness. Coprophilic fantasies involve watching people defecate, being defecated on, smearing their feces, and eating feces. There is a dearth of psychoanalytic research or theory regarding coprophilia, beyond the early analysts who linked these fantasies to ruptures in the anal phase of development.

In treating a coprophiliac patient, Karpman (1949) asks him to read Jonathan Swift's *Gulliver's Travels*, a novel rife with symbolism about bodily functions and the state of society. In the book, Gulliver urinates to put out a fire in Lilliput, meets a scientist trying to transform feces back into food, suffers the indignity of flies defecating on his meals, and encounters the Yahoos, a group of "filthy, dirty" brutes. Interestingly, the patient repeatedly misconstrues the novel, reversing Gulliver's disgust for the Yahoos as interest, such as when he observed of Gulliver, "when he saw what kind of creatures they were, and how dirty and filthy they were, and how much they liked filth and excretions, and how bold and free they were, and how they were left completely to themselves all the time, it was very inviting" (p. 166).

This total misinterpretation of the story is an example of this patient's wish fulfillment about his own desires. The analyst's choice of using *Gulliver's Travels* as a therapeutic intervention for this individual is notable. Beyond the motif of filth and dirtiness, the book satirizes government, religion, corruption, and morality, and also makes a statement about the dirtiness of the human condition. Written during the Enlightenment movement, which optimistically viewed human beings as enlightened, noble, and intellectually transcendent, its many dirtiness motifs also communicate that we are dirtier and less evolved or enlightened than we would like to believe.

Dirtiness of language

Words are the basis of most of our communication. Words convey our thoughts, ideas, emotions, wishes, and fears. They connect us to ourselves and to each other. Freud (1905c) writes, "Words are a plastic material with which one can do all sorts of things" (p. 34). Psychoanalysis depends on language to communicate, interpret, understand, and question. Without words, there is no "talking cure."

And what of dirty words? There are a plethora of phrases utilizing the word "dirtiness" in our cultural vernacular, including but not limited to: airing dirty laundry, digging up some dirt, dirty dancing, dirty little secrets, dirty magazine, dirty money, dirt poor, getting down and dirty, giving a dirty look, playing dirty, telling dirty jokes, and talking dirty.

In the English language, "dirty" may be associated with notions of purity/impurity, as in "unclean"; it may be a spiritually and morally neutral substance, as in "earth"; it may be associated with harm to others, as in "dirty talk"; or a value, as in the notion of "worthless" (Jewkes & Wood, 1999, p. 169). Swear words are often called "dirty" words. Stapleton et al. (2022) note that swear words fall into three categories: "religion (e.g., damn, hell); sex and sexual body parts (e.g., fuck, cunt, prick); and words related to bodily excretions (e.g., piss, arse, shit)" (p. 2). All these words involve societal taboos against discussing body parts, sex, rage, death, and more. Some words (e.g., oh shit, fuck!) are used when people are confronted with a sudden, unexpected, and upsetting situation that makes them angry, frustrated, or upset. Others (e.g., asshole, motherfucker) are used to degrade another person or to convey emphasis, as in "That movie was fucking awesome." Feldman (1955) recognizes that obscene words can be experienced differently depending on the interpersonal context. For an adolescent, saying "fuck" to a teacher, parent, or authority figure carries a different impact than saying the same word to a friend.

Dirty words are ubiquitous in most societies and they serve a psychological purpose. Ferenczi (1911) recognized that patients could speak in a distant, intellectual manner about emotional experiences, yet the use of obscene words often facilitated intense affect and emotionality. One of his patients could discus "flatus" in a calm manner without affect, but the term "fart" produced a strong emotional reaction. Ferenczi believed that using obscene words was vital to a successful analysis. He also suggested that for immigrants, using obscene words in their acquired language does not have the same impact as the words in their native tongue. According to Ferenczi, this is because words in one's original language are experienced as closely related or equivalent to the acts they describe, and therefore carry more affect. Obscene words make vivid the act and/or the body parts they describe.

Bergler (1936) sees the "peculiar power" of obscene words deriving from the idea that "obscene words have remained infantile and therefore retain their abnormally motor and regressive character" (p. 229). He says that "obscene words are, psychologically, *oral flatus*" (p. 230, italics in original). Although most of the literature on obscene words is general in scope, Stone (1954) studied the specific word "fuck" and suggests that this word is unconsciously related to the word "suck" and therefore related to oral aggression.

Arango (1989) writes that dirty words "constitute an authentic trigger of deep memories and ancient passions. They not only awaken dormant desire but also prohibition. They revive the great incestuous conflict and provoke trauma and hallucination. That is why they should never be written or uttered" (p. 34). Obscene words can also be used defensively, often with respect to anxiety. Intellectualization is one way of avoiding the myriad of conflicts underlying obscene words. One patient reported that her mother, who was highly intellectually defended and eschewed all conversations involving emotionality or sexuality, once caught some neighboring teenagers having sex in her backyard. She expressed outrage that the kids were "fornicating" on her property.

Language and its meaning are constantly evolving. For example, the word "fuck" has taken on a new meaning among adolescents. My fifteen-year-old daughter recently shared that the phrase, "I fuck with that" means something like, "I vibe with that or connect with that." She gave the example of Erewhon market, the upscale supermarket made famous by Instagram and TikTok celebrities. In her words, "It's like, 'I fuck with Erewhon' means I like it. Saying 'I fuck with it' communicates that it's a good thing."

Dirty language thus serves many functions. Dirty words unconsciously play a significant role in the creation and interpretation of jokes, as well as beliefs about money, as in the following examples.

Two other realms

While the foregoing discourse has covered a considerably wide terrain of human experience, there remain two more categories that need our attention. The first pertains to "dirty" jokes and the other to "dirty" money. The following passages address these two categories of dirtiness.

Dirty jokes

Profanity, which is also known as dirty language, is commonly used for emphasis and often is the basis of humor. The comedian Lenny Bruce was arrested several times in the 1960s for saying these words: ass, balls, cocksucker, cunt, fuck, motherfucker, piss, shit, and tits. Convicted of obscenity in 1964, he was sentenced to four months in jail, yet made bail and appealed against the verdict. In the following decade, another comedian, George Carlin, made headlines for a monologue about the Seven Words You Can Never Say on Television. This routine was also known as "Filthy Words" (1983, HBO Special) and "Dirty Words" (1978, HBO Special) and "Forbidden Words" (1978 HBO Special). The seven words were: shit, piss, fuck, cunt, cocksucker, motherfucker, and tits. Carlin's use of these "dirty words" facilitated a court case that went all the way to the Supreme Court, which ultimately ruled that the Federal Communications Commission (FCC) did indeed have the power to regulate broadcasts considered indecent but not obscene. This landmark decision challenged the protections of the First Amendment.

Yet, why do we find humor in dirty language? Freud (1905c) views the function of jokes as a means of releasing inhibition. As he puts it, "they make possible the satisfaction of an instinct (whether lustful or hostile) in the face on an obstacle that stands in its way" (p. 101). Legman (1968), in a comprehensive analysis of sexual humor, explicates the genesis and meaning of dirty jokes throughout many cultures, writing, "Under the mask of humor, our society allows infinite aggressions, by everyone and against everyone" (p. 9). He explores the aggression inherent in all dirty jokes, sometimes directed toward the teller of the joke, and its relation to the anxiety felt upon telling them. The categories of the book include: children, fools, animals, the male approach, the sadistic concept, women, premarital sexual acts, marriage, and adultery.

Each of these categories appears in "The Aristocrats" a raunchy and perverse skit that dates back to Vaudeville. The elaborate joke involves a family pitching their act to a potential talent agent, violating every taboo against incest, rape, pedophilia, bestiality, and more, including gross-out bodily humor. It ends with the reveal of the name of their act: The Aristocrats. This joke was the subject of a documentary (*The Aristocrats*, 2005) and is considered the dirtiest joke in the English language

(Denby, 2005). These days, the Aristocrats joke is rarely performed on stage and is instead told by one comic to another, as what Dougherty (2010) calls, an "acid test of talent, wit, and unflinching nerve, who can out-cringe whom?" (p. 251).

Freud (1905c) divided what he called "tendentious jokes" into four types: exposing or obscene jokes, aggressive or hostile jokes, cynical, and skeptical jokes (p. 115). He states that "the intentional bringing into prominence of sexual facts and relations by speech" (p. 97) is akin to "smut" and that "a person who laughs at smut that he hears is laughing as if he were the spectator of an act of sexual aggression" (p. 97). Sociologist and communication theorist Arthur Asa Berger has written extensively about the role of jokes in society. In his book *The Anatomy of Humor* (1993) Berger divides jokes into three main categories: release jokes, aggression jokes, and superiority jokes. Release jokes relieve tension and anxiety by allowing the teller and listener to temporarily escape from the reality of their lives. Aggression jokes are used to put down or attack a particular group or individual and are often used to reinforce stereotypes and prejudices. Superiority jokes are used to establish the teller as superior to the listener or the group being joked about. Not all exposing jokes are offensive, as in this example from Berger (1993):

> A man goes to Miami for a vacation. After four days he has a tan over all his body, except for his penis. So the next day he goes to a deserted area of the beach early in the morning, takes off his clothes, and lies down. He sprinkles sand all over himself until all that remains in the sun is his penis. Two little old ladies walk by and one notices the penis. "When I was 20," she says, "I was scared to death of them. When I was 40, I couldn't get enough of them. When I was 60, I couldn't get one to come near me ... and now they're growing wild on the beach!" (pp. 5–6)

Dirty money

Money is another topic that is often correlated with dirtiness, as evidenced by these idioms: Dirty money. Filthy rich. Obscenely rich. Stinking rich. The connection between feces and money was first postulated by Freud (1908b) as an outcome of the anal stage. Individuals who withheld their feces in this earlier stage are more likely to be miserly and hoard money as adults. They find it difficult to "let go" of money just as they once found it difficult to let go of their bowels. Those who were anal expulsive in childhood are more likely to be generous, given to emotional conflicts, rebelliousness, confidence, and artistic ability.

Sándor Ferenczi (1914) views mud as a fecal substitute, suggesting that playing with dark, moist mud represents the first stage in the sublimation of anal eroticism. Explicating Freud's belief that there is a connection between the outcome of the anal stage and the handling of money, Ferenczi proposes that the child's interest in fecal matter is first sublimated into playing with mud, then finger painting, playing with clay, and eventually collecting pebbles or marbles, which are primitive forms of money. The eventual outcome of the anal stage is the sublimation from stool to money, which appears in our vernacular as "filthy rich" or "dirty money."

Interestingly, dirty money may also be "laundered" which means concealing the identity of illicitly obtained money (as through drug deals or other criminal activity) and therefore making it "clean" and rendering its origins untraceable.

Haight (1977) describes the plethora of expressions referring obliquely to money and bodily functions. A financially conservative person is often called "tight" with money and a person who can't make a decision may be told to "shit or get off the pot." He notes that people may earn "a pile of money" and that those with a lot of money have "a cushion" or have "hit pay dirt." Those who lose their money are "wiped out" or "cleaned out." We also go to the bank to "make a deposit." He suggests that these linguistic connections between the language of the body and that of money are not coincidental, stating, "The key word in all this is 'dirt'" (p. 628). The repression of dirt leads to a neurotic obsession with its sublimated substitutes. In Haight's view, we are repulsed by dirtiness because dirt unconsciously reminds us of darkness and death, so it must be repressed and sublimated. He suggests that to create change, we must accept the cycle of birth and death, and such acceptance will create an outlook in which "money" will no longer be a dirty word.

Conclusion

This comprehensive survey of dirtiness in human life clearly demonstrates that it is thus a multidimensional concept that plays out intrapsychically, relationally, figuratively, and literally. The art and science of psychoanalysis involves delving into the dark corners of the unconscious mind to dig up the proverbial dirt, discovering that which is buried, disavowed, and repressed. Sigmund Freud compared the practice of psychoanalysis to archeology. His patient known as Wolf Man later wrote of his experience as Freud's analysand (1958), "Freud himself explained his love for archaeology in that the psychoanalyst, like the archaeologist in his excavations, must uncover layer after layer of the patient's psyche, before coming to the deepest, most valuable treasures" (p. 352).

Those valuable treasures of the mind may simultaneously illuminate and terrify us. As a patient declared, "We're uncovering all my dirty little secrets, even the ones I didn't know I had." Psychoanalysts dig into the past, seeking clues to solve the mystery of the current problem. Only by sifting through the dark and dirty recesses of the mind can we facilitate psychological birth.

It's a dirty job, but someone's got to do it.

CHAPTER TWO

Miserliness

Ann Smolen

The difference between being greedy and being miserly seems simple. The greedy person wishes to acquire more and more things such as money, houses, art, the list is endless; however, the miserly person wishes to keep all he has for himself. He is ungenerous of pocket, heart, and spirt. There is a dearth of psychoanalytic literature on the act of being miserly and its intrapsychic meaning. I rarely think in terms of miserliness when I think of my patients, so I was surprised that when I began to write on this subject several of my patients came to mind. First, I would like us to think about miserly behavior theoretically, after which I will support the theory with clinical vignettes. Since *greed* and miserliness are interrelated, I will begin with a very brief theoretical exploration of greed.

From greed to avarice

Klein (1952) locates greed in the oral stage of development, highlighting that greed is intensified by depravation, but stresses that there is a dynamic interplay between the innate aggressive drive and actual depravation. Klein states: "… children in whom the innate aggressive drive is strong, persecutory anxiety, frustration, and greed are easily aroused" (p. 62). When loving feelings prevail between the mother and her infant, then the child is able to feel gratitude toward the loving object. However, when there is gross misattunement and when the libido–aggression balance within the dyad (and in the infant's intrapsychic world) is tilted towards aggression, then receiving supplies stirs up more hunger and more anger; this angry hunger constitutes greed.

Anna Freud (1965a) describes how the young infant appears to possess an insatiable "oral greed" as she takes everything she desires. Greed by definition is inherently insatiable and will not be satisfied. When we call someone "greedy," we are disapproving and scornful. It is often said in annoyance and accompanied by an irritated tone (Boris, 1986). Both Boris and A. Freud do not view greed as pejorative, but rather as "an unresolved state of mind in which one wishes and hopes to have everything all of the time" (ibid., p. 45). By the beginning of the second year when the toddler acquires the use of the word "mine," "he begins to guard his possessions fiercely and jealously against any interference" (A. Freud, 1965, p. 117). Anna Freud points out that the concept of being stolen from comes into play much earlier than the understanding that the other's belongings are not for the taking, and in fact,

> ... oral greed, anal possessiveness, urges to collect and hoard, overwhelming need for phallic symbols, all turn young children into potential thieves unless educational coercion, superego demands, and with these, gradual shifts in id-ego balance work in the opposite direction, namely, toward the development of honesty. (pp. 117–118)

Winnicott (1986) also does not view greed as bad, but instead describes greed as a primitive love "that we are all frightened to own up to, but which is basic in our natures, and which we cannot do without" (p. 170). I imagine that the fantasy and wish to have every need met instantly and have everything all of the time is also a primitive wish to merge with the mother which produces a state of feeling high excitement and pure bliss.

Greediness is generated by the social and economic environment (Dodd, 1994). The American story of the road to happiness is to have more. The saying "keeping up with the neighbors" means individuals are valued by what they own and have, not by what they do. American society cultivates the idea that success or "getting ahead" is accomplished by having valuable things. The idea is these *things* will enhance self-esteem and contribute to lifelong stability (LaMothe, 2003). Nikelly (2006), states: "attachment to inanimate possessions becomes more important than recognizing and fulfilling inner emotional and authentic needs and deeper longings" (p. 69). Akhtar (2012) points out how Americans love to throw extravagant parties and shower their children and grandchildren with lavish gifts. He urges his readers to look deeper and writes: "One constantly hears of 'Southern generosity,' 'Italian generosity,' 'Greek generosity,' 'Indian generosity,' 'Armenian generosity' and so on. The question then arises whether there are ethnic groups that are less generous" (p. 669).

Salzman (2001), an anthropologist, describes how in hunter-gatherer societies, food and other goods are shared equally among everyone. This custom earns each individual admiration and distinction within the group. This reciprocity ensures that when one hunter is unsuccessful, his family is assured to eat. In still other primitive societies gift giving such as offerings to the gods had a spiritual meaning of giving back, which in turn, restored the balance of nature (Becker, 1975). In these societies, keeping excess to oneself separated that person from nature and disrupts the harmony within the community (Nikelly, 2006).

Lastly, many religions stress the virtue of generosity in their teachings. Christian religions, citing the King James Bible, teach: "It is more blessed to give than to receive" (Acts 20:35), and "God loves a cheerful giver" (Corinthians 9:7), and "Whoever is generous to the poor lends to the Lord and He will repay him for his deed" (Proverbs 19:7). The Jewish religion preaches the giving of tzedakah and Gemilut Hasidim. This is understood as an act of goodwill and generosity. Tzedakah is usually the giving of money to the less fortunate, however Gemilut Hasidim are acts of loving kindness. Before we can understand miserly behaviors, we must first explore what it means to experience gratitude.

I think it is important to clarify that miserliness is "unrelated to the financial state of the individual. Both the rich and the poor can be miserly, and both can be generous" (Akhtar, 2012, p. 670). Indeed, Klein (1957) states: "Inner wealth derives from having assimilated the good object so that the individual becomes able to share its gifts with others. This makes it possible to introject a friendlier outer world, and a feeling of enrichment ensues. Even the fact that generosity is often insufficiently appreciated does not necessarily undermine the ability to give" (p. 189). Developmentally, during the toddler years/anal phase/rapprochement phase, a bowel movement is a gift to the mother. From this gift of feces, the toddler receives a pleasurable response from her mother, which in turn, teaches the child that giving is virtuous and feels good. Later, during school age, adolescence, and young adulthood, the generosity of teachers, friends, extended family, and neighbors comes into play. These important figures in one's life become role models for generous behaviors toward others. In adulthood, professional mentors become import role models in giving back to the next generation, Akhtar states: "In the end, it seems, that the balance between normal and abnormal elements in generosity depends upon the ratio between early gratification and frustration, libido and aggression, and actual or imaginary identification, and finally, between the process of sublimation and reaction formation" (2012, p. 649).

The case of a miserly child

I have written elsewhere (Smolen, 2015) about one child as being consumed with greed. However, her analytic material is also an excellent example of miserliness. She accumulated objects and needed to keep everything for herself.

Seven-year-old Kay was brought for treatment because of night terrors, bed-wetting, and impulsive aggressive behaviors towards adults, other children, and small animals. Kay witnessed domestic violence, and on multiple occasions, her father threatened to kill his wife and abduct his children. When Kay was an infant, her mother burned Kay's esophagus by heating her bottle in a microwave oven. Kay's mother was obsessed with cleanliness and would wash the inside of Kay's vagina with a washcloth. When Kay was four years old through to age seven, she suffered a chronic yeast infection where her perineum would sometimes become so raw it would bleed. Kay had also been told by both of her parents that she was stupid, worthless, and fat. Kay's parents lost custody of their child and the paternal grandparents took over her care and quickly sought psychoanalytic treatment.

The beginning

In her first session, this pretty, slightly overweight little girl, with enormous sad green eyes, stood in the center of my playroom, unable to move, seemingly paralyzed with fear. I stood near her and explained that in this room she could do whatever she wished. Within minutes after my encouragement, Kay became bossy and demanding, insisting, in an abrasive and somewhat cruel tenor, that I sit next to her at the dollhouse and make up a story. She was unable to take part in the play, but instead became the audience to my production of her commands. In subsequent sessions she continued her imperious and taxing demeanor. The play quickly turned to abusive mother/baby pretend. Session after session I was told that my child got lost and I could not find her; my baby was screaming in hunger and I was unable to obtain food; my baby was sick and I was inept at getting help. As the months went on this theme remained but became more elaborate. Through this painful "play" she showed me the abuse she had experienced since infancy. She quickly went to her hurt and her pain. Kay gave herself a character and demonstrated how she used splitting as a defense against her pathological greed and miserly demeaner by sometimes being the "good" Helen and sometimes the "mean" Helen. However, she continued to participate from outside of the play. By this I mean that she narrated the story and I had to speak the lines of my character, but her character never speaks. For example, she would say: "Pretend that mean Helen hates you and gets all the townspeople to hate you, and your husband likes me better than you." I act out my despair and sadness and hurt over such treatment. Her response is: "Pretend Helen doesn't care."

The early phase of treatment

As the months wore on, Kay continued to have trouble connecting with other children her age or maintaining any type of meaningful relationships. She acted out aggressively and was bossy, manipulative, nasty, and extremely greedy both outside and in her analytic hour. In her play she showed me over and over how devastated she felt under her grandiose disguise. She always put me in her place, as she frustrated, tricked, manipulated, controlled, and humiliated me. She slowly began to tolerate the profoundly sad feelings that I expressed (in the play), but would quickly change the theme of the play when she was no longer able to tolerate my affect. For example:

K: "Pretend that nobody likes you and you have no friends and you try to be my friend." [I act this out and she rejects and ignores me and will not allow me to be her friend.]
A: "I feel so bad. I am so sad. I feel so alone. It is terrible that no one loves me. All I want is for somebody to love me."

She watched me, but in a sideways fashion, out of the corner of her eye, while demanding that I repeat the whole scene several times. Eventually these themes overwhelmed her and she would attempt to change the play to an unrelated theme, but this always failed as she ended up rejecting and hurting me in every game. I would be exiled to a corner of the playroom as she screamed at me chanting hurtful slurs and stating clearly that I was completely unlovable. These games were repetitive and tedious and I was left to feel devalued and helpless. At the end of our first six months of her analysis, she began to act kindly toward me at the very end of the session. We had begun a ritual where, when I told her it was almost time to end, she would help herself to mints that I kept in my desk drawer. Perhaps she worried that I would not give her a mint if she was not nice. One mint was never enough. Kay would graciously accept the one mint I offered and then quickly grab as many as she could and run for the door. She had to take everything I had and what I gave her was never enough.

Kay elicited strong countertransference as her demeanor was extremely obnoxious, manipulative, and unpleasant. Understanding my countertransference was very important in working with her. I often felt bored, sleepy, humiliated, frustrated, irritated, and worthless. I felt I was reacting to the emptiness in this little girl. It was as if she were dead, as if her soul had been murdered. However, for the most part I was able to feel empathy for the pathetic, devastated little girl that she had buried underneath her nasty, greedy, and miserly exterior.

After one year

Even though all of her presenting problems persisted in her outside world, I had a sense we were making progress. She had become more fluid in her play, would speak more readily about an event in her life such as a visit to her parents, and was able to tell me "You feel really sad" instead of making me insert the affect into the play. For example, in our "mean Helen" game, she would take everything from me, my husband, my children, all of my worldly goods, and instead of waiting silently for me to react, she would tell me what to feel: "I have everything, you have nothing! I get it all, you get nothing! You feel really, really bad!"

Kay's play continued to be monotonous and repetitious. The point of the play seemed to be to take everything from me, to keep everything for herself, and to frustrate me. For example, she set up a parking game using matchbox cars. The whole play consisted of making sure I never got a parking spot. She did this through trickery. Her demeanor remained bossy, demanding, and controlling. She often screamed at me in a high-pitched voice to do her bidding. I interpreted how important it was to her to treat me this way and I wondered out loud if she is treated this way in the real world. As she listened to my words, her features softened and she got a faraway look in her eyes, perhaps sadness. These interpretations were not responded to verbally but I felt that she was taking in my words.

Kay continued to act out her real-life dramas as she insisted that I act as an abusive mother who does not care for the welfare of her child. I am told to hit and demean my child, leave my child home alone sitting in her excrement, and at one point she wanted me to kill my child by drowning her in the ocean. At times she would join me and we were two terrible mothers who would go off shopping with our boyfriends. Her identification with her mother's lying and deceit was evident in her saying: "Pretend that we smile and seem happy in the stores. People can't tell how mean we really are. Let's pretend that we can take anything in the store we want, and nobody can stop us."

In another continuing drama, I am the little sister who lives with mean terrible parents. She is the big sister who has escaped. She has a loving husband and two beautiful babies with whom she is very nurturing. She sends me a letter, telling me I must sneak out in the middle of the night and fly on an airplane to her home. She sends me the plane tickets and $50,000. The game ends when I escape; she is unable to continue the game where there would be a loving relationship between the two of us. In this drama, she was telling me her story, one of escape to a safer home, but one where she still feels alone and isolated. Through the transference her greed, hate, and envy were worked through as this drama was replayed for many sessions.

Over time Kay began to play a lot of school and teacher games. This play demonstrated many levels of our relationship and her improved ego functioning. This play was used as another avenue, which she used to feel superior to me, as she was the better teacher, the most loved teacher, the smarter teacher, while I was left demeaned and alone with nothing. At times she used this play as a way to distance herself from me, perhaps as a defense against her fear of intimacy. At other times this play demonstrated her move into latency as she acted out age-appropriate scenarios where she followed rules and began to tolerate losing or not having everything all of the time.

As Kay's development improved, she became much more open verbally. She told me of her accomplishments in swimming and basketball. She spoke about situations while visiting her parents in which she was upset and unhappy. She told me when her grandparents punished her and how she outsmarted them. She seemed to become a bit less greedy and miserly. In the past, she had to use all the clay or all the paint or take all my mints from my desk. She began to show less compulsion to have it all and many times left sessions without depleting me of all I had. The fact that she no longer needed to rob me of my possessions in order to feel close to me indicated the growth of trust in our relationship. I thought that perhaps I was beginning to become internalized as a new developmental object and that she had begun to have some "object constancy" (Mahler et al., 1975), and thus no longer felt compelled to take a part of me home with her. This improvement also demonstrated new ego strength where she was better able to control her impulses. In addition, her hate, rage, greed, and envy were becoming modulated through our experiences together as she saw that these overpowering affects would not destroy our relationship, as she no longer needed to completely deplete me in order to feel okay.

The treatment deepens

Sexual themes entered our sessions as she began to bring questions about her feminine identity into her treatment. For example, she began a session by opening up a toy cell phone, removing the batteries, which had leaked, and washing out the interior of the phone. She used the phone to call a boyfriend who told her that he loved her. Next, she made a tunnel out of a toilet paper roll to drive little cars through. Later in the session as we were constructing valentines she told me: "Once I stuck a scissor in myself on purpose." She was unable to elaborate and changed the subject. She ended that session making necklaces for her siblings out of beads and she said: "I have a secret drawer where I keep all the things you have made me. If you come to my house, I will let only you see inside my drawer."

In later sessions she spoke about a boy who dressed as a girl and how she is excited by a particular boy who kisses girls on the playground. In all of these interactions I listened. If I had interpreted her erotic feelings in a more adult manner, she would have shut down, limiting the possibility for further exploration.

All of Kay's play themes demonstrated her intense grandiose fantasies that covered up terrible insecurities. Her need to be admired and lauded was a thin camouflage for her inner feelings of chronic emptiness and boredom. She was in constant search for beauty, wealth, brilliance, and power. She was in search of the perfect "all-good" object. Her play and behavior were exceptionally controlling, which I understood as Kay's way of showing me that she felt helpless, controlled, and powerless. This left little room for capacity to love and to experience empathy for others. She often behaved in exploitive and ruthless ways toward her grandparents, siblings, and her analyst. She successfully inflicted narcissistic injuries on others that she was terrified of suffering herself. Kay's play themes displayed her possessiveness, envy, jealousies, greed; and her impulses to kill rivals and frustrating figures had the potential of becoming nuclei for later dissociality. However, on Valentine's Day, I found a tiny valentine that she left on the floor in my waiting room for me to find at the end of my day. This tiny glimmer of light gave me hope for further progress.

Kay's play began to change. The monotonous, frustrating games of the previous year disappeared. She became more organized and contained. Her play became more creative as we built roads that had tollbooths that sent us off to magical destinations. However, even in this more advanced, creative play she made sure that I did not have enough money to get to the best most magical places. It seemed that her anxiety had diminished as she worked through her traumatic history, which allowed her creativity to come to the forefront. However, her envy, greed, and miserly behaviors remained. A turning point in our work occurred when she began a game in which I was a queen and she my daughter/princess. In this role play, she sat close to me and called me "Queen Mommy" as we made invitations to her royal birthday party. This play, which continued in different forms, represented an important change in the transference from the "bad" mother transference to the "good" mother transference. My countertransference also began to change as I felt caring, warm feelings for her. This shift occurred because of her increased capacity for greater intimacy. She could now reverse the roles and accept a "loving mother." For the next several months, school games dominated, but an important change took place. I was given the role of head teacher and she was now my daughter and my assistant. For months, we worked together in a warm cooperative manner, playing this game where we teach our children. Kay directed this play and we had music where we sang, art where we made creative projects, and academics where our children may have made a mistake, but we never ridiculed or hurt their feelings. In our pretend recess time in our school game, she made up a game called "silent ball" with many rules, which she wrote out on paper and hung on the wall. Some of our children were unable to follow the rules and they were given consequences with warmth and understanding. These games indicated that Kay was moving forward developmentally and had entered her latency phase.

Kay began to bring me objects from home to share with me. When Kay began treatment she had presented with a lack of gratitude and defects in the ability to express and feel empathy for others. At this point there was a shift as she began to acknowledge that she had received something good from me. At Easter she gave me a basket of tulips and suggested that they could also be Passover flowers, adding that her grandfather thought that maybe I was Jewish. Around this time she became interested in me and wondered how old I was, filling the whiteboard with numbers and playing a guessing game to figure out my age. In subsequent sessions she probed, asking me other personal details about my life. She wondered if I were married, if I had children, and what kind of house I lived in. As I helped her explore her feelings toward me she began to speak about herself and her family, but her inquisitive stance was an indication that she had begun to not only use me as a new developmental object and a transferential object, but was also viewing me as a real person with a mind of my own. She was no longer consumed by greed and envy as she seemed to now be able to experience loving feelings.

Working through

As her analysis proceeded, the school game gained a variation on a theme: sometimes we owned a pet store; sometimes a day care; sometimes a restaurant or bake shop. In all of these games, which became elaborate and filled the whole session, there were exact rules, regulations and proper ways of behaving. Most importantly she fully included me (I no longer felt bored or sleepy), and she was no longer bossy, demeaning, or humiliating toward me. The following segment of a session illustrates her latency-appropriate behavior and how Kay's ego functions had improved. She began her session by showing me her new outfit and new shoes and suggested I too, should go to this store and get new shoes for only $6.99. She set up school and stated that today will be "Fun Day" as she listed games we could play on the board. She settled on Dodge Ball and for the next thirty minutes we played this very physical game. She is very good at it, much better than I, and she played by the rules and was fair. She clearly enjoyed hitting me with the ball and became excited and overheated.

A: "I think you are enjoying this game very much. It seems that you like hitting me with the ball."
K: "I do! I do!"
A: "It also seems to be very important to you that you are better at this than I am."
K: "Yes, yes. I like being better at this game!"
A: "This is a very exciting game and you are getting very excited."

After I said this, she told me it was nighttime and we needed to sleep. She made a bed on the floor and we lay down together. She said she was going to have a dream.

K: "I'm going to dream that I go to an island that is made out of ice cream and I can eat all the ice cream I want."
A: "What a wonderful place. Who else is there?"
K: "You and me and my baby and you can eat all the ice cream you want and so can my baby."
A: "The baby too?"
K: "It's a dream, silly. Anything can happen in a dream! Now go to sleep!"

In our game, we slept past the alarm and had to hurry to school, where we taught the children about fire drills. She is kind and nurturing as she helped the children to not be afraid of the shrill alarm that, she confided in me, scared her. At the end of the session, she told me she was exhausted from our play and crawled under the easel where she discovered there was a small blackboard, and wrote "No Boys Allowed" and instructed me not to read it until after she had left. The above vignette demonstrates Kay's newfound capacity to feel empathy for others and her ability to be giving to others and not feel totally depleted in the giving. Also, as stated above, this session showed her entrance into age-appropriate play and latency feelings about boys.

After months of sessions like the above vignette, her bossy, greedy meanness, and miserliness came back. This regression was not unexpected as there are always ups and downs and reworking of the traumas, conflicts, and the transference. Once again, I was left helpless, rejected, and abandoned in the play. This game was short-lived and after ten minutes of this regressed play she announced:

K: "Enough of this. Let's play school."

However, in her school game I am left out again as we pretended that my children do not like me and leave me for her. She sent me from the school, never to come back. I was banished to a corner of the playroom.

A: "This feels sad. I'm all alone. Nobody seems to love me."

She needed me to repeat this over and over, and this scenario continued until the end of the session. She refused to help clean up and in a two year old's whiney voice announced that she refused to leave and could not understand why she just cannot stay all day! I addressed her difficult feelings, verbalizing how one day she can feel very grown-up, competent, and loving, and the next day all of the difficult mean feelings come flooding back. These play scenarios demonstrated what Akhtar (2014) has underscored about greed: "The individual afflicted with it is momentarily pleased with the attainment of supplies and then becomes unsatisfied, empty, and inconsolable" (p. 37). In Kay's regressed state, it was helpful to remember Winnicott's (1986) wisdom: "If we acknowledge the importance of greed in human affairs, we shall find more than greed, or we shall find that greed is love in a primitive form. We shall also find that the compulsion to attain power can spring from fear of chaos and uncontrol" (p. 213). In her next session, Kay went back to her newer behaviors as our games proceeded. Her grandiosity and sense of entitlement did not reappear until termination when it got replayed but with an important difference.

Termination

We decided to terminate for two reasons: the first was (as with many child cases) a necessity due to schedule and geographical distance. Kay needed to attend full-day school. She was entering the fourth grade and it would be detrimental to her further development both academically and socially if she was not allowed to attend school like the other children. Because her grandparents traveled an hour and a half to bring her to me it became evident that my schedule (and hers) would not permit this arrangement to continue. I had maintained an intensive relationship with the grandparents since the beginning of treatment, meeting with them twice monthly. These meetings, while difficult at times, had proved extremely beneficial as the grandparents valued my advice and worked very hard to help their granddaughter. I was confident that Kay had grown very close to her grandmother in particular and this woman was providing a secure, loving holding environment for Kay to continue healing.

I began an analysis with Kay because her normal progressive development had been arrested. Kay's clinical material suggested very clearly that she was back on track developmentally. This was supported by reports from the grandparents that her acting-out behaviors had stopped at home and at school, the night terrors were gone, and she no longer wet the bed. She was better able to understand her living situation and was coping better with her visits to her parents. She could now verbalize her fears, sadness, and tremendous anger, and she could speak about her disappointments in the parents she loved so much.

At first, Kay was displeased with the decision to end, but comforted with the choice to maintain one session per week. In almost every session during this ending period she went back to a play/drama from early in our work but with a significant difference—the endings were altered. She replayed the scenario of the poor abused little sister who needed to escape from her parents. The game was exactly as we played it over a year ago except when we got to the end. Now, she accepted me into her home and off we went shopping together. In this play, Kay retold her story, but now she felt intimate with me. She no longer felt abandoned, alone, and isolated. In another session, she replayed some of her earliest games wherein she built a car lot in the sand. The game retained some of its original monotony where I began to feel left out, bored, and sleepy, when she suddenly included me. In yet another session, she replayed a game where we were college students and I saw her from afar and I was bedazzled by her beauty. I was so taken with her that I followed her home and ask to be her friend because she was so beautiful, and owned a magnificent home and the most expensive car. When we played this game a year ago, she would end up rejecting and ignoring my desire to befriend her and the game would end with her being very nasty to me. This time she accepted my friendship; we became best friends who had wonderful husbands and beautiful babies. In all of these dramas Kay was retelling her story, but with new endings. She no longer felt as worthless and unlovable as she did when we began. Her grandiosity and greed remained to a degree and she continued to be easily narcissistically wounded, but her coping capacity had been greatly fortified.

In one of our final sessions, we played school once again. I was the teacher and she my student. She insisted that I give her difficult math problems, reading comprehension, and spelling tests. In the past, she would refuse to take any risk where she might fail. She could not tolerate the humiliation of being wrong. I was amazed as she attempted difficult problem-solving and was able to ask for help and was not mortified when she made a mistake. At the end of the session, she spoke of her excitement about going away with her parents on a vacation to another state to visit relatives, and her worries that school may be difficult this year.

Discussion

Kay had experienced abuse and neglect by her primary attachment figures. I speculate that Kay's mother, who was not at all attuned to her infant daughter's physical discomforts, could not provide emotional attunement. Kay's mother was unable to act as an auxiliary ego in order to support her infant's immature and unstable ego functions. Kay began life at risk, and learned early on that her world was an uncomfortable and hostile place.

There was some salvation for Kay, in that she had grandparents to stand-in and provide for her emotional and physical needs during infancy and her preoedipal years. I conjecture that she got enough nurturance to enable her to continue to develop in certain areas, as evidenced by her advanced academic skills. Between the ages of five years through seven years, during her oedipal years, she lived with her parents. During these years she experienced confusing physical and emotional abuse. These early impingements had the effect of disrupting Kay's ego integration, her sense of self, and her object relations. These early traumas led to a premature and pathological (although adaptive) narcissistic defensive organization. As an abused child she felt unlovable and worthless. She had internalized self-with-other as "bad" and "dangerous." She demonstrated what her experiences had been with adults in her life by splitting and being either all good or all bad. Kay's defense of splitting was maintained because of her rage toward her mother and father. She was unable to integrate and resolve both hating and loving her parents. Kay developed pathological narcissistic defenses to avoid feeling intense and unbearable pain and sadness. It is also my belief that her narcissistic self-formation, plus her free-floating sadism may have protected her from developing a major depression. As stated above, Kay's early traumas and maltreatment have interfered with the development of her ego and its functions. This, in turn, has influenced her adaptation to her environment. Her coping mechanisms suggested severe pathology as she had retreated into grandiosity and omnipotence as a defense against her poor self-esteem and her lack of trust in others. Kay demonstrated an understandably skewed sense of self, and her understandably intense need for my admiration, over and over in her games that demanded that I find her beautiful, smart, and powerful.

Kay suffered emotional and physical deprivation leaving her virtually starving, which in turn caused her to continuously search for anything and everything to fill her emptiness. Akhtar (2014) states: "The child then pushes the envelope of supplies, takes a lot, steals from his caregivers, and behaves in outrageous ways" (p. 45). In addition, her infantile omnipotence appeared untamed (Blum, 1991). When Kay stole from me, I understood this behavior as her need to "compensate [herself] for the earlier deprivation but also to hurt the benefactor who has come to stand for the depriving primary objects" (Winnicott, 1986, p. 45).

Considering the severe trauma that Kay experienced, why did she improve so dramatically in a relatively short period of time? The answer is multiply determined. As soon as Kay's grandparents obtained legal custody, they actively sought psychoanalytic treatment. They had deep concerns for their granddaughter and made a great effort to obtain the best treatment they were able to afford. They were supportive of the treatment and developed a positive working alliance with me. They were able to tolerate the intense relationship that develops between the patient and the analyst. It should also be noted that they made Kay's analysis a top priority, driving a great distance and altering school schedules. The grandparents attended parent sessions with me twice monthly and highly valued my advice and guidance. Slowly, over time, they altered their behavior and Kay's home environment significantly improved. Kay was court-ordered to have scheduled visitations with her parents. What became immediately imperative was that the grandparents needed guidance in how to handle these visits and how to get along with their estranged son and his wife. Improvement was notable when the grandparents began to accept and understand Kay's ambivalent feelings for her parents. It was difficult for them to comprehend that Kay had loving feelings for parents who had been so abusive to her. I was surprised and impressed when the grandmother began to relate positive loving stories to Kay about her father when he was a little boy. Most important and helpful was the fact that the grandparents no longer "trashed" Kay's parents when they began to understand that this was extremely damaging to Kay's self-esteem and reinforced the splitting that Kay was already expressing. It was also difficult for the grandparents to understand the necessity of appropriate limit setting for Kay. Part of this trouble was because they were her grandparents and very much enjoyed the grandparent role; however, over time, they came to understand that it was detrimental to Kay's development when boundaries were defined too loosely. Kay's grandparents understood that setting rules and limits and providing appropriate boundaries helped Kay begin to self-regulate. They heeded my concern that, left unchecked, Kay had the very real potential to develop an "addictive disorder—such as abuse of alcohol or drugs, or promiscuous, hyperactive sexuality—or tendencies toward exploitative manipulations of others, theft, and other delinquencies" (Blum, 1991, p. 296).

Kay, herself, demonstrated superior intelligence, creativity, and the ability to make use of symbolism and metaphor. I feel that Kay's innate intelligence and other strengths drove the therapy, particularly in our enactments, but given such a dramatic improvement over a two-year period, what led to progress was the working through of her trauma through reconnecting to the object. Through the use of the mirroring transference Kay could really see herself in our work. Mirroring of the child-as-victim but also victim-as-child was valuable. This was done by submitting myself to the process of working through over and over and over again. Intensive work with the grandparents combined with Kay's innate superior intelligence and other character strengths made Kay analyzable so the work could proceed.

However, the treatment as a whole was most responsible for her improvement. I became a new empathic developmental object and provided a safe play space where Kay was able to work through her traumatic experiences. She was able to make use of me as a new developmental object as well as a real object. She was able to tolerate my interpretations that linked her traumatic experiences to her reactions within the play and integrate them into her new developing sense of self. Trust in our relationship grew and she became confident that I would accept her no matter how terrible she treated me within the metaphor in the play. Kay was able to make use of the play and use metaphor. She told me her sad story over and over in her play/dramas and as long as I was able to stay within the play and help her feel the profound sadness and pain (within my play character) that lay underneath her demeanor of grandiosity, she began to feel accepted and understood. In other words, within the play, I made interpretations of her symptoms that were being played out, that she was able to accept. The working-through element in our work where she played out her life story over and over allowed Kay to develop ego mastery and was insight generating because together we put language to her deeply buried feelings. As her ego developed and she felt more confident in herself, she became capable of tolerating and recovering from my empathic failures, which gave her the opportunity to work through traumatic experiences.

The case of a miserly adult

James, a fifty-five-year-old white man, came into treatment in an effort to understand why he felt discontent with his life even though he was highly successful professionally, was married with twin sons in college, and felt he was a wonderful support to his wife both financially and emotionally. In his initial sessions he spoke of wanting to find his place in the community in an effort to do good deeds and pay back some of the tremendous wealth he had accumulated. I quickly learned that he was unable to follow through with any plan to contribute to a worthwhile cause, either by becoming a board member or doing hands-on projects. He claimed he could not understand what got in the way of his pursuing something that he thought every good member of society should do. Over time I learned he was actually very miserly with his wife, not only with money and material items, but he was unaffectionate, and he was angry that his wife complained that their sex life was almost nonexistent.

James was adopted into a working-class family when he was three months old. At age three years the family adopted an infant girl. James's father struggled with alcoholism and abandoned the family when James was eight years old. His mother worked a menial job to pay the bills, was gone from the home for long hours, and often had to work night shifts. James referred to himself as a "latchkey kid" and was put in the role of man of the house, babysitting for his little sister well before he was of an appropriate age to do so. James was lucky as he was gifted intellectually and thought of himself as a nerd all through elementary school and high school. He received a merit scholarship to a highly respected university and excelled there and in graduate school.

James was a collector of various items such as sought-after expensive watches, works of art, and antiques of all types, but mostly oriental rugs. It is interesting to note that he did not display these valuable items, but kept them hidden away in a room in his mansion that housed his coveted collections. James was able to spend large amounts of money as he collected more and more things, and he seemed to find pleasure in the ownership of so many beautiful works of art, rugs, and timepieces but he did not share them, and he alone visited these things that were all locked away. James was full of contradictions, that often left me surprised and confused as they came to light in his sessions. As noted above, he lived in a massive home yet refused to allow his wife to furnish it. A major conflict in the marriage was money. He insisted that his wife stay within a tight spending budget for the household, shopping in discount stores and second-hand shops. He insisted that his wife make use of coupons when food shopping. Over time, he shared with me that he enjoyed sex, watched a lot of porn, and was withholding with his wife. They rarely had sex and were not affectionate. She complained about this and divorce was discussed. His wife began her own personal therapy, and in addition James and his wife entered into couples therapy. He found the couples sessions unpleasant as he often felt ganged-up on and complained bitterly about the cost of therapy, including my fee, degrading our work.

Clearly James's miserly ways had become a torture to his wife, sons, friends, and to a lesser extent, me, and most importantly, to himself. It should be noted that James refused a more intensive treatment and would often miss sessions, ranting all the while that he had to pay for the missed time. However, to his credit, he sought out treatment in order to understand what got in his way of giving back to his community, which he began to realize included all of his relationships.

Discussion

James had few memories of his early childhood. What stood out was his isolation and loneliness. I speculate that he experienced a "profound and traumatizing lack of nourishment from his early caretakers and, in a move typical of "identification with the aggressor" (A. Freud, 1936), has adapted an ungiving attitude toward others" (Akhtar, 2012, p. 671). James's earliest object relations were lacking which left James with feelings of loneliness and worthlessness. This in turn made intimacy too painful to maintain. He filled his emptiness by buying and hoarding expensive objects of art. Luckily for James he wanted help and entered therapy. At first James did not think of himself as miserly or ungenerous. He rationalized and convinced himself that he was being thrifty and helpful to his family. In this way he was able to avoid consciously facing his inner conflicts and turmoil; however, his inner life was filled with anxiety and fear. All of his relationships were "permeated with sadism, even though he is consciously unaware of it" (Akhtar, 2012, p. 670). For James, the amassing of large quantities of valuable objects helped to conceal an unverbalized and unconscious fear of nonexistence. His expensive objects compensated for his poor self-worth. His objects were a stand-in for security and love. Akhtar (2012) summed it up beautifully: "Yesterday's victim has become today's perpetrator. The miser's self is split. A cruel and withholding adult triumphantly parades outside while a deprived child weeps inside" (ibid. p. 671). I often felt and saw the lonely little boy. There were moments when his eyes showed deep sadness as he fought back tears. In this way, James began to allow himself to feel vulnerable with me and slowly began to trust his wife by sharing his soft, sad inner self.

Conclusion

Kay and James were miserly, stingy people. Both had experienced early developmental trauma and deprivation. Neither was able to be generous to others and needed to take everything for themselves. Neither was given to as babies and young children and thus they were empty and had nothing to give back to others. Kay's treatment gives us a clear view into how working-through helped Kay begin to feel better about herself and in turn she was able to be more generous towards others. For James, rethinking his beliefs about money and expensive objects helped him become more self-aware. He slowly became capable of viewing his greedy behaviors and connected them with his most inner feelings of worthlessness and loneliness. His early identifications with ungenerous caregivers began to evolve as he identified with me. As we know, within therapy there are experiences and expressions of gratitude and love. It took patience and time, but both Kay and James ultimately expressed both.

CHAPTER THREE

Shyness

Jerome Blackman

When native English-speaking persons say someone is shy, they are describing a certain set of observable characteristics. I will attempt to describe these below with aplomb, which is in some ways the opposite of being shy.

As Kahlbaum astutely observed in 1888, observable features don't tell us much about what type of mental disturbance is producing these (pathology), no less than any potentially discoverable causes (etiology) of that pathology.[1] Parenthetically (or perhaps not), the *DSM*, in all its iterations[2] fails to even depict the observations clearly, and purposely eschews any indications of causality (see Blackman, 2016, for my criticisms of the *DSM-5*).

One of the better resources I used to unearth the multiple meanings of shyness in English was a Spanish–English dictionary

---

[1] "In 1888, German psychiatrist Karl L. Kahlbaum called for the meaningful classification of mental illnesses according to their course. He noted that counting only overt symptoms was useless because the same symptoms might accompany different diseases and vice versa" (Papiasvili & Mayers, 2013, p. 134).

[2] At the time of this writing, we have been regaled with *DSM-5-TR* (2022).

(Dague-Greene & August, 2020). Ironically, in attempting to break down the many potential meanings of the English word "shyness" to make it more understandable to the native Spanish speaker, this resource delineates the many possible nuances, I think, much better than the *Oxford English Dictionary* (2023).

Many origins of shyness exist. Beginning with the common-sense delineation of different types of phenomenological shyness, different psychoanalytic views apply depending on the underlying pathology. Once we investigate the pathogenic mechanisms causing each type of shyness, we begin to wonder about the causes in each case. Most psychoanalysts are aware of the complexity (Morin, 2008) of these assessments. Approximately 10 to the 63rd power worth of possibilities are available whenever we take more than a superficial look at a character trait or a symptom.[3] So the task of delineating and defining seems almost impossible. Nevertheless, using our synthetic functions and capacities for categorization and generalization, we can take a stab at the problem.

What I will present, in this contribution, derives from data collected from patients, students, supervisees, and extant psychoanalytic literature, as scant as it may be. It should be realized that the definitions can apply in more than one case. Even clear cases are complicated by metapsychological inexactitude (Abend, 1982) and the problem of intersubjectivity (Papiasvili, 2020). The "irreducible subjectivity" (Renik, 1993) of the evaluator, that is, even in proposing definitional clarifications, cannot be eliminated. In other words, even the most objective "reality assessment" based on "objective data" is never wholly objective (Arlow, 1979).

Notwithstanding that rather daunting caveat, let's proceed to examine both the pathology and potentially knowable etiology for each type of shyness. Of course, this list is still not complete, and the potential differential etiologies in each situation frequently overlap. Moreover, modern conflict theory requires that we consider that all factors described, technically speaking, should be considered layered compromise formations (C. Brenner, 1982). Finally, neuroscience can explain, perhaps, just a tiny bit of it (Solms, 2021).

---

[3] Blackman (2010, p. 58).

Definitions and explications

Although shyness is often considered the opposite of sexual exhibitionism, especially in females, this is certainly not the only meaning. The characteristic shyness in that sense is exemplified in the 1960 song, popular worldwide, "Itsy Bitsy Teenie Weenie Yellow Polkadot Bikini" (Vance & Pockriss, 1960). The song concerns the embarrassment of a young teenage girl who wants to exhibit her body but is self-conscious about it. In this situation, shyness occurs as a preconscious automatism (Hartmann, 1939). But let's go further and look at each origin of shyness individually:

Timidity

Generalized timidity, or lack of courage, is a character feature (a compromise formation including a sizable quantity of defensiveness) that makes unconscious the mental operations usually necessary to carry out a desire to act. In timid people, the desire to take action, which Parens (1973) termed "non-hostile, non-destructive aggression," is often confused with hostile-destructive aggression. Because of this confusion (actually a condensation), guilt may be engendered which causes the person to defensively recoil from taking any action. In addition, there may be transferences and displacements from other, prior situations, where the patient's ambitions had been rebuffed, causing pain, disappointment, and/or humiliation. In fact, timidity is a dangerous type of shyness, in that self-preservation is based on awareness of one's surroundings and must be connected to aggression (non-hostile/non-destructive or sometimes hostile-destructive) for survival (Blackman, 2010). In other words, in order to protect one's livelihood, hygiene, identity, and at times one's life, at least non-hostile, non-destructive aggression is needed to assert one's opinions, to feel self-confident, and to assure one's survival.

Faint-heartedness

This involves a slowness to warm up, as described by Chess and Thomas (1995). Such people do not engage in interpersonal reactions readily and are very slow to "get involved" in even slightly tense situations, regardless of the importance to them. The etiology of this type of shyness is, no doubt, inborn "temperament"—which can sometimes be traced to the earliest postpartum state of the newborn infant. Some parents are able to correct such an inborn tendency, but persistence of this type of reserve is common.

Inhibition

As noted above, when we look at wallflowers, we consider that, at least unconsciously, they wish to be the center of attention (oral desires) and to be admired for their sexual allure (beginning in the first genital phase and prominent in the second genital phase). The often unconscious wishes of such persons conflict with shame (see Akhtar, 2016); the shame then provokes inhibition to ward off (defensively remove from consciousness) the urges for those specific gratifications.

Unfriendliness

This is generally caused by a distancing defense, predicated on object relations difficulties. The object relations problems may be due to failures to develop self and object constancy during the first three or four years of life or failures to develop a stable identity during adolescence. Because of the resulting instability, the person uses emotional distancing and therefore does not relate with openness about feelings, ideas, or wishes for emotional closeness. In fact, the wishes for emotional closeness produce self–object fusion anxiety, leading to the distancing mechanism. The emotional distancing may be complicated by intact social ability, so these people often speak socially without meaning what they say, giving their interactions an air of disingenuousness. Ironically, in tense political situations, this type of speech may be adaptive. However, in interpersonal situations, one can think of a husband and wife sitting for two hours at dinner without uttering a word to each other.

Aloofness

This character trait also usually involves object relations pathology, more specifically regarding regulation of narcissistic supplies. The aloof person's self-esteem is based on maintaining a somewhat superior, condescending attitude which is complicated by emotional distance. Aloof people may avoid contact with others to some extent, but when they do have contact with others, they come across as supercilious, apparently without any external reality motivation for such an attitude. The etiology of the narcissistic defenses is often found in the early mother/child relation as well as potentially disturbed peer interactions during latency and adolescence.

Clinical vignette: 1

A fifty-five-year-old lonely heterosexual bachelor, due to this character trait, would automatically function in a polite but aloof manner on first dates with women. Any woman he dated would tend to misinterpret his quiet solicitude as genuine interest complicated by social shyness, and then proceed to dominate their interactions with all sorts of free associations regarding her own life. As the patient became more bored, the woman would typically become more ardently talkative. Invariably, when he did not call the woman after the date, he predicted correctly that the woman would call him, which he dreaded. (For more about this case, see Blackman, 2013b.)

Elusiveness

This word involves negativism in answering questions. When asked a question, the person involved will "skirt the issue"[4] or simply refuse to answer the question which has been asked.

Chronic tendencies toward elusiveness should not be confused with good judgment, which involves an assessment of the reality of answering questions which may be dangerous in certain situations.[5] Elusiveness as a persistent character trait prevents people from getting

---

[4] An admittedly anachronistic term deriving from women's "modesty" (see below) causing them to avoid frank discussions regarding sexual desire.

[5] Lois Lerner famously invoked Fifth Amendment protection against self-incrimination by refusing to answer a congressional committee's questions regarding her possible involvement in political influences on the IRS in regard to 501(c) (3) groups. Eric Holder, the attorney general during part of Barack Obama's administration, dramatically refused to answer questions from a congressional oversight committee regarding his involvement in a covert US operation code-named "Fast and Furious." He is still, as of this writing many years later, technically in contempt of Congress, but he evidently believes his elusiveness was necessary, even in that circumstance.

to know the elusive person, and therefore is a certain type of shyness. Usually, the pathology involved is a sensitivity to being asked anything. The sensitivity and anger often derive from adolescent identity diffusion problems, where any question is sensed as an invasion of autonomy and therefore repulsed. In other words, curiosity by another person is not experienced as an attempt to get closer or to know the person.

The etiology of chronic elusiveness is often found in families where parents did not allow their teenagers to lock their bedroom door. The teenagers therefore were constantly on the lookout for invasions regarding privacy (sense of self) and feared discovery of their masturbatory activity (Blackman & Dring, 2023).

Self-consciousness

Self-conscious people are embarrassed about the way they look and are persistently concerned with what other people think about them. This may not just be regarding dress, but the way they are standing, what they say, and other features of their self-image. The pathology of self-consciousness is often found in the superego, which is continually launching shame attacks toward the self-image.

Clinical vignette: 2

An otherwise successful professional woman sought help for fear of public speaking. While many determinants of this symptom were unearthed during the course of her treatment one particular memory stood out. As a five-year-old girl, she had taken a doll and held it to her chest as though she were breastfeeding. She recalled her mother yelling at her, "Shame! Shame on you! Put that down!" She then internalized the mother's scolding critique and this dynamic played a central role in her adult life inhibition.

Clinical vignette: 3

A middle-aged mother attending a school conference with her husband reacted with anxiety when he spied a coffee machine and offered to get her a cup. She warned, "The coffee pot may just be for faculty." Due to her concerns, the husband asked a nearby school official if the coffee was available for waiting parents. The official responded incredulously, "Of course! What did you think? It's obviously for everyone!" The wife's concern with self-consciousness, in this case, had actually resulted in the husband being mildly humiliated, which was exactly what the wife's self-consciousness had attempted to avoid.

Solitariness

Hermits are shy. They are shy because they are unable to form verbal relationships with others that have any meaning. They wall themselves up in their rooms, in their houses, or in their offices, and have little contact of a meaningful sort with other people. They may be good as radiologists or computer programmers, but their abilities to form a relationship are damaged, and they tend to prefer to be alone. This solitariness is generally caused by object relations problems (although a rare type may symbolically self-incarcerate to relieve unconscious guilt). Very often, there has been a failure to develop a warm symbiosis during the first several months of life, so that the usual glee of the infant, demonstrated by Beebe (2022) in videos of mothers laughing with their four-month-old infants, has not occurred.

Solitary people, if the history is available, barely made it through infancy without dying from anaclitic depression (Spitz & Wolf, 1946). Later relationships tend to reinforce the anxiety they experience in relating. They often, in adulthood, show characteristics of the "low-keyed" infants Mahler and her group described (1975).

Standoffishness

People who are standoffish will interact socially with others but when asked to participate in any activity, will generally refuse. The same pattern can be seen in people who socially warm up, but when they get into close relationships are highly reluctant to engage in sexual relations. The pathology in these cases involves a constellation of defenses. When seen as patients, they are seen to limit themselves to relieve guilt and shame; they also, consciously or unconsciously, take pleasure in rebuffing people who expect more from them (sometimes, these standoffish persons are identifying with someone who teased them).

The frequent sexual activity among teenagers that is, in slang, known as "dry humping" has to do with standoffishness about sexual intercourse. Teenagers will rub on each other, with their clothes on, become sexually excited and even may experience orgasm, but they are standoffish regarding the actual experience of sexual intimacy.

Unassertiveness

Similar to timidity, but not quite as severe, people who are unassertive will take action only if invited to do so.[6] However, they will not initiate action. Initiation of any type of activity is associated with reflexive fear of any type—for example, reality fear, fear of loss of the object, fear of the loss of the object's love, fear of damaging the object, fear of being damaged, fear of being punished or humiliated, and fear of humiliation should any ambitions become known.[7]

Clinical vignette: 4

> In a couple's therapy session, a wife complained that her husband would never initiate sexual activity "even if I parade half-naked in front of him." Her husband's value system, which had been imbued in him as a late adolescent by the high school and university he attended, was that initiating sexual activity without a female's explicit permission constituted a form of rape. Because of his cultural indoctrination, of which his wife had been unaware, and which he had not consciously considered for years, he had failed to initiate sexual relations with her, and she had been too ashamed to mention it to him. (For a masterful description of these types of unconscious shame dynamics, see Levin, 1969a, 1969b.)

---

[6] A satire of this type of shyness was instituted by the Society for the Preservation and Encouragement of Barber Shop Quartet Singing in America (SPEBSQSA), whose members are ethically proscribed from singing unless asked to perform.
[7] See Blackman (2010) for a list of the nineteen types of thought content which can accompany the unpleasurable sympathetic nervous system-based sensations in different types of anxiety.

Withdrawnness

People who are withdrawn are socially nervous. They will attend social functions, but barely talk. They will speak when spoken to, but otherwise, they do not engage in much conversation, and when they do it is superficial. This type of shyness is usually brought about by a particular defense: inhibition of an ego function (Blackman, 2004, Defense #48)—in this case, inhibition of speech. Inhibition of speech can occur when speech takes on symbolic meaning. If speech is unconsciously equated with something sexual, speaking may cause humiliation, which in turn engenders the inhibition. If speech has become emblematic (usually unconsciously) of destructiveness, this may cause guilt, which again results in defensive inhibition of talking. Speech may also have various gender meanings (Gilligan, 2009), which then may cause unconscious conflicts in the person, leading to withdrawal before the conflict is exposed.

Freud gave a remarkable example of this type of inhibition of speech (also involving repression). A single woman patient of Theodore Reik's reported she had been enjoying speaking with men at a party, but could not recall the name of a recent book she had read. Freud figured out that, in the language they were speaking, German, the name of the book, *Ben Hur*, had the same pronunciation as *[Ich] bin hure*, meaning "I am a whore." In other words, the woman would have revealed her sexual "invitation." Freud does not mention shame, since this example precedes superego theory. However, part of the woman's symptom occurred due to her inhibition of her speech function as a defense against that shame (Freud, 1901b).

Nervousness

Shy people who are "nervous" are overwhelmed by anxiety. The pathology involves damage to an ego strength known as affect-tolerance (Blackman, 2010, ch. 7) or "affect-regulation" (Bretherton, 1992). The prototype of this type of person is found in the character Don Knotts portrayed on the *Steve Allen Show* (Knotts, 1960s), who was always very jerky in his responses to people though he humorously, while shaking, screamed that he wasn't nervous. Rather than the pathology being primarily defensive in nature, this type of shyness is associated with being overwhelmed by affect. According to attachment theorists (e.g., Bowlby, 1983), weakness in affect regulation derives from failures, during childhood and adolescence, to develop secure-organized attachments. The ensuing developmental delay results in the observed weakness in containing social anxiety, which in turns interferes with simple interpersonal communication.

Unsociability

This type of shyness is due to a pathological lag in the development of the ego function I call social skill.[8] People like this may be warm, they may be friendly, and they may not even be timid. However, they don't like going to parties, engaging in group discussions, or being in any situation where socializing is required. They can't "network," and typically despise normal activities where social alliances are formed. The usual etiology of this difficulty is a failure to learn social skills somewhere along the way. Unsociable people tend to have parents who did not instruct them about rules of etiquette. Their friends may not have been sociable people. During adolescence, perhaps, they did not get in with a group of other children who were flexibly able to interact with each other (e.g., they hung out with "Goths"). There are different developmental delays which may have contributed to the problem, but they wind up with an attitude which used to be called "antisocial," until that term was expropriated and twisted by the *DSM-III*.

Wariness and distrustfulness

This particular type of shyness is seen in people with paranoid personality disturbances and with paranoid versions of psychotic illnesses—including delusional disorders and paranoid schizophrenia. Since basic trust vs. basic mistrust was described by Erikson (1950) as an epigenetic development during the oral libidinal phase, we know that difficulties during the first two or three years of life may lead to the trust element not developing adequately. Kleinian (1945) theoreticians might formulate

---

[8] For more about this see Blackman (2010, ch. 6).

that the child never moved from the "paranoid/schizoid position" to the "depressive position." Early childhood disturbance in consistent soothing, regardless of one's metapsychological predilection, is destined to cause disturbances in the capacity to trust (Akhtar, 1992, 1994; Blackman, 2017) seen in the adult pathological entities known commonly as schizoid, paranoid, and borderline personality disorders.

Disturbances in soothing seem necessary but not sufficient to describe these etiologies of shyness, however. Mistrust is also caused by poor self and object differentiation during the first several years of life, often amalgamated with other traumatic experiences in simple social situations thereafter. Invasive or neglectful parents during adolescence also cause mistrust (Masterson, 1981). Teenagers growing up in dangerous, unpredictable environments (Meers, 1970) will likely find trusting others difficult.

In our current understanding of paranoid schizophrenia, mistrust seems to occur because there is congenital damage to the integrative function (although the exact etiology of that remains unknown).[9] Because of the difficulty in integrating concepts, reality testing is later damaged, and self and object differentiation does not occur adequately. Balint (1968) called persons with these problems "philobats."

Those who back out

This peculiar kind of shyness is evanescent in its appearance in one individual. People with this type of character do get involved with other people and they do become involved in activities. But at clutch times, when they need to do their part, they withdraw or do not keep promises previously made. This oscillatory shyness is most often due to pathological ambivalence about any type of interaction. Sometimes the etiology of this ambivalence can be found in people who harbor "superego

---

[9] Some of the more persuasive research on this matter has been done by Burket and Deutsch (2019) and implicates various intracerebral glutamate and glycine metabolic pathways. MacLean's (1990) *Triune Brain* illustrates how millions of cells, having different mammalian and reptilian anlage, no doubt act in conjunction with each other to produce both normal and abnormal thinking. This exponentially complex, and no doubt more accurate approach to human mentation has been admirably pursued more recently by Inna Rozentsvit (2023).

lacunae" (Johnson & Szurek, 1952) or, alternatively, an "unintegrated" superego (Ticho, 1972). Clinically, such individuals welch on their responsibilities without remorse[10]; that is, they "shy away" from reliability, resulting in an attitudinal problem which can disturb all their relationships and sometimes get them in trouble at work. People who cheat on their spouses but are highly moral in other areas of their lives fit this pattern (see Blackman, 2018). Object-coercive doubting (Kramer, 1983) is not only seen in children but is characteristic of adults suffering with obsessive-compulsive personality disturbances (not complicated by borderline personality organization or psychosis (Blackman, 2013a)).

Those who get scared off

Certain types of shyness are healthy. When an adult has made a judgment about danger, that adult may "shy away" from an activity which, in reality, is likely to be dangerous. This type of decision making, based on intact functions of judgment, relationship to reality, anticipation of consequences, and executive functioning, should not be confounded with the persistent character trait of shyness (which could be based on one of the many pathologies described above). Specifically, people who are not scared enough in certain situations may be denying a danger (Blechner, 2007), yet still experience unexplainable phobic-type anxiety. In more complex situations, counterphobic defenses exacerbate denial by way of an act (A. Freud, 1936). By definition (Blackman, 2010, ch. 6), judgment, reality-based anticipation of consequences, and the executive function (decision making) are late developing mental functions which can undergo inhibition or destruction under certain circumstances, leading to tragic endings. Paul Schilder, a famous neurologist-psychoanalyst, for example, was unfortunately killed when he was run over by an automobile in New York City. He was not sufficiently assessing the danger of standing off of the curb, on a street in Manhattan, where taxis drive wildly. Possibly better known is the incident of John F. Kennedy, Jr., who flew his private plane at night although he had had no instruction about "flying on instruments."

---

[10] For a scholarly dissertation on remorse vs. regret, and other variations, see Akhtar (2017).

He, his wife, and other members of his family tragically died in the ensuing crash, which apparently was brought on, at least partly, by his failure to use judgment about the real danger.

Tentativeness

Again, being tentative about something may be a healthy function. "Fools rush in where angels fear to tread" (Ricky Nelson's 1963 take on the poem of Alexander Pope) is a song that depicts the problem if someone is not tentative. Assessment of consequences, judgment about danger, using executive function regarding aggression and sexuality, employing impulse control and using fantasy as trial action—all are functions which reasonably should be brought to bear before deciding to take any particular action.[11] Without these components of tentativeness, human beings face considerable danger.

Camera shyness

This is a particular symptom concerning resistance to having one's photo taken. Sometimes the shyness about this begins as a resistance in early childhood, when parents are taking too many pictures of their child and the child feels invaded and controlled. In later situations, during middle age, people may have anxiety about a particular activity being documented, whether realistic or not. In octogenarians and nonagenarians, I have noticed conscious resistance to being photographed, in particular in women who don't feel they have maintained the type of beauty necessary for a photograph to be taken. They hate looking at themselves in photographs because they are no longer the youthful person they had been decades previously. In other words, their avoidance of being photographed is a defense against depressive affect. The depressive affect, in turn, combines grief over loss of beauty with narcissistic mortification. Camera shyness in younger people may be due to a reaction formation when shame conflicts with a grandiose and/or sexual wish to be well known and admired. The etiology of camera

---

[11] How quickly the concatenation and integration of these functions occur varies from person to person.

shyness, to summarize, can be due to rebelliousness, due to a defense against depressive affect over loss of beauty, or due to defenses against shame over drive-related wishes.

"Once bitten, twice shy"

This means that once people have had a particularly bad experience, they will likely be hesitant to try something that in any way resembles that painful experience. The exaggerated nature of their avoidance, however, even though based on a reality experience, can be quite an interference in their lives. This phenomenon is seen very often in later middle-aged people who have had a horrible divorce. They may stay sociable and interact with people, but they avoid dating. They resign themselves to a future sexless existence.

Other common examples of this type of shyness occur in people who have suffered trauma. One of my maternal uncles had lived through the massive, insane inflation of the Weimar Republic in Germany.[12] Although Jewish, he also survived the Nazi horrors by working as a stone mason, in Germany, from 1937–1945. He was not bothered by the Nazis because he had a round face and red hair, therefore not comporting with the bigoted stereotyped image the Nazis had of Jews. After World War II was over, he emigrated to the US where he married my mother's sister and began an ultimately successful business. Throughout his work in the US, he shied away from using banks and kept the bulk of his money "under the mattress." One might attribute this type of shyness to transferences from the Weimar Republic and Nazi Germany, where no one could be trusted. His exact dynamics were never clear to me, but he consciously acknowledged that his mistrust of governments had caused him to be leery of trusting banks.

Feminine modesty

Certainly not universal, but very common, most women are shy about undressing in front of other women. This is true of preadolescent and, in particular, early adolescent girls. If forced to undress in the locker

---

[12] For an excellent depiction of that terrible period in history, see Taylor (2015).

room at school, they often hide or find some way to skip gym class. They are vulnerable in their self-esteem regulation and worry about other girls being critical toward them. The criticism is often in regard to competition about ideas of beauty, but beauty is ill defined and may be based on the prevailing social presentations in fashion magazines.

Commonly, these girls are overwhelmed by shame about their bodies, especially after menstruation has begun. Even after decades of positive feminine encouragement in the US, negative attitudes about menstruation persist (Stubbs, 2008). In particular, the sense of smell, which is more sensitive in females than males, makes girls concerned about genital odor.[13] Many girls become disgusted with the menses (superego elements of self-criticism associated with early childhood concerns with being "clean" during toileting). They may then project self-disgust onto others and imagine that others are disgusted with them. A more unconscious element of feminine modesty may derive from the girl's awareness that no matter how beautiful she may wish to be, she will never win her father from her "more beautiful" mother. The recrudescence of such unconscious competitive strivings was discussed by Blos (1966).

In most cultures, mothers and fathers also worry about their daughters' burgeoning exhibitionistic adolescent pleasures. Adults know that male sexual predators exist and may attack a naïve young girl. Statutory rape laws also have this reasoning behind them. In the US today, most subcultures have jettisoned the teaching of modesty to girls, based on a philosophical challenge that females should be accorded the same autonomy and freedom of sexual expression historically given to males who "sow their wild oats." The ultimate results of this cultural change are not, as of this writing, entirely clear.

Socially appropriate restraint

A certain degree of control is required in social situations. Not saying things that offend others, not using foul language, and not being insensitive to other people's feelings all require a certain degree of conscious

---

[13] For decades, commercial companies played upon women's sensitivities to this in marketing such products as FDS, a mildly perfumed "feminine deodorant spray."

control which could be seen as a type of shyness. The opposite of this normal social functioning would be obnoxiousness.

Shyness in new groups

Groups, usually of more than two or three people, present psychological challenges to a new member. These are described by David Levy (1950) in his interesting paper, "The strange hen." Open groups, where there are a lot of new members, often do not present as much of this particular phenomenon. Slavson (1964) perspicaciously formulated that the more cohesive a group is, the longer people have known each other, and the more they know about each other, the more difficult it is for a new person in the group to be included. Almost automatically, most new people in established groups will be shy—that is, somewhat restrained in their verbalizations and offering of opinions.

Most new Federal Cabinet members in the US, most new medical school department heads, and most CEOs begin their terms of office by saying something like, "The first thing I'm going to do is listen to everyone. I need to understand everyone's concerns." Whether this statement is true or not, new leaders tend to say things like this because they are entering a position in a relatively new group, where they may be rejected if they offer their opinions or their attitudes too quickly. In the summer of 1973, as a member of the US Army National Guard Reserves, I was sent to Fort Sam Houston in San Antonio, Texas (Brooke Army Medical Center), to spend my required two weeks on active duty. On the first day, I showed up on time and reported to the colonel, a physician who was the chair of the psychiatry department. Within minutes, there was a department meeting attended by about twenty-five professionals. I sat in the back, quietly.

The meeting proceeded, about what I have no recollection. The colonel did not introduce me, and no one else noticed me. I thought about Levy's "strange hen," realized that the group had not noticed me, and began daydreaming of spending the rest of the day playing tennis and sitting by the pool.

Finally, the meeting ended, and still no one noticed me. I was stoked. The colonel was out the door when one lagging woman glanced behind her, and startled, asked the colonel, "Who is that!?" He then recalled, and haphazardly said, "Oh, Blackman, go down to the clinic; we have some extra patients who need to be seen." I did not make it to the pool that afternoon. But almost.

Conclusion

Shyness can be a conscious, healthy approach to new groups, dangerous situations, or invitations to act which are not clear. On the other end of the spectrum, shyness may be caused by paranoid delusions, where any type of interaction is seen as dangerous, and the person pulls away.

Between these two extremes of normalcy vs. psychosis, there are a variety of situations where people may become shy, and that shyness can have different meanings and will require differential diagnoses. The pathological mechanisms involved may produce character traits or symptoms which can be periodic (preconscious automatisms) or chronic (character traits).

I have attempted to illustrate the many different types of dynamics which can result in the phenomenological trait of shyness. I have also made an effort to explain the wide variations in etiology that can apply. Some types of shyness seem due to damage to object relations development in early childhood or adolescence. Other etiologies of shyness include compromise formations that form at different stages and may coalesce, acutely or chronically, during middle and late adulthood.

CHAPTER FOUR

Outrageousness

Lois W. Choi-Kain

Outrageousness, as a personality trait, has gained an undeniable presence and power in the social, cultural, and political world. Outrageous behaviors capture public attention, escalate visibility, and mobilize robust emotional and social reactions more effectively than almost any other human tendency. Yet there is a notable absence of a coherent definition of what constitutes outrageousness and what are its origins and consequences.

In this contribution I will first attempt to clarify the complex phenomena that constitute outrageousness and then elucidate its ontogenetic roots and evocative aims in contemporary relational scenarios. Following this, I will present a case in detail where outrageousness and its painstaking amelioration played a very significant role in the clinical work. I will conclude by summarizing what I have offered and noting a few areas that require further attention.

Descriptive characteristics

The *Merriam-Webster Collegiate Dictionary* (1993) identifies three main definitions of the word "outrageous," all of which emphasize transgressions of usual expectations and realistic constraints. The first and third emphasize "exceeding the limits of what is usual … not conventional or matter-of-fact" and "going beyond all standards of what is good and right … deficient in propriety and good taste," while the second entry in *Merriam-Webster* includes a "violent or shameful" quality (p. 521). An absence of usual restraint, defiance of social norms and conventions, combined with disregard for factual reality depict what constitutes outrageousness in human functioning.

A global electronic search of the terms "outrageous" and "outrageousness" on the Harvard Online Library Information System (HOLLIS) yields many thousands of entries, spanning artistic, historical, cultural, and legal literatures. Many of these entries are published in the lay press, and many are about notable personalities throughout history. Such entries commonly mention popular culture celebrities (e.g., Zsa Zsa Gabor), stand-up comics (e.g., Don Rickels), and political figures (e.g,. Donald Trump), whose outrageousness fueled their popularity, charisma, and power. In the case of Donald Trump, outrageousness contributed, paradoxically, to his influence over the masses despite grave skepticism about his credentials to serve the public. Political tactics of late have utilized *outrage* rhetoric (Berry & Sobieraj, 2016). Hyperbolic and emotionally provocative, these maneuvers employ fear mongering, flattery, mockery, and conspiracy theories to ignite outrage. While these strategies often incite dysfunctional behavior, they nonetheless succeed in dominating political dialogue.

Only two search entries on HOLLIS appeared from clinical journals. The first of these entries (Welner et al., 2022) proposes an inventory of extreme and outrageous behaviors. Entitled "Distinguishing everyday evil," it defines extreme and outrageous acts in terms of the significant distress or harm caused, legitimizing legal liability for emotional damages. This article's authors conflate outrageousness with evil. The second entry (Billow, 2013) describes a group process in a conference demonstration, reporting how a group therapy expert employs unexpected behaviors to provoke spontaneous interchange among group members. Although the terms "outrageousness" and "outrage" make up the title of this article, these terms are not directly defined, nor do they refer to outrageousness in clinical cases.

The sparseness of clinical description, theorizing, study, and intervention is practically outrageous given that this essential quality of human personality functioning has occupied center stage in the popular and lay press, driving major political and social forums. Outrageousness is also frequently encountered in clinical situations. Consider the following vignettes that outline some specific qualities of outrageousness that highlight its unique dimensions:

Clinical vignette: 1

An accounting professional who is well-compensated frequents a high-end fitness facility. Every few months, he steals a credit card from a stranger's locker to buy a slice of pizza, returning the credit card to its original locale every time.

Clinical vignette: 2

A patient in residential treatment calmly rides in a van to a medical appointment. Upon approaching the office, she screams suddenly and jumps out of the van while it is moving at low speed. Staff fan out looking for her frantically. She is found an hour later cheerfully ordering a pumpkin spice latte at Starbucks, neither distressed, nor concerned.

Clinical vignette: 3

An MBA candidate sees her family therapist after returning from a trip. She politely offers the therapist a postcard of the destination of her travel. The therapist is shocked and outraged to look at the postcard, which is of male pornography.

These vignettes illustrate outrageous behaviors that transgress usual expectations and boundaries, but are not necessarily evil, violent, or impulsive. Consistent with *Merriam-Webster*'s definition, these outrageous behaviors surprise, alarm, and shock others because they "exceed the limits of what is usual," "go beyond all standards of what is good and right," and are "deficient in propriety and good taste" (p. 521). Such behaviors can be evident in the realms of (i) *body* where piercings, tattoos, and sundry alterations can, at times, represent outrageousness, (ii) *attire* where outlandish outerwear with a certain cocky buffoonery can betray underlying outrageousness, (iii) *language* where idiosyncratic acronyms, deliberate mispronunciations, and impish neologisms can be manifestations of outrageousness, and (iv) *interaction* where provocativeness, generational disrespect (e.g., a medical student addressing the school's dean by his or her first name), and misplaced seductiveness can be signs of underlying outrageousness.

A critical feature common to all these manifestations is their production of outrage in *others*. Those who behold outrageousness find the disregard for reality, reason, usual boundaries, and consequences bewildering. It often leaves spectators uncertain of how intentional or clueless such actions are. Because of this, it propels feelings of needing to do something due to the lack of concern or insight the outrageous individual appears to have.

Three psychodynamic configurations

Psychoanalytic Electronic Publishing Web (PEP-Web) is a magisterial compendium consisting of citations from 125 years of psychoanalytic literature. Surprisingly, however, it yields only one article with the term "outrageousness" in its title. This is the paper "Outrageousness, compliance, and authenticity" by Masud Khan (1986). In it, Khan describes outrageousness as an "affective ego state" (p. 629) which should be considered a discrete clinical syndrome. He presents a clinical case of a fastidious and contained patient who elicited a countertransferential outrage, with his combination of outward compliance and an active concealment of authenticity. Khan interpreted the patient's tendency to be "quietly spiteful … provoking others to be outrageous" (p. 648) as rooted in an early experience of abrupt maternal demands to be contained, independent, and tidy. Notably there was an absence of overtly outrageous behavior in Khan's patient; instead there was a transference dynamic involving outrage. Khan distinguished outrageous behavior from what is prone to be labelled as narcissistic or psychopathic:

> I have come to the conclusion that the restriction of spontaneity in infant/child care results in adolescence in outrage/outrageousness, whether it is a devious affective ego state which cumulatively gathers, not all that unconsciously, in a person, and expresses itself in various ways which are erroneously labelled psychopathic character, narcissistic neurosis, etc. It is the clinical handling of these patients that is so difficult, because interpretation is an alibi the analyst uses to cover his incapacity to cope with the patient's conduct. (p. 643)

According to Khan, these acts are generally not amenable to traditional interpretation, but call for "hold[ing]" and a restraint of interpretation.

A broader search of mentions of the "outrageous" in PEP-Web yields mostly irrelevant entries, many of which ironically discuss Masud Khan's personal outrageousness (Goldman, 2003; Guarton, 1999; Hopkins, 1998; Orcutt, 2019) or that of other historical figures including, to wit, Freud and Lacan (Dorsey, 1992; Luepnitz, 2009), and generally outrageous behavior in politics (I. Brenner, 2021; Prince, 2022). Many papers explicitly describe this or that behavior in treatment as outrageous but none of these addresses outrageousness as a distinct clinical phenomena.

Three of the articles yielded in the search were contributed by Akhtar (1995, 2014, 2015a). He noted that borderline patients use self-harm and outrageousness "as both an attempt at self-delineation and hostile connection with others" (1995, p. 585). He also related outrageousness to Winnicott's (1956) concept of the "antisocial tendency," as a reflection of unconscious hope in actions that powerfully invite the environment to respond in a reparative way.

Anchoring my proposals in these ideas as well as in Kernberg's (1970) psychoanalytic classification of character pathology, I suggest that "outrageousness" can emanate from three different levels and embody three different aims. These are, (i) guilt-ridden masochistic aims, (ii) growth seeking optimistic aims, and (iii) destructive narcissistic and sociopathic aims.

Masochistic outrageousness

This type of outrageousness is occasionally evident in otherwise stable, mildly "neurotic," and "higher-level" (Kernberg, 1970) personalities. Their identities are intact and their defenses revolve around repression. Their conflicts arise from unresolved oedipal strivings including prohibited sexual object choices and profound conflicts with authority. The dynamics of such outrageousness was actually detailed by Freud (1916d) in a section of the paper titled "Some character-types met with in psycho-analytic work." The pertinent section was devoted to individuals Freud thought had become "criminal from the sense of guilt." Freud proposed that such people carried deeply buried guilt (over their incestuous and parricidal wishes) and deliberately committed objectionable acts to get punished by proxy.

While Freud emphasized the oedipal roots of unconscious guilt in such individuals, the fact is that other roots of guilt (e.g., survivor guilt, separation guilt) can also result in their punishment-seeking behaviors. Regardless of the etiology, most such individuals respond well to dynamic psychotherapy and a select few might be suitable for psychoanalysis proper.

Optimistic outrageousness

The second variety is perhaps most commonly encountered in clinical practice. This type of outrageousness is associated with the "intermediate level" (Kernberg, 1970) of character pathology. It generally arises from loose interfamilial boundaries and from a deprivation trauma that leaves the child (and later, the adult) searching for reparation and repair.

What Winnicott (1956) called the "antisocial tendency" probably best describes the development and interpersonal relevance of such outrageousness. What defines acts constituting this outrageousness is a grotesque transgression of social norms and expectations. The most extreme of these actions can be criminal or illegal. But not all criminal or illegal behavior is outrageous. Rather, outrageousness, like the "antisocial tendency," "is characterized by *an element in it which compels the environment to be important*" (p. 309, italics in the original). Overtly, these behaviors may challenge interpersonal connectedness. Winnicott, though, emphasizes that these actions are object seeking, or at their core interpersonally active, and therefore an expression of hope.

Assessing outrageousness clinically is helped by an understanding of the antisocial tendency, which is a reaction to an object that becomes depriving or disappears altogether from the child's interpersonal orbit. Knowing this can distinguish outrageousness from more malignant strains of narcissism or sociopathy. Even with such knowledge, our reflexive tendency to reject, rebuke, or withdraw from such behaviors challenges our capacities to maintain a hopeful position. Psychotherapy alone is therefore not a solution to this problem. A combination of a supportive realistic environment (e.g., familial, occupational/academic) and psychotherapy is critical to providing adequate holding for the outrageous individual. Such holding not only supports the weak, action-prone ego but also helps resume the developmental process by which a person can evolve the capacity to contain their impulses, reflect upon them, and act in more socially acceptable ways.

The challenge to this holding function has to do with the paradoxical tension between attachment-seeking and destructiveness inherent in the outrageous act. The outrageous person is looking for a basic need to be met, but does so maladaptively, straining the stability of the environment to contain it. These tendencies manifest as a nuisance, that is making a mess of things, that disrupts the implicit order of how the world works. A child, though, needs to be supportively socialized to bear the failures of the environment and the realistic sacrifices of growing up. In Winnicott's (1956) words,

> Briefly, the treatment of the antisocial tendency is not psychoanalysis. It is the provision of childcare which can be rediscovered by the child, and into which the child can experiment again with the id impulses, which can be tested. It is the stability of the new environmental provision which give the therapeutics ... [W]hen the patient is a deprived child ego relatedness must derive support from the therapist's side of the relationship. [I]t is the environment that must give new opportunity for ego relatedness since the child has perceived that it was an environmental failure in ego support that originally led to the antisocial tendency. (p. 315)

Winnicott's explication of the *nuisance value* of these tendencies as hopeful might engage therapeutic curiosity and patience enough to not squander the hopeful developmental opportunity at hand.

Another important contribution in this context is that of Casement (1985). He admires the way patients intuitively seek the support and opportunities they need for recovery. Such "unconscious hope" is healthy, distinct from "hope which is projected—when one may 'carry' hope on behalf of another ... [or] unrealistic expectations" (p. 293). Rather, it is "an unconscious search (or hope) for what is needed to meet unmet needs, and that parents and analysts are given clues to what is needed in behavior, and even in some forms of defense or pathology" (p. 293). Under such circumstances, the job of the therapist lies in containing the outward behaviors and attendant affects related to such needs, by tolerating being used as a good and bad object without "collapsing or retaliating" (p. x). Some examples Casement offers illustrate the needs children have of others in the context of their growth. Risky behaviors may elicit a needed proximity to ensure safety while a child is discovering his or her mobility. Tantrums require parental firmness, stability, and containment to aid tolerance of frustration. Parental attention is the solution to this unconscious search for meeting a need to be attended to, but enacted in a way that temptingly invites punishment and hopeless rejection.

Conflicts derived from developmental failures are repeated and worked through via the role-responsiveness of the therapist, who will need to retread the path of caregiving failures to express rage and protest to enable the patient to reflectively represent an earlier experience. Projective identification is another means of a need to share difficult aspects of self-experience that "cannot be managed alone" (p. 304). Whether what is projected is hurt, despair, or other intense affect states, the therapist will need to manage the resulting countertransference to sustain hope in the challenging moments of treatment. "What the patient needs is to find someone who can bear really being in touch with the patient's extremes of personal difficulty without having to give up, someone who (without being unrealistic or trying to be omnipotent) can find some way to see the patient through" (p. 307). In simple terms, Casement reminds us that seeing a patient through difficult times, understanding their hopeful search for unmet needs, and helping them bear the disappointments of such needs and reality more broadly, contributes to a process whereby unconscious hope is met.

Sadistic outrageousness

This type of outrageousness is associated with "lower-level" (Kernberg, 1970) character pathology. These are individuals with severely disturbed identities, defenses centering upon splitting, and egos suffused with destructive aggression. Malignantly narcissistic and antisocial characters (Kernberg, 1984, 2007) display a callous, exploitative, and hostile outrageousness that borders on becoming criminal. Any attempt at treating such individuals must subsume measures to "spoil" the pleasure (conscious or unconscious) in their ego-syntonic ruthlessness.

Only then might that become amenable to traditional psychotherapeutic interventions. Even then the involvement of social and legal agencies in their management might not be avoidable.

A detailed clinical illustration

Thomas was amid applications to transfer schools while on medical leave from university, where he had completed two semesters. An only child, he had been very gifted compared to his peers in his hometown. Thomas had been recruited by several schools for his national rankings as a top fencer, as well as his unusual aptitude at learning obscure foreign languages. He had been accepted to his school of choice in "early decision," in a binding agreement, while simultaneously being heavily recruited by other schools. Thomas neither returned his "early decision" paperwork nor did he withdraw his applications to other schools. His parents and school counselors became frantic. Despite the pressure his parents and school counselors put on him, he could not make a confident decision and delayed filing required paperwork past all deadlines, only to decide to fulfill the early decision agreement as a path of least resistance.

In the fall of his freshman year, Thomas had trouble fitting in socially, failing to find a social group in which he felt he belonged. Insecure and lonely, Thomas called his parents several times daily, frantic for direction about how he was to complete his assignments. His mother spent a considerable amount of time and energy coaching him over the phone. Despite his panic, Thomas was able to make the Dean's List in his first two semesters. Yet, he decided to go on medical leave for depression at the end of his freshman year. He was referred to me for a consultation during this time.

When I first met Thomas, he was attractive and well-dressed. He presented casually, but in an effortful way. He was aloof, waiting for me to take the lead. He answered my questions honestly, but with little expansion or spontaneous conversation about any topic explored. He described being unable to settle a decision around returning to university as well as any alternatives he might pursue instead.

After this very sparse conversation, Thomas decided to move into the area to be able to pursue more intensive treatment. There was an absence of adequate discussion of the treatment, its framework, and our respective roles and expectations. The first few months of treatment were chaotic. Thomas undertook projects and plans, some of which he did not start and all of which he did not finish. He had recurrent difficulty being on time for appointments, at times being more than an hour late. Initially, he was staying with relatives at quite some distance and had to drive to my office. Then, to make attending appointments easier, he attempted to live with friends in a local college dorm. He concocted a bizarre solution to not having key card access to the building, and asked his friends to take turns leaving their identification cards in crack between bricks in the building. There was a cycle of reinvention of solutions doomed to fail, and onslaughts of advice by parents who expressed more anxiety and frustration than Thomas over the situation.

These difficulties were not exactly described by Thomas but did became obvious gradually. He repeatedly sought direction, with poor follow through. Over time, his individual therapy was overrun with reporting of crises regarding his participation in treatment as well as his applications for transfer. His treatment was more observational than therapeutic in the sense that very little progress was made by either of us reflectively. He never managed to overcome his indecision, but rather the decisions seemed to happen by external processes. In the treatment, things just seemed to unfold. But, we were able to observe the tendencies of the patient, specifically in his interactions with his family and other environments. We learned the following from the family therapy, which was mostly attended by Thomas's mother and rarely by his father.

The parents were both educated and successful professionals. Michael (the father) grew up in a well-resourced family and had few complaints of his early life. Jennifer (the mother) described growing up in a situation of neglect and had diminished her professional activities later in her life when they had Thomas. She wanted to provide Thomas a childhood that was the opposite of hers, one in which she had felt she was unnoticed and unimportant. Meanwhile, father's career was booming, while his physical health was unstable. With most of his energies devoted to his work, Michael was frequently absent from the home. Jennifer and Thomas were tightly bonded. Jennifer was a devoted mother and Thomas thrived in most activities he pursued. But there was one area of concern. At bedtime, Jennifer continued to tuck Thomas in at night through almost all of his life into puberty. He insisted she lie down in his bed to help him sleep, no matter what time it was. At times, he went into his parents' bedroom to get his mother for this reason. According to Thomas, around the time he was struggling to make a decision about college, he entered his parents' bedroom seeking his mother for their bedtime routine. Both parents became frustrated and attempted to make him leave, ending in a physical struggle between Thomas and his father. He expressed feeling deep pain when his parents, in the heat of the moment, exclaimed hating him and wishing he was never born.

This nighttime family conflict occurred in the spring of his senior year of high school; Thomas was seventeen years old then. The next day, Thomas agreed to the early decision university verbally, when school officials called seeking an answer on the spot. When he started college, he developed a habit of being in touch with his mother, talking to her nightly, around bedtime. The more depressed he became, the more involved his parents were. Thomas described feeling completely immobilized at his first university, and felt anxious socially. His mother spent hours each evening helping him write papers and complete assignments. When this became unsustainable, his parents arranged medical leave for Thomas.

Family therapy was incorporated into his treatment. His parents' anxiety exceeded that of Thomas's; they were prone to both be outraged by Thomas's disregard for deadlines and needy indecisiveness. Dr. S the family therapist mostly focused on encouraging Jennifer in establishing boundaries with Thomas, which became fraught with angry and desperate protests by him. It was clearly very challenging for both of them to manage separation. Michael would respond logically, critically, and without much affect about what Thomas should be doing, but his contributions were generally disregarded. Frequently, Jennifer rolled her eyes when Michael spoke, which he would do slowly and without affect.

Thomas was accepted by a handful of other Ivy League universities for transfer, but did not reply to any correspondences or deadlines for enrollment. Somehow, he managed to enroll in both a new university while also reversing his medical leave at his prior one. Outrageously, Thomas attended two universities—located in two different cities—at once in the first month, strategically scheduling flights, trains, and Ubers to travel the distance between them.

It was not until this became totally unsustainable that he settled on transferring to the new university. There, he met a woman in his class who introduced him to the social scene there. They started dating for the entire course of his time there. At this second university, Thomas began thriving socially and academically. He did not experience another depressive episode. While he remained anxious from time to time, he did not continue with treatment while at this second university. He graduated with a very large network of friends, some maintained from high school, many developed in college, across diverse social cliques. He accepted a good professional position in a financial services training program locally, moved back to the area, and moved in with his girlfriend.

During the COVID-19 pandemic, Thomas contacted me again. Now twenty-six, he had become depressed again. His college girlfriend had broken up with him, complaining that his dependency was exhausting. Thomas was unhappy with his professional position and anxiously seeking a new, better job. He was back on the job market, while applying a minimal amount of effort in his ongoing position. Jennifer resumed regularly coaching him through these difficulties with his work and his girlfriend, strategizing different approaches to meeting his goals.

When Thomas resumed treatment, all clinical work was occurring remotely due to pandemic restrictions. It took some time to establish a workable frame for treatment as we all adjusted to the shifting demands of working from home in transitions between total and partial lockdown. Over time, I realized Thomas was online for other work meetings on mute while on sessions with me. His management of sessions became more regularly irregular. He had sessions while driving, taking the subway, and walking around the city. In the sessions he did attend, he would ask for directions or skills, with very little introspection or reflective consideration of his experience. He remained aloof, detached, and concrete in his dialogue with me, but was eager to change and answered my questions honestly.

After six weeks of increasingly erratic and outrageous excuses for his poor or delayed attendance to sessions, I told Thomas I was skeptical treatment could be successful in the way it was going. I reset the treatment framework, requiring predictable attendance at sessions, indoors and in a quiet place where he was able to talk more freely without distraction. I re-involved his parents as well, who were even more worried about

Thomas than when he was in college. His continued dependency on them was more concerning than before, and took on a more outrageous flavor. When he visited home, he was intrusive and needy with Jennifer, but domineering and bullying towards Michael who already had a number of medical issues, having received a diagnosis of cancer. Michael was demoralized and frustrated with the family situation, stating he felt like an occupant in Jennifer and Thomas's house. He yearned for a better relationship with his only child. While he was prone to be indecisive in his own life, Thomas was dictatorial and rigid about what he and his parents ate when together or where they went on vacation, often selecting obscure restaurants and geographical destinations that were exotic and poorly suited for Michael with his physical limitations. By this time, Jennifer was more cognizant of and bothered by the way Thomas occupied a wedge between her and Michael. Michael's prognosis involved a likely decline in five years and mother felt more conflict about not taking better care of her husband when busy tending to Thomas. In our discussions of Thomas's ongoing problems, Jennifer was quick to say "It's my fault" in a declarative and non-reflective but guilty way, as if she occupied not only all the responsibility for Thomas's outrageousness, but also as though there were finally no solution.

After involving his parents, and intermittently meeting with the three of them to help them understand his needs, and the developmental process of helping him bear the times such needs go unmet, Thomas became more concerned about his behavior towards his father. He expressed more clearly not wanting his parents to know he was grown up. Thomas found his own bullying act towards his father exhausting, but did not know how to manage himself otherwise. At times, I felt outraged by this, given that his father was so physically frail. Thomas wanted to relate to his parents differently. I advised the parents to be more curious about what emotional rather than material or problem-solving needs Thomas was seeking when being a mess or a nuisance.

Thomas was hired into a new firm, and faced negative feedback from his first position upon leaving it. He was stunned and resentful that his boss had been negative about his performance, attributing it to anger that Thomas had decided to leave. We discussed the reality of his disengagement, tendency to pretend to be working at times when he was not, and resultant unresponsiveness and unreliability. When he transferred to his new position, Thomas made efforts to be more responsible and invested, prioritizing being available to work on projects when needed, instead of being aloof and elusive. He slowed down his frenetic social activities, and spent more time alone. He expressed more shame and distress about his tendency to make a mess of things, and was more tolerant of thinking about the meaning of these problems rather than constantly seeking solutions to them. Thomas began to decline help from his mother increasingly, expressing to her that he needed to cope with his own problems. Freed up a bit from his dependency on her, Jennifer spent more time with Michael, as did Thomas intermittently. Then Michael retired from his job and his parents decided to spend winters in a distant location with better weather. Thomas and I discussed this transition, working on containing his urge to dictate their planning. While he expressed little sadness or anxiety directly tied to their imminent move away, he began to describe feeling unrooted in life. He expressed this more directly to his parents who appreciated more meaningful dialogue with him. They were increasingly less anxious and guilty about leaving for the winter, and without crisis from Thomas, were able to do so.

Back to theory

Thomas's case confirms the two foundational assumptions of psychoanalytic understanding of psychopathology (i) *the principle of overdetermination* (Freud & Breuer, 1895d) which states that all human behavior is the product of many causative elements and not the result of one simple antecedent, and (ii) *the principle of multiple function* (Waelder, 1936) which states that all human behavior has many purposes and leads to many consequences.

More specifically Thomas's case illustrates that three types of outrageousness (i.e., masochistic, optimistic, and sadistic) cannot be surgically separated: mixed forms are frequent and Thomas's case contains the elements of both masochistic and optimistic types of outrageousness. His behaviors were not impulsive, generally illegal, or intentionally malignant. However, his disregard for deadlines, formal procedures, and basic expectations was bewildering in the face of many well-developed islands of high functioning. His outrageousness was obvious to few, but represented his ongoing resistance to taking care of himself, and was consistently met with the re-involvement of his parents. Thomas's behavior was always more distressing to his parents than to him, and effectively *compelled them to be important*. The problem was that his outrageousness would involve them in a regressive way that they tended to resolve for him, instead of helping him learn to manage differently. Initially, the family were not reflective and could not discuss this beyond concrete terms. But confrontation and interpretation in the individual work with Thomas was ineffective, and like with his parents' problem solving, represented in me an intolerance of his behavior and a directive to stop making a mess of his life. In line with Winnicott's (1956) observation, individual therapy could not in and of itself be sufficient to help Thomas. Facing disappointing limitations of reality, related to his own potential, his family's ability to erase his problems, and my inability to change him was a realization that was contained by upholding a consistent treatment frame while also supporting the family to maintain boundaries in a way that was neither retaliatory nor collapsing.

Maintaining this "holding environment" (Winnicott, 1960) with a patient and confident attitude that Thomas could take better care of his affairs and find a way to grow up was challenging. It was difficult to discern covert optimism in his decisions, and much easier to express alarm, skepticism, and even outrage in the face of his usual ways of managing responsibilities. While his narcissistic issues made it tempting to focus on his personality pathology, maintaining a view that his symptoms were as Casement (1985) indicated, an intuitive opportunity to seek out health through resolution of an unmet need proved more effective in fostering an engagement in treatment that could be reparative. Refraining from criticizing, punishing, or protecting him from his obvious destructive potential was necessary to minimize rejection as he was still needing the devoted care of his parents, in the pressures to grow his autonomy and accept their inevitable unavailability. His reluctance to accept being grown up and transition more responsibly to university or jobs, was only fueled by the outrage, anxiety, and disapproval his behavior generated despite his clear potential and capabilities.

Thomas's adolescent-like push and pull between regressive and progressive ego trends recapitulated what were most likely his childhood difficulties with attachment and separation (recall his early difficulty in falling asleep and needing his mother's help to do so). There was perhaps also an oedipal element to his psychic make-up. A "weak" and rejected father and a desired and indulgent mother perhaps fueled Thomas's oedipal defiance, rendering him to be an indolent victor who did not need to make much effort to achieve his goals. Nonetheless, unconscious guilt at such victory resulted to self-destructive behaviors that existed in parallel with barely suppressed irreverence.

This brings us full circle back to the fact that outrageousness as a dimension of personality is not diagnostically specific. Thomas's problem had both preoedipal and oedipal roots. It was more isolated and contained than that of most individuals operating at a borderline level of personality functioning. He was able to develop meaningful stable friendships, be devoted to a romantic partner, and be himself socially. However, in transitional moments in his life, Thomas demonstrated outrageousness in the process of increasing his autonomy while also signaling to his parents a sort of helpless and hostile dependency. What I feel he and his family needed was assistance to rework and better navigate these moves towards independence with diminished acts of intervention and increased patience, hope, and confidence. Both parties (Thomas and his parents) needed to firm up their own intrapsychic separateness but also their interpersonal (specially generational) boundaries. Important in this process was a confidence too that Thomas could survive making mistakes and learning from them, so long as the parents did not continue to feel responsible and therefore outraged at his repeated nuisances and messes. This helped Thomas see the messes as his own, be more concerned about himself, and reflect more on what he wanted to do about them.

Coda

Outrageousness remains an unlit dimension of human functioning and social interchange. Irreducible to basic temperament or a categorical diagnosis, it represents a psychological signal of unmet needs and an opportunity for reparative experiences to complete the process of growing up. It can also reflect oedipal defiance perpetuated by poorly enforced generational boundaries in the family. While the clinical literature remains curiously limited on this subject, this chapter has aimed to provide a review of the important directions of clinical thinking available, predominantly using Winnicott's concept of the "antisocial tendency" and Casement's concept of "unconscious hope." These clinical scenarios challenge empathy for the patient's dilemma by provoking outrage and related impulses to punish or rescue. But what is required is openness to retread a developmental dilemma and reflect more faith and confidence in the possibility of growth with proper holding, limit-setting, and benevolent provision of ego support.

Before concluding, two other matters need to be mentioned. The first pertains to gender and the second to culture. While knowledge of how outrageousness is affected by these two variables is lacking, it is tempting to speculate that owing to greater propensity for action and outward discharge of aggression, males might show more outrageousness than females. Similarly, one can assume that a behavior regarded outrageous in one culture might not be deemed so in another. Insofar as this is true, there might be more phenotype variations of outrageousness than we are aware of. Such caveats notwithstanding, the fact is that outrageousness exists and is hard to overlook regardless of its appearance in social and clinical circumstances. Indeed, to ignore it, even under the guise of being tolerant and forgiving, might have adverse consequences. However, all is not doom and gloom in this realm. A proverbial silver lining to the cloud is provided by the fact that a modicum of outrageousness, in the setting of talent, can enhance creativity. W. H. Auden's quip that "there is no creativity without audacity" represents this very perspective. It opens up the possibility that myriad forms of creativity, ranging from the perspectival juxtapositions of Pablo Picasso and George Braque to the magical surrealism of Gabriel Garcia Marquez and Salman Rushdie, might be the products of that paradoxical capacity of the mind that one can only designate "civilized outrageousness."

PART II

Mostly private

PART II

CHAPTER FIVE

Shallowness

Michael Civin

My first lesson in psychoanalysis came at six years old or maybe seven, standing next to my father at the edge of the shockingly deep blue waters of Crater Lake in south-central Oregon. Generally, his passion for mathematics—hen-tracks scribbled across every possible piece of paper—led him into abstractions so obscure that they bore no direct connection with my daily life. However, when we were hiking in the mountains or on vacation, he loved to explain the physics behind things like the blueness of the lake's water. I was six and naturally, I had no ability, let alone desire, to understand a word of what he was describing. Still, I remember one thing very clearly; he said that the lake had no inlet or outlet and that rainfall and melted snow filled a crater that plunged into the interiors of the earth, the remnant of a volcano that had erupted eons ago. And, he told me the lake was unfathomably deep. Of course, I had no idea what "unfathomably" meant, only that he often said to my mother with unmistakable contempt, "I can't fathom what it is you're talking about," so I gathered that it must have something to do with not being able to understand. Tentatively I slid my foot toward the water, bent down and reached in. I imagined my arm growing longer and longer, even longer than my father's, stretching into the interiors of the earth. But the water hadn't even reached my elbow before my fingers jammed into slimy gook covering sharp stones underneath. I yelped and, arm still in the water, defiantly announced to my father that the water of the lake wasn't deep at all. Quite patiently, if not more than a bit patronizingly, he explained that here, near the shore, the water was still quite shallow, but that if I were to move out toward the center of the lake, the bottom of it would get deeper and deeper and that by the time I reached the center I would be so far above its depths that I would have no idea where its bottom might be. Just then, from some distance behind us, I heard my mother shouting, "Paul, get his arm out of the water! It's dangerous! He could fall in! Who knows what's down there!" Before my father could speak, I yanked my arm out of the water. I remember that I shrank back in terror for a moment, forgetting my father's words and my own experience, and imagining myself sinking into the "unfathomable" depths of a lake with no bottom or having my arm swallowed whole by some monstrous creature.

However frightened I may have been, it couldn't have lasted more than a few seconds, because my attention almost immediately shifted to hundreds, maybe even thousands of brilliantly colorful bugs skipping endlessly back and forth on the surface of the lake, each leap creating a tiny ripple in the deep blue water. And behind them, jutting out of the water like an iceberg, the peak of Wizard's Island defied everything my father had told me.

This vignette from my childhood illustrates that even a six or seven year old intuitively experiences "shallow," "superficial," and "deep" to signify fundamentally differing phenomena. "Superficial" can exist at the surface over shallow or deep, while "shallow" suggests that nothing deeper lies below and surface spreads out above. This is the topography that we know in our everyday wanderings.

Freud (1915b) wrote, "Life is impoverished, it loses in interest, when the highest stake in the game of living, life itself, may not be risked. It becomes as *shallow and empty* as, let us say, an American flirtation" (p. 290, italics added). Even if, perhaps, it may stray a bit afield from Freud's intent, when we follow this single sentence we stumble onto a pathway that leads to a panoramic psychoanalytic vista overlooking a crisis in our contemporary world and its significance, not only for psychoanalytic practice, but also for a psychoanalytic contribution to attenuating this societal emergency, at least for our patients and those others whose lives they touch.

My aim here is to explore complex relationships among differing versions of "shallow" and risking "the highest stake in the game of living, life itself." I propose that: (a) "shallow" in the sense of my childhood experience at Crater Lake is Euclidean in nature and, as such, stands at variance with the "shallow" of psychic topography; (b) at least in the sense of Freud's first topography, no human being is topographically shallow; (c) and as a corollary, from a psychoanalytic perspective, "shallow" stands in stark and significant contrast to "superficial"; (d) remaining superficial has alternative forms, one that involves "operational thinking" (Marty & de M'Uzan, 1963, p. 345) and one that repudiates thinking altogether; (e) the latter increasingly describes an unfortunate way of being, perhaps more prevalent here in America than elsewhere; (f) the "shallow and empty" of Freud's American flirtation derives from a virtual vacuum, left in the plunder of the "paternal order" and absent of representation, below superficial in its relationship to deep, and (g) from a psychoanalytic perspective, this absence in "shallow and empty" differs fundamentally from the "shallows" of vibrant preconscious activity, the potential space of vitalizing experience that resides at the heart of psychoanalysis. I use clinical and literary vignettes to flesh out these ideas.

The Euclidean "shallow" and the topographic "shallow"

In the first six books of Euclid's *Elements* (c. 300 BC, pp. 1–156), he articulates the fundamental principles of plane and, in books XI through XIII (pp. 367–449) those of solid geometry. The specific postulates of his theory of geometry figure less here than the backdrop to them, what we now think of as the X, Y, and Z axes of the three-dimensional world in which we locate our experience at any point in time. In this Euclidean construction, space is definitively defined. Three numbers, one for a position on each axis, are together necessary and sufficient to locate any person or object. If we were to articulate the superficial, it would be the plane in which Y = 0, while X and Z extend without limit in all quadrants. While shallow is perhaps not quite so specific, presumably it would be constituted by something like $-a > y > -b$, where $b > a > 0$, with X and Z still extending without limit in all quadrants. Odd as it may seem in a psychoanalytic chapter, this algebraic intrusion highlights the cold precision of the Euclidean. In other words, less mathematically symbolized through axes and coordinates, a three-dimensional view of "shallow" articulates some space below the surface but with a hard-stop limited depth. This is the Crater Lake that I experienced near the shoreline and, as a rule, water's border with land captures this concept clearly. In Ingmar Bergman's (1951) stunning tragic-romance, *Sommarlek* (*Illicit Interlude*), Marie, now an older successful ballerina, re-experiences her first love. As a fifteen year old, she enjoyed a brief frolic through life that came to an abrupt end when her young lover, Henrik, dove off a cliff and suffered fatal injuries because the water below was too shallow. We will return to this vignette shortly.

The post-Euclidean

Time

Beyond Euclid, the idea of adding a fourth dimension has a long history, but, of course, it was Albert Einstein, in his articulation of the special theory of relativity (1905, pp. 253–274), who left the world with the indelible imprint of complexities of *time* as this fourth dimension. If in fact Einstein's descriptions of *spacetime* complicate a straightforward appreciation of X, Y, Z, and T, they compel the location of a person or object to include time.

Quite mysteriously, after a particularly difficult time in her professional life, the contemporary Marie receives a diary in the mail. Opening it, she discovers that it is Henrik's diary from years before, leading up to the time immediately prior to his death. She is shocked into a world of recollections of the past, including the events of Henrik's accident, diving *back then* into the far too shallow water.

Cause and effect

The concept of cause and effect in Western thought dates back at least to Plato: "Everything that becomes or changes must do so owing to some cause; for nothing can come to be without a cause" (c. 360 BC,

28a4–6, c2–3). Plato's focus was on the causes that produce the effect of being. Aristotle (1984) developed the notion further by introducing the "negative" logical stance: "something without which the thing would not be."[1] If Henrik had not dived from the cliffs that day and in that place, he would not have plunged to his death in the shallow waters.

The first topography and "shallow"

Up to this point, I have focused on the Euclidean/post-Euclidean version of "shallow", the shallow near the shore of Crater Lake and off the cliffs of that Swedish island. If we turn our attention now to Freud's first topography, the model of the mind he first set forth in *The Interpretation of Dreams* (1900a), we find an entirely differing concept of "shallow." In his foundational paper "The unconscious" (1915c, pp. 159–190), Freud tells us about a topographical model that describes a *depth psychology* (p. 173) and that clinical experience reveals an Unconscious with neither time nor space.[2] "To sum up: exemption from mutual contradiction, primary process … timelessness and replacement of external by psychical reality—these are the characteristics which we may expect to find in processes belonging to the system *Ucs*" (p. 187). Ironically, but unavoidably because it must be communicated through the written word, the description of this first topographic model is incontrovertibly Euclidean. But this depiction of

---

[1] *Aitia*, as he termed them (borrowing from a long history in Greek thinking), are the inferred structural facts responsible for an outcome and are opposed to *prophaseis*, which are the observable antecedents that in and of themselves have no causal inferential status. Of course, the concept of causality has progressed through many twists and turns within Western philosophy, notably via Aquinas, Descartes, Newton, Kant, and Mill, with relatively recent challenges to its essential nature through the quantum physics built on the foundation of Einstein, Bohr, and Heisenberg.

[2] In *The Unconscious as Infinite Sets* (1975), Ignacio Matte-Blanco describes, in exquisite detail, the relationship between the logic of the Unconscious and that of the Conscious. André Greene arrives at a very similar conclusion: "The primary process, even in its seemingly most primitive aspects, remains governed by logic, not, of course, the logic of the secondary process or that of reason, but nevertheless a form of symbolic logic" (1974, p. 419). See also Civin (1990) for a functional comparison of the preconscious and potential space in their intermediary roles "linking" the logics of the unconscious and the conscious.

the human psyche is anything but Euclidean. As we know so well, there in the depths of the psyche, there amid the drives and the repressed, Freud unveils a different system, an unconscious in which X, Y, and Z dissolve into total interchangeability, in which "now" is "then" and "when" is "was" or "never" or "always," in which the cause can be the effect and the effect the cause, in which John is John and John is Tom and what Tom is doing to John he has already done to Sally, himself, to anyone, or everyone. The integrated logic of our conscious being disintegrates in the unconscious. On the one hand, we have a system of laws, of rules, of clarity, of understanding, of regulation, while on the other hand we have a system of disorder, of chaos, of lawlessness, of a constant pressure of sexual and aggressive forces waging guerilla warfare against any form of restraint.

On that particularly difficult day, with the unresolved mystery of the source of the diary and the realization that it was Henrik's diary from all those years earlier, Marie's world is shaken to the core. Or, Bergman hints, perhaps the difficult time at the ballet happened as some presentiment of receiving the diary and having her world upended by a trip back to the island of that initial love and tragedy. In that trip, she experiences herself in the midst of the frolic and its fate *and* she experiences herself on the island as an older woman reliving both. Was it an actual trip back to the island or a trip back to the island created through the words of the diary? Was there a diary at all, or was the diary (hinted by Bergman to have been sent by the older man with whom, perhaps, she had an affair after Henrik's death) the breaking through of the idea attached to some repressed guilt, and, if so, about what was she actually guilty—her youthful sexuality, her affair with the elder man, or something much earlier, something unknown, something oedipal, in her psychic life? Is the cleric who lingers about quite gratuitously an actual cleric or an ideational representation of the guilt resulting from her forbidden sexual drives? But, of course, Marie is a two-dimensional image cast onto the screen for us to make of it what we will (in two dimensions if we fail or decide not willingly to suspend disbelief; in four dimensions if we live the movie concretely and accept the diary as a diary and the trip to the island as a trip to the island; or in untold dimensions if we drift in and out, simultaneously or disjointedly, among all of these), and she *is* Marie and she is Bergman's creation and she is Maj-Britt Nilsson, the actress, and she is our sexuality, the destructiveness of our own desires, our guilt, and our plunge toward death.³

These systems, the conscious and the unconscious,⁴ have no way of communicating with each other. They aren't like English and French, languages that we can translate with a fair amount of accuracy; these are systems governed by dramatically differing laws with no isomorphic relations. When something of the Ucs (i.e., ideation which, if conscious, would expose the undamped pleasure-seeking ferocity of the drives) pushes toward consciousness against the forces that bar it absolutely from arriving at its destination, the Pcs has the potential of doing the work necessary to transform that forbidden ideation into a representation that is adequately disguised for the Cs to accept, if and only if that system exercises the forbearance to pay attention to it: "… it devolves upon the system Pcs to make communication possible between the different ideational contents so that they can influence one another, to give them an order in time, and to set up a censorship or several censorships; 'reality-testing' too, and the reality principle, are in its province. Conscious memory, moreover, seems to depend wholly on the Pcs" (Freud, 1915c, p. 188). The preconscious has access to the Euclidean and post-Euclidean system of consciousness and it has access to the symmetrical⁵ system of the unconscious (ibid., p. 188).

Freud also makes it clear that in our psychical apparatus Pcs is topographically closer to Cs than it is to Ucs. In our conscious functioning, we retain a capacity to drift into the preconscious and form connections, thoughts, or representations, even those of extraordinary complexity that suggest links among felt experiences of the here-and-now, the then-and-there, and the somatopsychic mind–body. Similarly, in the preconscious, these same felt experiences are rearranged, regrouped, reformulated, revised and relocated on a case-by-case,

---

³ As another interesting Bergman play with the unconscious, the Swedish title of the movie and the Swedish word for sexual intercourse are strikingly similar ("Sommarlek" and "Sammanslek").

⁴ Freud used the abbreviations Cs, Pcs, and Ucs to distinguish these elements of his first topography from the commonplace use of the words.

⁵ For Matte-Blanco (1975) "symmetry" is the form of logic that prevails in the unconscious, consistent with Freud (1915c), whereas "asymmetry" is the form of logic of consciousness, consistent with Freud (1915c).

individual-by-individual basis. The logical order of the Cs is twisted and turned, warped and distorted, bent but not entirely broken, transformed in manner that prepares it to disappear into the impenetrably molten depths of the Ucs. Looked at this way, the relationship between Cs and Pcs more closely resemble the "logic" of chaos theory than the "logic" of either Cs or Pcs. In chaos theory, large differences in some causally, but apparently randomly, subsequent states are exceptionally sensitive to an initial state, a phenomenon well known by the meme of the flapping of a butterfly's wings in Tahiti causing a tornado in Arkansas (Lorenz, 1993). If my father and I had taken a boat out into the waters between the shoreline and Wizard's Island, and if I had extended my arm down beneath the interwoven ripples of the boat and thousands of bugs skipping over the surface, I would still, in the shallow waters beside the boat, have been able to observe something that might be some unpredictable, perhaps distinguishable, version of an arm. Below the shallows, in the "unfathomable" depths of the waters, there is not even a "nothing" to see.

No human being is topographically shallow

In "The Unconscious", Freud (1915c) writes that

> … our assumption of the unconscious is necessary and legitimate, and … we possess numerous proofs of its existence … It is necessary because the data of consciousness have a very large number of gaps in them; both in healthy and in sick people psychical acts often occur which can be explained only by presupposing other acts, of which, nevertheless, consciousness affords no evidence. These not only include parapraxes and dreams in healthy people, and everything described as a psychical symptom or an obsession in the sick; our most personal daily experience acquaints us with ideas that come into our head we do not know from where, and with intellectual conclusions arrived at we do not know how. (pp. 166–167)

In "The location of cultural experience" Winnicott (1971) builds on another allusion to water, the famous quote from Tagore, "On the seashore of endless worlds, children play." At the beginning of life, the sea is the mother for every child and every child is "spewed out upon the land" (pp. 95–96). The thalassic mother of endless worlds, the unknowable infinity of our origins, represents the initial unconscious for every child. Of course, as the child plays on the seashore, he or she picks up pebbles, plays with them only to leave them behind, along with castles built of sand, to be washed back into the sea.

Regardless of the unique subsequent experience of every individual, after the primary narcissistic, unexpected, unrepeatable, and forever unknowable discovery of satisfaction at the breast, the infant's subsequent hallucination/dream of it marks the origin of preconscious transformation. As we will note later, the fate of this preconscious may vary in profound ways, but in this moment of primary erotogenic masochism both it and the endless worlds of the unconscious remain at the foundation of living for every one of us. Citing Bion's (1962a) work the transformation of beta particles into alpha particles through the containing function of maternal reverie, Akhtar (2022a) arrives at the same conclusion from a somewhat different perspective. "Psychoanalysis has revealed that while the capacity for thinking might be hardwired, the actual act of thinking is a developmental achievement, acquired through the early interactions between a child and his parents, especially the mother" (p. 125). From the earliest moments of existence, the topography of human experience inscribes itself in every being. Comatose states aside and psychopathology notwithstanding,[6] we all walk about in our individual worlds in a conscious constellation of time, place, person, mutual contradiction, and cause and effect. For a human being to be topographically shallow, none of this could be the case; there could be no unconscious in the psychic depths that underlie our conscious beings and since everyone has an unconscious, no one is topographically shallow. Even when we find slime and stone near the shoreline, the unfathomable depths of endless worlds remain.

---

[6] In severe psychotic states the foreclosure of consensual conscious life exists only in contrast to it. Just as does the unconscious, consciousness remains in sickness and in health.

Shallow as opposed to superficial

The conclusion that no human being is topographically shallow doesn't preclude the possibility of an individual patient presenting such a generally superficial life that we can be tempted to deem our new patient shallow, despite our training in the topography of the human psyche. In my experience, supervising relatively inexperienced trainees, listening to more seasoned analysts present their cases and, of course, thinking about my own, I have observed a frequent tendency to allow this frustration to turn into a judgmental attack on the shallowness of the patient's psyche. On a better day, we take a step back from the "shallowness" of allowing our superego to cloud our judgment and we recognize this judgmental stance as a reflection of some aspect of the patient's internal landscape, what Racker (1968) defines as a complementary identification. "The complementary identifications are produced by the fact that the patient treats the analyst as an internal (projected) object, and in consequence the analyst feels treated as such; that is, he identifies himself with that object" (p. 135).

Clinical vignette: 1

> Arturo had been suffering from panic attacks for almost two years when I met him. In the previous month, he made three visits to the ER, convinced he was having a heart attack. For the first half hour, he chronicled the doctors he saw and the tests he had, finishing up with the neurosurgeon who, finding nothing to doctor, referred Arturo to me. In that first session, he had neither past nor future. His present consisted of such preoccupation with his physiological symptoms that he could barely drag himself to work. Without a hint of sadness or concern, he reported that all his friends, even his long-term, unnamed girlfriend, had grown so impatient listening to him fret about his complaints and fears that they left the room, hung up the phone, or stopped texting back. With the same unmodulated tone, he told me about his work as an accountant in one of the major international firms. He lived frugally, stashing most of his earnings in savings accounts. The day that he made the appointment, his boss had complained about Arturo missing too much time and coming in late too often. He explained that he had been late for work because

every morning he had to check if he was having a heart attack. His pulse grew ever faster and he always felt that his heart was skipping random beats. Even though knew he should be worried about the misses and lateness, because he would have no way to survive if he lost his job, he was equally concerned that he would collapse and die in the office. Like the waters at the surface of Crater Lake, Arturo's life had neither inlet nor outlet, shallowness nor depth; his body skipped hither and yon like the colorful insects, leaving only endless superficial ripples colliding with each other—nothing else.

Clinical vignette: 2

Andie seemed to have been dragged into couples therapy by her live-in boyfriend of many years. He complained loudly that he "couldn't reach her"; she, with apparently insouciant silence, ironically demurred. The boyfriend was, by his own description, a gym-rat, broad-shouldered, thin-waisted, and stretching his black t-shirt to its limits. Andie was tall and slender, green-eyed, and red-haired with hints of grey and colorful tattoos that ran up one arm and down the other like a compromise between an expressionist mural and a comic strip. At a glance, he looked the younger by at least a dozen years. Their sessions together lasted no more than six weeks, every meeting beginning and ending with the bulging blood vessels of his neck in stark contrast with the statuesque impenetrability of her tattoo-armored body. Near the end of their final session, and almost without a hint of inflection, she suggested that he pack his things up and move out. To my surprise, as she trailed behind her now ex-boyfriend, Andie, still with no inflection in her voice, said, "I will be here next week … alone."

Andie was born and raised not far from the deep blue waters of Crater Lake, the only girl and by far the youngest child in a tie-dyed, acid-inclined hippie commune. She described herself as "almost home-schooled," sitting alone among stacks of dog-eared books randomly selected from curbside discards. When her parents weren't bickering with each other or having loud sex in the doorless room next to her own, her father tended his field and greenhouses of marijuana, while her mother threw endless clay cups, bowls, and vases that they sold, along with the pot, in open-air markets.

For three seasons of the year, they wandered hither and yon from Salem to Santa Rosa, often sleeping in jerry-rigged vans and eating leftovers, traded for pot with other vendors. Always with neither inflection nor a hint of complaint, Andie spoke fluently about the details of her early years. She recalled the shabby, soiled clothes and cramped nights, almost always sweating or shivering. She described sitting for endless hours alone, reading her books or playing with half-broken toys that had also been collected from the discards, or hiding in the nooks and crannies she found in every market, pretending that her parents were not "not there." At sixteen, wandering about in one of those markets she met a twenty-five-year-old graduate student. "I didn't have to run away. I just left. I think they barely noticed."

Always on time, always with the same uninflected whisper, Andie left me with almost no sense of why she kept coming. Despite the stark drama of her childhood, my countertransference gave me no clues other than, perhaps, to suggest that she had little awareness of being alive.

Back to clinical vignette: 1

In the weeks and months, perhaps years, before I first met him, Arturo rarely leant himself to anything that might stand out as "thinking". He focused his attention almost entirely on his somatic ailments to the exclusion of anything else. Prior to that, at least as he related his earlier years to me two arduous years later, Arturo's only interests were sports, video games, and mathematics. An only child in a small remote town in western Massachusetts, he had few friends growing up. His parents divorced when he was seven, following an acrimonious relationship for as far back as his memory extended. His father was remarried almost immediately to a woman with a son exactly Arturo's age. Arturo remembered looking forward to the weekends with his father and the other boy. Eventually, as his disavowal waned, he began to realize how much he dreaded the three-block journey back to his mother's every Sunday night. At home with his mother, her life was only he, and he lived in such oxygen-deprived subjection to her that, in a retrospective, reconstructed fantasy, he found the unthought image of her stretched out on the hospital gurney of his hateful asphyxiation. In the endless days between visits to his father, mirrored so exquisitely in the endless hours of his sessions, Arturo dutifully followed his mother's every lead, tiptoeing on the eggshell thin surface of existing and learning how to think without feeling anything. At thirty-one, he had never had a serious relationship with a woman before Sophia, the younger sister of one of his video game partners. Even thinking back on it, Arturo couldn't reconstruct how the relationship came into being or progressed to the point of her moving in with him. What hindsight eventually did tell him was that within days of her commandeering his solitary homeostasis, the old, ever-so-familiar sense of asphyxiation returned. If he wanted to watch a football game instead of chatting with her, shopping together, or heading off to a party at one of her friends, she collapsed into a life-threatening meltdown. And so, Arturo turned from the operational thinking (see below) of his previous life to the thoughtless superficiality of his symptoms.

I have commented elsewhere about the relationship between the capacity to experience difference and thinking.[7] Freud (1915c) writes: "To have listened to something and to have experienced something are psychologically two different things, even though the content of each be the same" (p. 125). To experience, as contrasted with merely to listen, requires differentiating between the content and what is not the content. To differentiate requires thought. I suggest that for our inquiry, we might break down the concept of "thinking" into three categories[8]: (1) a form of "doublethinking" (Orwell, 1949) that largely, if not totally, disavows difference through a pervasive commitment to emptiness (e.g., Andie); (2) a form of "operational thinking" that recognizes difference, but deals with it in a concrete, analytical manner (Arturo); and (3) a form

---

[7] Civin, M. (2023), "... whatever ..." in *The Search for Pleasure in the Contemporary World: The Turning of the Screw.*
Civin, M. (2022), "No body talk, nobody talk," presented at the 9th Delphi Psychoanalytic Symposium: Delphi, Greece, August 25–28.
[8] Clearly, of course, the notion of "thinking" can be approached in many other ways. I am using this particular approach, not only because it helps us expand on the central theme, "shallow," but also because I hope to demonstrate that it proves helpful in clinical work.

of thinking that facilitates representation (an analytic patient, capable of free associating, sharing dreams, and displaying curiosity about their interiority) (Marty & de M'Uzan, 1963, pp. 345–356).

Difference and thinking

In discussing his reluctance to spell out particular examples of transitional phenomena, Winnicott (1971) explains that "It is rather similar to the description of the human face … the fact remains that no two faces are exactly alike … as soon as there is animation they become different" (p. xii). In his foundational paper, "Transitional objects and transitional phenomena," Winnicott (1971) tells us that "the term transitional object gives room for the process of being able to accept difference and similarity" (p. 6). Similarly, in "Hate in the Countertransference" (Winnicott, 1958a), he cautions that the analyst must preserve the capacity to hate as well as to love, in other words to honor the unimpeachable significance of our capacity to think about these differing affective states.

The relationship between difference and thinking is pervasive in Freud's canon. For example, "The function of judgment is concerned in the main with two sorts of decisions. It affirms or disaffirms the possession by a thing of a particular attribute; and it asserts or disputes that a presentation has an existence in reality" (Freud, 1925h, pp. 236–237). In his treatise on "The 'Uncanny'" (Freud, 1919h), Freud devotes great attention to the *difference* between heimlich and unheimlich in his quest to locate an aspect of heimlich that is *identical* to its antithesis. Elsewhere, Freud (1937d) writes of constructions in analysis, phenomena presented to the analysand by the analyst that facilitate the analysand's capacity to represent that which has been forgotten in contrast to that which is remembered: "it is a 'construction' when one lays before the subject of the analysis a piece of his early history that he has forgotten …" (p. 261).

Searles (1960) highlights the ability to differentiate between animate and inanimate (human and non-human environment) as fundamental in normal development while failures in the development of this capacity may generalize into psychosis.[9] Searles's thoughts on this

---

[9] See Civin (2001, pp. ix–xii) for a detailed description of the application of Searles's thinking to contemporary issues surrounding the influence of technology in human functioning.

also run parallel to Bion's early notion of a "proto-mental system", a system or matrix "in which physical and psychological or mental are undifferentiated" (Bion, 1961, p. 102).

A few more words about clinical vignette: 1

> For month after month, Arturo spoke rarely of anything other than the drab details of his physical state, doing better some days and worse others, or the equally dull headlines of his daily life. Then one day, perhaps seven or eight months into treatment, he came in and, for the first time, spent at least five minutes in silence. Across from him, I felt tense, outweighing boredom as the strongest counter-transference reaction that I had experienced to date.
>
> "My fantasy football draft is on Friday evening after work."
>
> "Fantasy football?"
>
> "We get together and pick the players for our teams for the season."
>
> Feeling even more strongly this remarkable new tension, I wait through another prolonged silence.
>
> "It's been the thing I look forward to the most for years."
>
> Still waiting through even more tense silence.
>
> "My girlfriend's good friend is having a bridal shower in Norwalk and the guys are supposed to take her fiancé out at the same time." Then, after an interminably long pause, "Whatever ... Not that big a deal. I'm just going to do this with her and give up the draft."
>
> Arturo remained unaware of the implicit connection to his early years of subjection to the experience of his mother's requirement that he keep her alive by self-sacrifice, and his girlfriend still didn't have a name.

Klein (1950) suggests that "Failure in working through the depressive position is inextricably linked with a predominance of defences which entail a stifling of emotions and of phantasy life, and hinder insight. Such defences, which I termed 'manic defences', although not incompatible with a measure of stability and strength of the ego, go with shallowness. If, during analysis we succeed in ... diminishing manic defences one of the results will be an increase of *strength* as well as in *depth of the ego*" (p. 46, italics added). And later on she continues, "It is evident from my description that mental health is incompatible with shallowness. For shallowness is bound up with denial of inner conflict and of external difficulties ... if it is predominant it results in lack of depth because it prevents insight into one's inner life and therefore real understanding of others" (p. 270).

Encouraged and supported by that first boyfriend, Andie got a GED and, working at her studies day and night, graduated summa cum laude from a local, well rated college. She and the boyfriend separated amicably, but for reasons Andie couldn't explain. She reported that, after that, she drifted across country through a long series of jobs, drinking and drugging constantly without misplacing a tireless work ethic in every job, no matter how menial; she spoke also, almost as a footnote, of an even longer string of forgettable relationships with her self-proclaimed icy femininity shrouding every superficial sexual encounter in a manner that made her indispensable through the almost ignored lens of her rearview mirror. Landing eventually in New York, she used her striking appearance to garner a secretarial job in a medium size investment banking firm where, before long, she was working as a highly paid, totally disinterested but nose-to-the-grindstone junior executive. By the time I met Andie, she was approaching fifty, childless and with a battalion of revolving-door acquaintances with whom she clubbed almost nightly. She still drank, although now a bit less often to excess; however, for the first time since her pre-teen years, she gave up drugs altogether after learning that her father had died at his own hands, alone in the almost deserted commune after his wife left him in the middle of the night. She said that she had no inclination to locate her mother nor any interest in whether she was still alive. In March of 2020, when her job and her therapy went remote and her clubbing ceased, she told me that she barely noticed the change. And yet, almost a year later when we returned to my office, she surprised herself by realizing she had missed it and that she felt tired; for a flickering moment, she seemed curious that she didn't understand why. Then, with a shrug of her tattooed shoulders, she began an unmodulated narrative about her return to the office.

Both of these young people, who appear to function without preconscious representation, led what we might quite easily classify as superficial lives: Andie with her "predominance of (manic) defences that entail a stifling of emotions and of phantasy life, and hinder insight" (Klein,

1950, p. 46) and Arturo with his operational thinking and somatization. Functionally, the observation of their superficiality seems fair enough, and yet, with the subtle shift in their psychological presentation that these vignettes suggest, we might speculate about a different way of understanding what we are witnessing, a way that sheds a great deal of light on the larger social phenomena that face us while at the same time providing us with a bit of guidance in our psychoanalytic practice.[10]

Recalling the conclusion I drew above, that no human being is topographically shallow, I am suggesting that we explore the significance of considering, through the lens of Freud's topographical model, exactly what he referred to as "the 'American flirtation'" in which "[L]ife is impoverished, it loses in interest, when the highest stake in the game of living, life itself, may not be risked ... it becomes shallow and empty" (1915b, pp. 291–292). In very different ways, in order to avoid the overwhelming anxiety complicating the subjectively felt risk involved in the game of living, both Andie and Arturo sacrificed Eros in favor of the homeostatic inorganicity of differing forms of Thanatos. Merely to pathologize this tilt toward superficiality leads us far afield of the psychoanalytic significance that we witness in our contemporary consulting rooms. What we see now is not so much a form of psychopathology as it is a reflection of a contemporary manner of being. These people number, among the long queue at our office doors, these contemporary disaffected patients for whom both libido and aggression have given way to a life beyond the pleasure principle, a life dominated largely by the death drive. To be clear, there is nothing new about this way of living other than its steadily growing pervasiveness, with addictions and suicides on the rise and sexual intercourse on the decline. In the large study sample (Herbenick et al., 2022) the investigators used detailed measures of sexual behaviors in an attempt to address the decline in coital (penile–vaginal) frequency. They report "significant decreases across all partnered sexual behaviors assessed and, for adolescents,

---

[10] Akhtar (2022a) articulates this dilemma, so commonplace in our contemporary world, especially clearly: "This [the normal process of psychoanalytic work based on analytic listening] is true when the patient has the words to express inner contents. But when the patient lacks the ability to denote this or that affect, the analyst has to provide him or her with the correct words" (p. 131).

decreases in the proportion of adolescents reporting solo masturbation in the prior year" (p. 1423). In May 2022, the CDC released data that confirmed not just a rise in the number of drug overdose deaths in the US but also that, in 2021, the United States had the highest annual death toll from drug overdoses ever recorded (Desai, 2024, p. 207). It seems sadly ironic that this trend may, perhaps, have been heralded by Nirvana,[11] arguably the most influential rock group of the 1990s, whose creativity came to an abrupt halt with the suicide of its cofounder and lead singer, Kurt Cobain. If *carpe diem* leads to suicide,[12] why "stay alive," emotionally and even, unfortunately, altogether too often physically, for the risks of "poetry, beauty, romance (and) love …"

It is in the shallows of the preconscious that "[We] come nearer to the id with images, and call it a chaos, a cauldron of seething excitement" (Freud, 1933a). The preconscious does its work in these shallows, close enough to consciousness to endure and bind the conflicts of Eros and Thanatos that emerge from the unfathomable chaos of the depths, the work of disguised dreams and phantasies, of intertwined parapraxes, of transgressing censorship.

Yet, for Andie and for Arturo, as for so many of our contemporary patients, this preconscious cannot bear the burden of deadly anxious risk that accompanies these conflicts. For them the preconscious remains virtually (both figuratively and, nowadays, concretely) empty, barely flirting with the Damoclean sword of conflictual chaos.

Implications for psychoanalytic technique

Jacques Lacan (e.g., 1982, p. 218), along with others,[13] repeatedly emphasized the consequences of a dissolution of the "third" in the oedipal triangle. Arguably, the absence of this "paternal order" of

---

[11] Here, I am clearly alluding to the Nirvana principle popularized by Freud in *Beyond the Pleasure Principle* (1920g, pp. 55–56). It seems unlikely that the rock group had Freud in mind when Cobain settled on a name that was "kind of beautiful or nice and pretty" (Azzerad, 1994, pp. 61–62).
[12] This fate is so poignantly illustrated in the 1989 film *The Dead Poets Society* with Neil's fictional suicide; and then tragically replicated with actual Robin Williams's suicide many years later.
[13] Notably Aisenstein in *The Dead Father: A Psychoanalytic Inquiry* (2009, pp. 65–74).

the third lends itself to the substantiation of the chaos of the depths in the four-dimensional, lived experience of consciousness. Where limits defined by the paternal order eviscerate, the proliferation of the limitless, infinite, third-less expanses of the digital bear witness to this dissolution. In the emotional desert of this domain, we face this terrifying syllogism—without a limit, without difference; without difference, without thought and representation. For example, where we might, in past years, have delved into an analysand's masturbatory fantasies, with our more contemporary patient we learn what categories of porn they prefer; not only that, but ever increasingly we learn that these preferences, even the viewings themselves, no longer hide from the prohibitions and taboos of a third and the castrating consequence of trespass. In the past few years, I have witnessed that, among my younger patients, with the absence of this castration anxiety,[14] watching porn has given way to watching horror movies and shows in which some semblance of anxiety remains. Both porn and horror movies come ready made, served up with the click of a key, without the work of fantasy or dream—without flexing the muscles of an atrophying preconscious. When individuals speak of "hooking up," not with the romantic phantasy of becoming a couple, but rather with a partial-drive/partial-object vagueness that resonates even more with instinct than with drive, we often have a difficult time deciphering what or with whom they have enacted. The preconscious suffers a solar eclipse in a parallel manner with addictions, somatizations, video games, deep dives into internet "information" bleeding from one topic into the next, "social" media, commercialized cloning in the sky that dictates desire and creates the "subject" from "above," disinformation, political splitting that veers so far from discourse-motivating exchange that voluntary servitude and anti-eros supplant thinking, doublethinking censorship of language, rampant "canceling" unhindered by due process, xenophobic obliteration of Otherness that criminalizes difference and annihilates thinking, and so on—Freud's nirvana in a limitless expanse of undisguised bathos.

We might imagine Arturo, Andie, and their Other-less cohort dwelling in the thrall of some mother's screams at the shore of Crater

---

[14] For Lacan (1962, p. 53) the idea of the absence of castration anxiety in this context is that "the lack is lacking."

Lake, each one with an arm yanked from the shallows in abject terror. The shallows would still be there, but for them they would be empty. Of course, all of us suffer our own echoes, and yet, hopefully we locate a transitional battleground for our preconscious conflicts; in our days and nights we dream, we find our parapraxes intriguing and when we situate ourselves on the analytic couch, or in the analyst's chair, we enjoy the liberation of relatively free association and become curious about its limitations and prohibitions.

For Arturo and Andie, it seemed that they could not endure the chaotic cacophony of their private echoes. In their sacrifice of Eros, their effort to temper every hint of overpowering threat in a plunge toward the inorganicity of nirvana, they disavow the conflicts of the preconscious. Arturo's operational thinking, which might easily be mistaken for more neurotic obsessionality, and his somatization, divert the drives from the preconscious to the body and machinery of living. Andie's drives are equally diverted from the preconscious. For her, the vehicle is through addictions to substances, partnerless sex, and empty-minded, all-consuming work. My practice, and the practices of the fairly large group of clinicians with whom I work, have become flooded with patients such as Andie and Arturo, even more so with the limitlessness of technology and the ravages of pandemic isolation and deadening fear. As psychoanalysts, recognizing the radical compression of the preconscious among so many patients we encounter, we face the imperative to develop an intermediate form of our work. Our new disaffected patients have been raised in a society that seems progressively to have undermined the capacity for representation. These people are inherently no more "shallow" than the people who entered our offices years ago. As disaffected as they may appear, they retain a vestigial capacity to think, to represent, to fill the empty shallows of their preconscious. At the individual level, we need to develop a way of working that transitions these people into patients. Whether that way of working is more didactic, more conversational, more active, more relaxed, or more rigid remains to be seen; but the problem needs to be addressed or psychoanalysis cannot do its part to help change this tendency. From the perspective of the analyst's office, we have a front row seat to witness America flirt with emptying the shallows of our collective preconscious.

CHAPTER SIX

Indecisiveness

M. Sagman Kayatekin and Z. Emel Kayatekin

The process of decision making is ubiquitous; it is a process of choosing what we do, write, or say. Choice options are infinitely variable, from mundane daily decisions to strategic choices of our lives. The decision-making process can be conscious or unconscious, it can be rooted in intrapsychic conflict or may have no connection to it. Uncertainties regarding one's decisions might be remediable by "reality testing" or might be too deeply anchored in existential anxieties to be easily corrected. Here is an example of the former type. The Apostle Thomas, "Doubting Thomas," was undecided on the question of whether Jesus had been resurrected, so Jesus invited him to touch his stigmata, upon which Thomas Dubitus decided that Jesus had indeed come back to life. Thus the "doubting" adjective. It is significant that the etymology of "dubitus" is rooted in the Latin *duohabeo*—held as two or double. And the other name for the Apostle Thomas is Thomas Didymus, which is of Greek origin and is a reference to twinship. Again, the implication being there are two to choose from (Flanagan, 2001). Thus indecisiveness can be resolved by an act of will, exercise of ego autonomy, and the capacity to choose. In contrast, the following passage from

Shakespeare's *Hamlet* depicts indecisiveness that is unshakable and firmly rooted in existential anxieties.

> To be, or not to be, that is the question:
> Whether 'tis nobler in the mind to suffer
> The slings and arrows of outrageous fortune,
> Or to take Arms against a Sea of troubles,
> And by opposing end them: to die, to sleep. (*Hamlet*, Act III, Sc 1)

In this most famous of lines, Hamlet is musing about his indecisiveness. In fact, as we will see in the section on psychoanalytic approaches, "to be or not to be," the fear of annihilation of the self or of the object can be the unconscious source of painful, paralyzing indecisiveness. Before delving into psychoanalysis, however, we will provide a brief review of the pertinent literature from related fields.

Observations from related fields

There are innumerable publications and research on decision making and indecisiveness and these come up with interesting observations and deductions. To name just a few: there are cultural differences in indecisiveness (Ng & Hynie, 2014); individualism and collectivism are prominent explanatory factors of indecisiveness (Yates & Oliveira, 2016); indecisiveness and impulsive decision making may coexist (Barkley-Levenson & Fox, 2016); contemplation and indecisiveness are important factors in identity construction (Newark, 2014), and abundant other themes suggest a wide range is being explored under the concept of decision making. Military decision making is also a heavily explored, centrally important, and manualized area (MDMP, 2015).

A pervasive trend in contemporary society is the assumption that indecisiveness is a symptom to be cured, eradicated. This, having a grain of truth in it, nevertheless is an oversimplification, because the personality traits that lead to indecisiveness have the same roots as refined analytical thinking and decision making, and even perhaps for creativity as some studies suggest: "Neutral style of rumination (reflective rumination) and indecision aided the creative process and were consistent with previous studies that found that individuals who ruminate excel in creative fields" (Cohen & Ferrari, 2010). This research supported by common-sense observation clearly suggests that there are maladaptive and adaptive self-reflective ruminations, and the latter are connected to efficiency and creativity. And it gives guidance on how to approach ruminations in a more sophisticated way instead of lumping them together and aiming to clear the mind of all ruminations.

It is also worth noting that indecisiveness and decisiveness have very strong connotations within the entrenched, old, work worshipping morality of the Western world. In earlier times, a soul not occupied by reading the sanctified Bible or consumed by the daily chores of our lives was considered by Judeo-Christian morality as sinful ("sloth"). In the age of modern liberal capitalism running amok, idleness is treated like a medical illness, where "sitting" is viewed as the new epidemic (DeFalco, 2016). In our contemporary psychiatric *Weltanschauung* of continually expanding the range and concept of mental illnesses, ordinary human emotions like anxiety, elation, sadness, fear—the capabilities that have survival value, are facing the risk of being considered as symptoms of illnesses in need of treatment. Similarly, ordinary human confusion, indecisiveness that can actually be helpful in decision making or creativity, can be seen as a problem in our sanctified workplaces and our worshipped ethos of hard work. And thus, indecisiveness, this transitional, preparatory frame of mind, runs the risk of being pathologized and attacked by consultants, therapists, and sometimes even via medications. Differing from the intellectual/political trends of Thomas Szasz (Roberts & Itten, 2006), anti-psychiatrists and their like of the late twentieth century, we are of the opinion that mental illnesses and pathologies that need treatment do exist, but the problem is that psychiatry is slowly invading all aspects of ordinary human mental experiences through the porous boundaries of the adaptive and pathological. We are naming permutations of ordinary human mental experiences as illness. And the second risk is, what can be seen as pathology that is in need of cure and extirpation, can be harnessed through treatment as a strength of the human ego, as the cases discussed in this chapter will try to demonstrate. Thus, there may be valuable lessons on the potentially important, adaptive functions of indecisiveness. In a 2004 interview with *The Paris Review*, author Haruki Murakami in his eloquent style openly states how he stays away from conclusions and leaves everything, in a somewhat self-generating spontaneous way to all possibilities that may come alive with the process (Wray, 2004).

Although writing (fiction, poetry, and especially screenplays), paintings, sculpture, movie making, and politics are all arenas that involve conscious and unconscious decision making; for the sake of expediency, we will focus here on the world of business. This is an area that has some commonality with a psychoanalytic approach on human groups and organizations (Ünsal & Kayatekin, 2022). We have journals dedicated to this shared area (organizational and social dynamics) and the A. K. Rice Institute of the Tavistock tradition is one of the organized psychoanalytic bodies that has an ongoing, systematic approach to the field. Psychoanalytic clinicians are also invested in this field of "organizational consultation" (Mann, 2012).

Daniel Kahneman, a Nobel laureate with a cognitive psychology background, is a founder of behavioral economics and established the concept of "unconscious decision making" in business thinking. He had a brief but important summer internship with the renowned psychologist-psychoanalyst David Rapaport (Kahneman, 2019). His central finding is about the two different systems of human mental functioning around decision making.

Intuitive decision making (System 1) is the system which human beings rely on for frequently returning decisions that can be made without serious deliberations. Examples would be what to take for a meal, and whether or not to take a cab when going out. System 1 is fast and energy efficient, relies on heuristics, and is the most common decision-making system. The problem with this system is, despite being a very efficient way to utilize the ego capacities, it is prone to making mistakes and it is the source of unconscious assumptions, "biases" that inevitably give a distorted view of the world. And a person can never recognize or learn about his or her own biases, whereas others can recognize them quite rapidly in group settings. This is perfectly in tune with our experiences in individual and group psychoanalytic work.

Rational decision making (System 2), by contrast, is slow, requires substantially more effort and energy and is less likely to produce suboptimal outcomes. System 2 is not required for frequently returning decisions, but is useful for infrequent, important, or especially difficult questions. Examples are buying a house or inventing an electric car.

Usually, this system functions as a controller, evaluator of the system 1. In psychoanalytic literature the marginalized and undervalued concepts of "primary process" and "secondary process" thinking, probably have some resonance with these concepts (Soldt, 2006). Kahneman and his team created a twelve-item checklist that can be used to detect biases, especially in high revenue, high-risk decision-making moments (Kahneman et al., 2013). Systematic utilization of this checklist is a tested evaluation of the decision-making process.

A prominent business consultant, Ram Charan (2006), makes a powerful statement that definitely has a psychoanalytic touch when he states "dialogue" as a key element in the success of organizations; he describes executive group meetings when "silent lies" and lack of closure lead to decisions that are in essence false. He notes that the common denominator in these ineffective decisions is a failure in mutual connection and engagement. He takes us through a lively vignette of a multinational corporation's decision-making process where the CEO claims, validates, and critiques the proposal of a team. He is a good reader of personality structures, aware of dangers of creating irreparable fractures in the organization. He is informed about human personality organization and group dynamics. He advises in a creative, non-shaming, thinking-together way, and helps in refining the thought processes of his juniors. The impact is clearly effective. The team follows through the final plan with success: it is noteworthy that the team leader identifies with the style of the CEO as demonstrated by his adoption of a similar interactional style with his subordinates. Ram Charan asserts that the central characteristics of meetings that lead to efficiency and creativity in the decision-making moments of organizational life are: (i) *openness*—answers are sought, not predetermined; (ii) *candor*—the participants are willing to speak the unspeakable, articulate their real opinions; (iii) *informality*—conversations, presentations are not scripted; (iv) *closure*—this is an element that imposes discipline. And thus, you can balance the freedom of openness, candor, and informality with a goal in mind.

Another business consultant, Sabrina Horn (2021), in an interesting twist, focuses on the interpersonal world of a CEO and gives what sounds like psychoanalytically sound advice. Her main theme is the "loneliness" of leaders as an impediment to decision making.

She suggests cultivating connections with a group of select individuals, avoiding turning the leadership team into an insulated bubble, using peer groups, creating a personal "silent advisory board." Nonetheless, the loneliness of the CEO as the ultimate decision maker remains an omnipresent, defining element at that level of management.

Psychoanalytic understanding of the roots of indecisiveness

Strikingly scant attention is given to decision making and indecision in the psychoanalytic literature (Kanwal, 2016). The major, perhaps the only, theoretician in this area is Leo Rangell. The astute observation he made more than half a century ago still has validity today:

> Deriving its original impetus from a motivation of salesmanship, the theoretical literature on decision has remained intimately attached to hard questions of practical application in business, commercial, and military life. Until today it is more abundant in the journals of mathematics, economics, business, and applied statistics than in the behavioral sciences, game theory, but has also found its way into psychology, philosophy, and sociology. Psychoanalysis, however, is conspicuously not represented. (Rangell, 1971, p. 425)

He emphasized that, as a historical understanding of the current in the context of the past, psychoanalysis would make unique contributions to related and important areas such as international politics; with the cautionary remark that we should not leap from the information gathered through our work in offices to larger groups. Rangell stated that decision making is of interest in all analyses, with varying degrees of importance. In this area the findings of psychoanalysis can complement the findings from other disciplines that have a common interest in the process (Rangell, 1969a). He personally wrote an incisive book on Watergate (Rangell, 1980).

In the clinical context, Rangell observed that the role of the ego, as the mediator between the id and superego and the external world, has a central function, whereas the specific role of the ego in decision making has not generally been explicitly stated in important psychoanalytic publications and documents. There is no parallel thinking to Anna Freud's classical concepts on the mechanisms of defense (Rangell, 1969b). He placed "the decision-making function of the ego" at the center of intrapsychic ego capabilities and paid systematic attention to this theme throughout his long and productive life (Lynch & Richards, 2010).

He gave a micro analysis of the decision-making process in twelve steps, utilizing structural theory and defensive operations of the ego (Rangell, 1969b, 1971, 1986, 1987). Following is a summary of this interesting formulation: a precipitating stimulus coming from within, or the environment, impinges on the psychic equilibrium and an instinctual temptation is aroused. The ego is in between this increased instinctual demand, superego, and external figures. This is the moment where, in the classical Freudian structural model, signal anxiety initiates the mechanisms of defense. However, Rangell complicates the mechanisms initiated (perceiving, defense, integrating, choosing) and adds another layer to the sequence. He proposes that, at this juncture, the ego permits only a slight amount of discharge of the instinctual tension, sampling the gratification which ensues and ready for the consequences emanating from the superego. Superego response is immediate, automatic, and again in limited dosage, in proportion to the cautious and small amount of instinctual pleasure that was permitted. Rangell names this "the minor preliminary phase [during which the ego processes] a miniature controlled sample of the conflict which might ensue if the entire dose were to be permitted" (Rangell, 1969a, p. 66).

The ego receives, judges, and reacts to these preliminary signals and decides whether there is a danger situation or safety; and if there is danger, whether it is mild or severe. If the danger is deemed mild or nonexistent, the ego can allow lenient gratification. The ego may, however, judge an appreciable danger from the superego, or the external world, or from the strength of the instincts. This is for Rangell the true stage of the signal anxiety. Thus it is the "major phase one," intrapsychic conflict, which is the beginning of the "decision–dilemma conflict." Ego is confronted with what to do next with this intra-systemic decision-dilemma. It initiates a certain amount of defense and decision making. This then initiates the next phase of conflict, involving an inter-systemic conflict between the ego and the instincts. This is now the better-known "opposition" type of intrapsychic conflict.

This phase, which Rangell calls the "second major phase" of the conflict, supersedes and outlasts the first decision phase, and will continue after the latter may have come to rest, until a final point of relative stability is achieved. Under less favorable circumstances, however, the instincts will not be so easily put off, and there is a next intermediate phase en route to symptom formation which the ego undergoes in its successive and continuing steps toward an attempt at resolution. The possible developments from this point on are too complicated to follow.

Rangell emphasizes the "doer," "mover," active, initiator functions of the ego, along with the utilization of unconscious free will. He explicitly states that cure has to be initiated as an action by the patient and has to go through a prolonged phase of " working through." The resistance, negative therapeutic reactions are parts of this complex, forward moving phenomenon. "The cure does not follow automatically from the gaining of insight; the patient must finish the work. The patient has acquired new levels of knowledge, which brings with them new ownership along with further possibilities. But along with these accrues a new level of responsibility." In his formulations Rangell uses case material to demonstrate his points. As he personally states, putting the decision-making capacity, and thus will, at the center of the ego is his main theoretical contribution to the psychoanalytic theory (Rangell, 1971, 2009).

A thorough review and critique of "will," decision making, and related concepts that we refer to in this chapter was also done by Meissner (2009). Rangell added a commentary to this work, highlighting the repeated disappearance of this central issue from psychoanalytic literature. And he predicts the same fate is probably awaiting Meissner's scholarly review. He draws a parallel between this significant omission and Gray's concept of "developmental lag" in psychoanalytic technique (Gray, 1982). The relative absence of Rangell's contribution from the curriculum of analytic trainings is probably a good testament to his observation, which he interprets as "transference to theory" (Rangell, 2009).

To expand on Rangell's sophisticated theory, I will add that the ego's capacity for decision making is centrally important in the assimilation and partial decathexis of the internalized old scripts that motivate repetitions. It is also centrally important in the creation of new object relational templates that will break the repetitive cycles through expanding the conflict free zone of the ego, enabling increased capacity for unconscious or conscious willful choices. To put it differently, in psychoanalytic work, recognizing and analyzing the transference and countertransference patterns and enactments are of central importance. Once we understand it, moving out of the role we are prescribed as a therapist initiates a cycle of maturation in the patient. It is a process of mourning and liberation: from early object relational scripts that motivate the repetitions, to new relationships, and thus new representational scripts, that allow more freedom for a willful choice. This is a process Freud (1933a) so aptly coined as "where id was there shall ego be." Or as Loewald (1960), more in tune with the German "*Wo Es war, soll Ich werden*" would, in his uniquely evocative prose, say the ghosts that haunt and dictate us are turned to ancestors that we can draw from.

On a related issue, in the matter of psychoanalytic technique, we are in the habit of constantly making decisions. We listen through the lens of transference and countertransference, pay attention to fantasies and bodily gestures of the patient. And just as listening is an active process, a decision is as well; we make decisions on when to speak and interpret. We can decide to speak to the "maximum point of anxiety," "genetic linkage," "shifts in the narrative." Most of the time our speech action is intuitive or happens spontaneously. And each choice means not choosing some other approaches. In contrast to the generally favored free floating attention, modern ego psychologists have a clear focus, with the "close process monitoring" (Gray, 1982) approach where the analyst is systematically attuned to the shifts in the narrative. These are seen as moments of defensive functioning of the ego, attempting to impede the emergence in consciousness of an unconscious conflict. The analyst's attention is thus selectively drawn to the sequence of words, the flow of associations, tone, and affect in order to trace the path of instinctual derivatives thwarted in their aims by the ego (Barahona, 2018). Finally, there is an interesting debate in the literature on explicit vs. implicit psychoanalytic theories, where we act in accordance, idiosyncratically, with our deeply personal theories unrelated to the psychoanalytic schools we think we belong to. This adds another dimension to the process of decision making in clinical interventions (Silvan, 2005).

Illustrations from clinical practice

In discussing the following cases we will rely upon Kernberg's (1970) psychoanalytic classification of the levels of personality organization. We will present two cases in detail and then three others rather briefly. The first case represents Kernberg's "higher level" or neurotic personality organization and the second case reflects a "lower level" or borderline personality organization.

Clinical vignette: 1

Patient S, a man in his early thirties, was in a four times per week psychoanalysis with one of us (MSK). He had obsessive character organization and sought treatment because he was becoming very inhibited, almost paralyzed when pursuing a woman. When attracted to a woman, he would develop a systematic, algorithmic planning on how to approach her. This script would become so detailed that he would inevitably fail at some point and abandon the pursuit. Or if he managed to date a woman, he would lose interest fast and leave the relationship. His obsessiveness was immensely helpful in work because he would prepare religiously and collect all the available data before making a decision, a trait which opened the road to fast promotions. On the other hand, in his personal life, this became an obstacle. For example, he would find himself compelled to read all the handbooks that came with a new car before even getting behind the steering wheel. He had a long-term girlfriend who was becoming frustrated because despite their plan to move in together, he was constantly delaying it for a number of excuses: he didn't have enough money, was working long hours, it would be embarrassing if their families back at home would hear about it. But they were excuses, nevertheless, attempts to rationalize his ambivalence. One evening someone knocked at his door, he opened it and saw his girlfriend standing at the doorstep with her luggage. Enraged with his indecisiveness, she unilaterally decided to move in with him. And they started living together. That was how the problem was resolved.

The memories of an ex-girlfriend whom he deeply loved, who abruptly abandoned S, and the deep longing for his family left behind in his country continue to resurface. The mourning deepens.

Thinking about their times together he cries. Following this period of open mourning he reverts back to his cocoon, ruminating about his day. When I point out to him this shift from mourning to ruminations he sleeps. When he awakens, I then point out the sequence of moving from mourning to rumination and then to sleep and ask for associations. He does not have any. Having used all the technical tools from Kohutian "empathic immersion" to Grayian "close process monitoring" to no effect, I recognize that I am getting bored in the sessions. As I repeatedly point to the absence of his fantasies, dreams, he tells me that he thinks they are a waste of time. With the help of peer supervision, I recognize more clearly his "trench war"-like stance, his opposition, and his dismissiveness. When I offer these as interpretations, he says he doesn't feel that way. My invitations to play with his associations are initially accepted with some joy but end up in his retraction to his obsessive/schizoid cocoon. I have a fantasy that I am besieging him with my ongoing fruitless efforts, and the city is resisting to surrender. He tells me he's scared most of the time, he is afraid of making mistakes: "If I make a mistake then it is irreparable," he says. He has associations to being locked in a cellar by his father after biting the leg of his mother at age four. His decision on not to play has good historical reasons I notice.

We recognize that he has internalized his parents. He is thinking and talking about himself in the way they would do. It is painful but it keeps him in good company. There is no one around to guide him or criticize him. Connecting the theme of his loneliness with my recurrent wish to give advice, I ask him what he thinks about my not giving him any advice on his decisions. He states, "Yes I would love to hear some advice from you. I would argue with my dad, but trust his advice one hundred percent. He was right about many things. I miss him. He is moving further and further away." He dozes off as he recognizes that he's becoming more emotional. It is becoming clear by now that a root/motive for this countertransferential boredom and his maddening indecisiveness is an invitation for me to take sides in his ambivalence and decide on behalf of him. A decision he will fight with either way.

I recognize that, in a slow but steady fashion, he's catching his dissociative defense structure earlier on. We uncover some regressed relations with his parents. His parents gave S the impression that if they didn't guide him, he would create an irremediable disaster. He's doing the same to himself now. He feels like a cripple who lacks a sense of initiative. He and his mom would get into heated arguments where mom would accuse S of embarrassing her in the eyes of neighbors. He misses those fights that he hated while he was still in his home country. He feels like he has lost his anchoring. He recognizes that if his parents are not around, then the only thing he knows is to behave like them. I point to his dilemma: "If they didn't guide then you will fail. If you give in to your desires, then again, you will fail. Thus, you fought with them but didn't feel alone. It sounds like you carry your mom and dad with you." He agrees. We attempt to further clarify the roots, feared consequences of his decision making and acting. His decision/indecision is becoming more meaningful in his personal history.

S feels these sessions are a block of time that belong to him but at the same time feels guilty; he is conflicted about our conversations. He feels relieved on the one hand and embarrassed at the same time. In addition, he's afraid that he may sound stupid to me. In his usual style, in between the lines S tells me he's getting very tired of his perennial indecision. Observing that he sounds tortured, I invite him for exploration. He doses off. I feel lost. When he awakens, he tells me he can't trust people, he has been taking care of things by himself for so many years. He protected himself from depending on others. He recognizes that we are both getting old and will die one day.

In the case of S, indecisiveness, while it is a resistance to progress, also has adaptive sides to it. His un-decisions are rooted in avoiding the abandonment of old object relations and finding new ones, new attachments, loves. There is significant ordinary human jealousy and a sense of betrayal related to progress and thus the resistance presenting as indecisiveness. Mother and father were also involved in decisions by S; all were in a partly undifferentiated relationship with some symbiotic colorings.

What S teaches us is that the acts of defense and thus resistance can be seen as decisions and actions initiated by anxieties and other affects and are motivated towards reducing them. These anxieties involve the basic "danger situations" (Freud, 1926d)—abandonment, loss of love, castration, and guilt. The ego is the active agent in this decision-making process, not as a mini homunculus but as a substructure of the mind, with the capabilities for decision making and will and agency. Of significance is the dyadic nature—as in his relationship with his current girlfriend or the analyst; he invites the advice, actions, and decisions of others. Decisions to push oneself into his apartment and life, like his current girlfriend, or push oneself into S's mind by making a decision for him (Kayatekin, 2016). Ongoing analytic treatment offers the possibility of expanding the conflict free zone, zone of will, and the patient has the chance of utilizing unconscious voluntary decision making, in comparison to the repetitive, driven, almost compulsive decisions of the past scripts.

In classic psychoanalysis, individuality, the concept of taking the individual as the basic unit, is a common denominator of formulating human beings, and decision making is thus seen as an individual act. With a subtle but powerful shift, this core individualistic formulation is challenged in psychoanalysis and many related disciplines related to human mind and behavior. In tandem with this paradigm shift, and taking the risk of oversimplification, we can assert that decision making almost always includes others in the process; others as represented in our minds, and as real persons in our human ecologies. This is ubiquitous but more marked in individuals with "partially internalized conflicts" (A. Freud, 1965a) or "object relations conflicts" (Dorpat, 1976). Such conflicts involve a psychic structure that is less differentiated and antecedent to id–ego–superego demarcation. The individual with such conflicts experiences opposition between his own wishes and his internalized representations of another person's wishes. This is in contrast to a proper "structural conflict" in which both vectors of the dilemma are experienced as fully belonging to oneself. In Kernberg's (1970) scheme, the predominance of object relations conflicts reflects a borderline personality organization.

Clinical vignette: 2

> T was admitted to a psychotherapeutic hospital with a history of failed treatments. Hospital felt like the last resort to the exhausted members of his family but nevertheless, they all were having serious doubts about whether this was the right decision for him. He was hopeless, saying he did whatever he was asked to do, and "nothing was helpful." Noticing the power of these doubts, and to locate an

island of agency in him, we, the team, offered an early formulation/ interpretation. We suggested that he shouldn't do anything others ask him to do or what he thinks he should do; instead, together with us, explore and understand his doubts before any decision action. He was surprised with our therapeutic invitation and agreed to give it a try. It was a major move; through action, we wedged ourselves into the primitive intrapsychic and family dynamics. And, if we could get a foothold, it could provide a nidus for an expansion of a sense of autonomy in T and hopefully would have similar ripple effects on other members of the family. It was of note that we were inviting him to think together, staying away from the paternal abandonment of "he should make his own decisions" as well as the maternal intrusion into his mind by taking over his thinking and decision-making capacity. This formulation of course was initially mostly intuitive and became clearer, conscious, and articulated as his treatment progressed.

During the night of our review of medications, I, his psychiatrist (ZEK), got an angry message from his mother, who was upset that the medication regimen was decided without her involvement. She believed her active involvement in every step of his treatment was crucial, as she was "the only person who kept him alive." She was resisting our attempt of increasing the autonomy of her son; the roots of her resistance would slowly become understandable. It confirmed our hypothesis that, with the intuitive action of deciding just with T, I had wedged myself into the primitive dynamics of the family.

The next day, I called the mother in T's presence. I explained the rationale for the medication regimen and stated that it is important for T to make informed decisions for himself. I was trying to keep the parents in the "neighborhood" of our treatment—a neighbor who is respectful and informed about what is going on, but not intruding, like the mother, or disappearing, like the father. T acknowledged our discussion and his agreement on the regimen. Mother was clearly not satisfied but tentatively agreed.

My interference with the family system continued to evoke strong responses from the mother. Even though the team strongly encouraged her not to visit T this early in his treatment, mother was insistent that T needed her comforting; she came and spent the whole weekend with him. The symbiotic tie was too hard to break on both ends. Resistances emanating from self and object relationships were understandably very strong and at the root of T's and mother's indecisiveness. And further, they were also actual interpersonal resistances, not just intrapsychic. It is of note that T was not passive in this process but was an ambivalent and active initiator and participant.

Following his mother's visit, T reported a conflicting set of responses; he felt comforted, confused, and frustrated. He felt overwhelmed for "needing to entertain" his mother all weekend. He was also surprised to learn that, even though he was just a few days into this treatment, his mother had developed a detailed aftercare plan. She was convinced that the hospitalization would be harmful and he would need to discharge soon, thus they needed to think about aftercare options at home. Lack of inclusion of a third (a therapist or his father) was quite striking. They were used to operating in regressed dyads.

We decided to involve his father, as a "third." We thought he must have felt excluded from this intensely close relationship and his involvement could help T stay in treatment. We were trying to create a triadic structure in the context of treatment.

T historically had a distant relationship with his father and believed his father didn't like him. Father seemed happy with getting involved. However, he was hesitant about supporting anything against T's expressed wishes. He believed it was important for T to make his own decisions. This, as we had surmised, was the exact opposite of mother's attitude of deciding on behalf of T.

Now, the "absence" of the father was becoming more meaningful—he had not disappeared but was present through his absence, by surrendering to the powerful, possessive jealousy of the mother. Further, by abandoning or obliterating the ego capabilities of T, father and mother were jointly resisting the initiation of the treatment. The split between the parents was the strong bond between them. The regressed dyadic pairs—mom and son, dad and son, mom and dad—could not create a threesome. The immediate therapeutic goal was to help this stuck family to come up with an understanding on why they were so ambivalent, undecided; the multiple roots, and meanings of their stuck situation; understanding how their indecision had protective and maladaptive sides to it. Our style of accompanying T in the analysis of these ego processes would set an example on how to use a nonintrusive, non-abandoning "other" in utilizing and understanding one's mind in the action of evaluation and decision making.

In family therapy, while trying to explore the relational dynamics between T and his mother, the therapist was getting intense resistance from both. Finally, after her persevering with therapeutic presence, a turning point came. T took the challenge, he talked about how everyone in the family "plays it nice and no one discusses the nitty gritty." His mother added that she shouldn't be his main relationship. T countered with the observation that while she says so, her behaviors don't match up with her words. It was a moment where mother and son were freeing themselves from the stereotypical repetitive narrative and a therapeutic, honest conversation was beginning to form. Then came another moment of shift outside of the usual repetitive, projection filled object relational scripts that allowed the search of a new decision making in the mother. In a surprising way, she shifted away from resistance and asked T directly, "What do you need me to do?" for which he had no response. It was a different question because mother was not projectively, pathologically sure of what needed to be done for her son but she was inquisitive. When the family therapist wondered about T's need for space and the mother's need for time off from worrying about her son's life, T jumped in and said he wanted to limit phone calls, as he felt it left no time for him to interact with others. The mother started crying, saying he was cutting her off, and how hard it would be for her, because she misses and worries about him.

Despite having developed considerable insight into his dilemma and expressing a desire to change the dynamic (at least being ambivalent about it), after talking about these issues, T was regressing further, isolating, and having long conversations with his mother about aftercare plans at home. Here the role of the larger hospital setting became critical.

The hospital milieu was a great laboratory for T, for the repetition, exploration, and maturation of his object relational scripts. And centrally important, it was a place where he could play with and practice making some decisions without endless vacillations. One important learning was his recognition that decision making was not a process, unfolding in the loneliness of the individual, but needs using the other as a sounding board, someone facilitating the process; that we make our own decisions, in the presence of and with the help of others. Even in our older years, we still need the minds of others to function efficiently. Yet the nature of this dependency shifts from more infantile, as in the case of T, to more mature forms that he was trying to find.

Gradually, with several team members, T started talking about his concerns that colored his ambivalence in treatment, thus indecisiveness on staying. He felt he needed to go back home for his mother; he feared, without him, she might die. He reminisced how, on several occasions, she became suicidal and got soothed only by him. It was clear that this mutual, regressively dependent attachment was the main source of his indecisiveness and immobilization.

What eventually seemed to help break this cycle of two steps forward, one step backward was art therapy. Through the medium of painting and discussing his paintings in individual and group settings, he was able to distance his internal world from himself and reflect on it as an object of study. The art was not as capable of evoking paralyzing emotions, conflicts, and splits as much as speech or writing did. So, he became freer to explore himself and others. Art therapy allowed developing an "observing ego" for T. In contrast to his difficulties in relating, talking, articulating in large groups, T was very active and spontaneous in art therapy groups. He had finally found an avenue to his interpersonal and intrapsychic world (Thuketana & Westhof, 2018). Art therapy, in the context of the containing atmosphere of the hospital (for not only T but his parents as well) and several other venues of treatment, allowed T and his parents to gradually free themselves from their worries they had about each other, and authentically focus on their own individual and couples issues, in the presence of therapists, which helped make the decision making easier for each one of them.

In clinical work such as with patients S and T, we pay special attention to intrapsychic and interpersonal object relational, psychodynamic roots of decision making. Patients like S, described in neurotic psychoanalytic treatment, continue with their lives despite an underlying painful indecisiveness. But theirs is a trait; even though it presents as a handicap in their interpersonal relationships, in other fields of their lives this thinking style increases their professional efficiency. For T, on the other hand, despite the internal object relational roots of his indecisiveness (which also are fed by actual, current interpersonal relational dynamics), he is incapacitated to a much more severe degree because his regression is triggered not just by a conflict but split defensive structures. Under these circumstances, choices evoke annihilation anxieties, are cathected with Hamletian "to be or not to be" fears for his self and object poles of representations. Thus, his more persistent inability to make important decisions about his life and treatment necessitates a multimodal intervention as in the holding atmosphere of the hospital.

There is yet another group of patients, who require a different approach; I call these obsessive-hypomanic personality organizations. At baseline, they are very driven, have obsessive character traits with a core identification with their professional selves. They are highly successful professionals, researchers, political or military leaders. What I (MSK) will write about is from my experience as the director of a special inpatient program designed for these kinds of patients.

Clinical vignette: 3

> A patient who was in his mid-forties and in a four times per week analysis with one of us (MSK) described an important defensive/adaptive aspect of his excessive work poignantly: "I wake up with a deep sense of sadness and grief. After taking a quick shower and having my breakfast, I immerse myself in my work and all these painful feelings disappear. I work excessively and methodically till I exhaust myself and others around me." He would work without any weekends or vacations for many years in a row, seven days off in seventeen years to be exact. Through exploration, somewhat foggy memories of his early teens emerged and he became more aware of how fond he was of his family until his father abruptly left and his mother fell into a depression. This necessitated him to be the main breadwinner of the household. He managed to work menial jobs,

go to school, become a top-notch student, and subsequently rise to professional prominence, but this, partially repressed, traumatic change was the main route of a painful and deeply embedded sense of loneliness and distrust in people.

Clinical vignette: 4
A fifty-year-old man in hospital psychotherapy had built a multimillion-dollar company and after achieving this goal had lost all interest in it. This pattern was repetitive. He developed goals, then accomplished them, and finally fell into a state of aimlessness and depression. He would miss the challenges he loved to overcome and goals he strove to reach. In one session, he said: "There is something very attractive about working and being successful at it. It is as if work has a way of expanding by itself, intruding into the person's life once the fulfillments are there."

These patients have some common developmental patterns; adolescent developmental tasks around socialization are often bypassed with a very early love relationship. Everything they do targets a perfect result—as a professional or a parent. They display a fiercely independent intellectual functioning. There is usually a history of early loss and unresolved grief that fuels the hypomanic style.

The most common context for severe regression for these patients is work related; being extremely successful or unsuccessful, getting promotion or being fired, change of fields or retirement, and many other significant recent changes in the aspects of life that shape them—their work. Once regression sets in, their core, work-centered self-definition crumbles, they complain of having lost the sense of "who they are." The hypomanic/obsessive style deteriorates to a ruminative, depressed style. The obsessive elements in their personality organization lose all of their impressive analyzing/problem-solving qualities; they shift to a deep, incapacitating ambivalence, ambitendency, and ruminations, and may even evolve into pre-catatonic, and in rare instances, catatonic states. Finally, they evolve into deep sadness, apathy, preoccupation with guilt-ridden reproaches, and extremes of dependence which is the polar opposite of their usual functioning self.

Clinical vignette: 5

One of the earlier observations that initiated my (MSK) thinking on this clinical presentation was a seventy-year-old patient who fully retired after a successful career. He was observed as "stuck" in the doorway to his room in our professional treatment unit. He stood at the doorway, took a few steps into the bedroom, and then walked out of the bedroom, took a few steps towards the hallway, and continued with this intriguing behavior repetitively. When we inquired about this back and forth, he said he was torn between wanting to go into vs. out of his room. He thus repeatedly stepped in and out. As a seasoned clinician I knew quite a lot about ambivalence and ambitendency but had never seen it this concretely and demonstratively.

On a more profound level, the case exemplifies the regression to a tormenting state of ambivalence. It took the patient more than a year to make up his mind and physically bring himself for admission. Once physically in the building, he could not walk in through the doorway of the admissions office, and after about a full day of conversations with the admission staff, he signed himself in. Once in the unit, despite daily requests to leave, he managed to keep himself in the program but wore down the staff's patience by constantly, repetitively asking for guidance on ordinary daily chores, such as which clothes to choose or which foods to eat. With intense treatment, he slowly cleared from this depressive/obsessive/indecisive pit.

For many patients, painful ruminations flooding their minds when regressed were rooted in productive, useful aspects of their cognitive organization. Their prominent obsessive personality structure, with their meticulous attention to detail, capacity to collect a wide range of data and weigh them, and ability to choose, was such that they were admired for their analytical skills and precise decision-making capabilities. However, this solution-oriented cognitive functioning began displaying a "broken record" quality when decompensated, and there was no processing but endless and futile repetition of similar themes (Kayatekin et al., 2024).

In clinical work, the most problematic phenomenon associated with these presentations is ambivalence. Even though it is tied to obsessionality, ambivalence is a ubiquitous human tendency, and according to some, a central aspect of the human mind (Cooperman, 1983). In the patients I described above, ambivalent indecisiveness increases to a level of severe incapacitation. Obsessive ruminations flood their minds, interfering with making ordinary decisions, leaving no space for any other thoughts. This is a point when the indecision and ambivalence seem to lose their object ties and meaning, when there develops a pre-catatonic, psychotic-like quality because of the unremitting intensity. Arieti hypothesizes that catatonic symptoms are primitive attempts to avoid taking responsibility for willful actions. He formulates that the future patient develops a vicious cycle of fear of making decisions, which he defines as "willed activity," the pre-catatonic develops a fear of willed action and catatonia freezes all of their decision-making capacities (in Johnson, 1984).

Unlike S and T, where we need to get out of the role we were pulled into in the script of enactment and offer new object relational templates, here the therapeutic task is different. During the early phases of treatment joining the enactment actively on issues of the daily decisions—like guiding, encouraging taking medications, eating, and mingling with their peers—is essential. In a way initially we need to make various decisions for the patient. And the patient slowly identifies with our capacity to make decisions and tolerates the risks we are taking. We initiate an alliance of co-deciding egos with what seems a wearing patience on our part and slowly wean the patient off of our symbiotic decision making for him or her. It is noteworthy that these patients come in with severely stuck symbioses, almost a fusion with another person, who has become their alter ego on even the minutest decisions of the day. It is a state of infantile dependence, and our task is initially to repeat that relationship, take that function over, and slowly give it back to the patient.

Discussion

In this chapter we have focused on psychoanalytic aspects of decision making and indecisiveness. It is clear that giving this relatively neglected ego function its well-deserved centrality among the capabilities of the ego is in order to have more precise formulations of the human mind.

The available theory, as provided by Rangell, still seems to be a relevant foundation. Yet, as I tried to show in these vignettes, the individual impacted by and impacting human relationships is missing in his powerful individual formulations. As Rangell suggests, pathology can be a great teacher of the normal. Through our now extensive experience with the "widened scope" patients or "severe pathology," we do know that with increased severity of pathology, characterized by a regression from conflict to splitting, from repressive defenses to projective ones, such a condition universally evokes (or occurs in the context of) dyadic and family regressions. All of these make the individuality of a person less clear, and the basic units, in our attempt at the decoding of human psychic functioning, inevitably include others. And further, during our development, from very young ages on, we display powerful capabilities to evoke and induce various roles in the others that are important to us, and in regressed states these come back in full force. This, in fact, is somewhat peripherally present and dormant in neurotic levels of pathology and "normalcy."

We are of the opinion that Rangell, the main theoretician of the ego, will, volition, and decision making are rather inattentive to this aspect of human functioning. Even though his case descriptions clearly describe his working with these templates, his formulations shift to the drive, the energy sublanguage of the psychoanalysis of his times that sometimes needs translation. But our main critique is that he is not fully cognizant of what the severe pathologies, the "widening scope" has brought to mainstream psychoanalytic theorizing. This is an attempt that is already initiated, and such attempts of synthesis need to be further expanded on (Akhtar, 1999; Kernberg & Caligor, 2005).

Conclusion

The ego, the decision-making structure of the human mind, has the capability to mediate between different aspects of the structures and functions of the mind and the interpersonal world. It controls, mediates, and monitors the infinitely complicated world of human motives in the way they are both represented internally and played out in the real human niche that surrounds us. Therefore we should strive to develop a formulation of the individual ego, not mainly as an internal regulator, but equally as the regulator of the relationship of the internal world to the external reality. A structure thus defined would have the capacity to shape, and be shaped by, the external and internal imperatives, and the potential of choosing (consciously or unconsciously) those "shaping actions" (Schwartz, 1986). It will impart to us a more nuanced and realistic understanding of the human mind as the defining aspect of our species as a social entity.

CHAPTER SEVEN

Restlessness

Nilofer Kaul

In his last years, my father took to shorthand, communicating his state of mind by scribbling scraps of poetry, on what used to be ubiquitous blue inland letters. Of the peculiar restlessness of old age, he quoted tellingly from Yeats's "The Tower" (1928):

> What shall I do with this absurdity—
> O heart, O troubled heart—this caricature,
> Decrepit age that has been tied to me
> As to a dog's tail? (p. 218)

He did not send me the next lines:

> Never had I more
> Excited, passionate, fantastical
> Imagination, nor an ear and eye
> That more expected the impossible … (p. 218)

Perhaps the lines that follow were implied. Or perhaps they did not suit his humor. Old age exacerbates the frustration, as we see the end closing in on us and all the roads not taken, vanishing furiously away. In the interstices of our conscious and unconscious lives, there is a continuous hum of another life, a longing to have a second stab at life, the so-called midlife crisis, the reinvention narrative, the trope of awakening, the call of distant lands. We often carry a curious and unexamined mix of these narratives and they course through the confused choices we make through our lives.

Adam Phillips's (2014) *Missing Out* is an evocative meditation on how the unlived life is always peeking out, crossing our paths, as we go about living the one we choose. All the while the roads not taken continue their phantom beckoning. Within the life we choose lie the embers of another life. And our disappointments, rejections, and failures therein stoke these to soothe us into believing "if only …" or else "some day …" (Akhtar, 1996).

Sometimes it fills us with bittersweet regret of that other path not taken. At still other times, it acquires a vice-like grip on us and we give in to the lure of taking another stab at life. It is sometimes like a pale ghost outside the window, at other times, a voluptuous lover, and yet other times, the nagging thrum in our ears. Often with age, the Shelleyian skylark's trill—inviting us to abandon it all and give it another go—gives way to a subdued melancholia. These Romantic gestures that have drained into cliches are mocked memorably by Larkin (2013) when he imagines us hearing "fifth hand" about how "he just chucked his old life" and perhaps lauding this "elemental, purifying move."

Envy, admiration arise like evil twins and beget mockery. Now why would he do that? Pathos clucks its tongue, "poor thing." And yet whichever side of the equator we might be on at that precise moment, ghosts of that other life wave to us: sometimes seductively, at other times ruefully.

Restless or restive?

Historians refer to the past characterized by a pervasive idea: as Dark Ages or the Age of Enlightenment, or the Romantic Age, or of Industry or of Empire. But every age has perhaps also been described as: "restless for" or "restless about." Restlessness for change leads to the conflict between those who want the change and those who don't: faith vs. doubt, peasants vs. patricians, feudalism vs. capitalism, and so on. Modernity casts this, not without reason, along the axis of progressive/regressive, or conservative/liberal.

The word "restless" itself is an adjective which comes from the Old English *restleas* "deprived of sleep"; and the Germanic compound (cf. Fris. *restleas*, Ger. *rastlos*, Dan. *rastlös*, Du. *rusteloos*)—meaning "stirring constantly, desirous of action" is attested from the late fifteenth century. The *Merriam-Webster Dictionary* defines it as "lacking or denying rest: Uneasy, a restless night; continuously moving: Unquiet, the restless sea; characterized by or manifesting unrest especially of mind, restless pacing; also changeful, discontented." The spectrum of meanings—uneasy, unquiet, changeful, and discontented—come together to strike the note we have come to associate with restlessness. According to the dictionary, the first known use of "restless" is before the twelfth century, signifying most commonly, uneasiness. The word "uneasy" itself was mostly associated with being disturbed in the mind.

The word "restive" that is used almost synonymously with "restless" enters the language three centuries later from the word *rester*, to resist. Although the oldest sense of restive ("balky") has not died out completely, it is overshadowed by the more recent one ("fidgety").

The two words have very different origins, as one comes from the absence of rest, while the other is linked with resistance. Yet the fact that they are used interchangeably also brings us to an overlapping spectrum—as though we were viewing the same proclivity through different vertices.

Religious poetry

Religion is often a refuge for the restless and the restive. People go to places of worship, they pray and chant for peace, for reprieve from restlessness. But it is in and of itself often a cause for restlessness. The vicissitudes of living create doubt in the believer.

In this vein, a lot of religious poetry follows the pattern of morality drama between restoring faith (God) on the one hand, and doubting (being of the devil's party) or despairing, on the other. Many poems have an epiphanic structure where doubt of the object causes a storm and an insight then brings a climax and restores belief. The arc of these poems often begins with the torments doubt brings, while they end on a conciliatory note. There is an encounter with the Big Other, the primary object who is experienced as overpowering; love and faith in this Other is disturbed. Gerald Manley Hopkins, who became a Jesuit, recorded his tormented wrestling with God. Doubting God is despair for a believer, for instance: "Not, I'll not, carrion comfort, Despair, not feast on thee; …" (Hopkins & Smith, 1976, p. 54).

Here Hopkins equates despair with deriving comfort from carrion or akin to feeding off the decaying flesh of animals. Doubting God, and feeding off despair makes him "most weary." We may notice here the repetition of "not." In fact, the poet has reached the end of his tether: "cry I can no more." The poem ends by moving away temporally from the memory of the torment:

> That night, that year
> Of now done darkness I wretch lay wrestling with (my God!)
> my God. (p. 54)

This is not unique to the Victorian Jesuit poet Hopkins, but John Donne, nearly two centuries before him, uses violent language to bring himself into a state of surrender/belief:

> Batter my heart, three-person'd God, for you
> As yet but knock, breathe, shine, and seek to mend. (Donne & Gardener, 1957, p. 85)

The subject who wishes to submit to God is constantly tested by the suffering. How can one reconcile God's love with the suffering he inflicts? Faith attempts to restore by understanding these to be God's ways of testing love. Being without the belief in a good and omnipotent figure is being abandoned to a violent desert. The poems often end like George Herbert's "The Collar":

> But as I raved and grew more fierce and wild
>   At every word,
> Methought I heard one calling, Child!
>   And I replied My Lord. (Herbert & Gardener, 1957, p. 135)

The obviously forced closure here brings the poems to a state of repose momentarily, a "false climax" to use Winnicott's language which I will discuss later.

The lunatic, the lover, the poet

> Lovers and madmen have such seething brains,
> Such shaping fantasies, that apprehend
> More than cool reason ever comprehends.
> The lunatic, the lover and the poet
> Are of imagination all compact: … (*A Midsummer Night's Dream*,
> Act I, Sc 5, ll 5–9)

Theseus in *A Midsummer Night's Dream* brings together three figures marked by restlessness: the lunatic (the delusional/psychotic), the lover (neurotic), and the poet (with some immodesty also occasionally the psychoanalyst). They all possess an extravagant imagination or as he terms it "imagination compact." The lover and the madman have an excess that makes them see things that cool reason hardly "ever comprehends."

Theseus recognizes the differences between these restless figures: the madman "sees more devils than vast hell can hold," the lover sees "Helen's beauty in a brow of Egypt," while the poet looks at "the forms of things unknown" and "turns them to shapes and gives to airy nothing/A local habitation and a name." He suggests that these three figures are bearers of strong imagination, and that the moment they experience something intense (joy or fear), they attribute this intensity to an object as moving it, an anthropomorphizing. Theseus concludes that flights of fancy or restless imagination point to an object in the mind, such as a lover or a persecutor.

On a related note, Akhtar (personal communication, February 17, 2022) notes in Urdu, "restlessness" can be variously called *bechaini*, *betaabi*, *beqarari*, and *bekaali*. These terms may be translated as without peace, without patience, without composure, and without solution. There are nuanced differences between these but as Akhtar points out, these are all prefixed by "be-" which signifies "lack of." For the unconscious, something missing slides into someone missing, he observes. The mind, unable to bear absence or intensity of any sort, quickly creates a shape out of "airy nothing." The idea of airy nothing is quite intolerable to the mind, and an object may be falsely attributed to a state of mind.

Freud (1909d) says something strikingly similar when he implies the need to attach our stronger emotional experiences to events that may correspond in intensity, for without this, they will be psychically suspended:

> We are not used to feeling strong affects without their having any ideational content, and therefore, if the content is missing, we seize as a substitute upon some other content which is in some way or other suitable, much as our police, when they cannot catch the right murderer, arrest a wrong one instead. (p. 176)

The question of course that arises is whether restlessness (is it primary?) seeks a theatre where it can be staged/explained or is there a fatal flaw (what Aristotle calls hamartia) that inheres causing us to be restless (secondary restlessness)? For instance, does ambition cause restlessness or does restlessness seize upon ambition as a canvas upon which it can express itself? Is restlessness a symptom or a cause?

Overreaching

When Minos held Daedalus and his son Icarus in captivity, the gifted craftsman Daedalus created two pairs of wings made of wax and feathers for them to fly away with. But he warned Icarus against the danger of flying too close to the sun, for the wax could melt. And if he flew too close to the sea, the feathers would get wet. Intoxicated by his flight, Icarus soared too close to the sun, and sank into the sea as his wings melted.

Icarus was to be the great cautionary myth of the Renaissance; a lesson against greed, ambition, and overreaching. Overreaching was the great theme of the sixteenth and even seventeenth centuries: human acquisitiveness had no bounds and this could only lead to tragic endings.

The kinship between restlessness and ambition is seen in *Macbeth*, and arguably, in its two most famous insomniacs. While we cannot assume any causal link between restlessness and ambition, we may see what Bion (1965) calls "constant conjunction." This is to say, these (restlessness and ambition) are often found in each other's proximity but are not therefore causally linked. Insomnia is often a way restlessness announces itself.

Macbeth staggers in on stage presumably disoriented:

> Methought I heard a voice cry "Sleep no more!
> Macbeth does murder sleep", … (Act II, Sc 2, ll 34–35)

He appears not to notice Lady Macbeth's questions about what and wherefore, but in an obvious "waking dream" (Ferro, 2004) continues:

> Still it cried "Sleep no more!" to all the house:
> Glamis hath murder'd sleep, and therefore Cawdor
> Shall sleep no more; Macbeth shall sleep no more. (Act II, Sc 2,
> ll 40–42)

Macbeth cannot sleep in his bed, it is true, but he is awake to the terror of having done something irrevocable, and bloody retribution is afoot. He cannot tell the difference between being awake and asleep; between voices inside and those outside his mind. This ought to have been a nightmare, as also perhaps, the opening scene with the witches. But it isn't. Soon after chiding him for being so white with fear and proceeding to smear the guards with blood, Lady Macbeth cannot stop walking and talking while "asleep." Macbeth sleeps with his eyes open and Lady Macbeth wakes only in her sleep. By day she can pretend that blood has no meaning and like any grime can be cleansed simply by washing hands; but at night she is awake to the horror. In a chilling scene we watch her intimately, through the eyes of the doctor, washing her hands in her nightgown, talking aloud to her husband who she scolds for being so fearful: "Fie my lord!" But admits obliquely that it is not easy to get rid of taint: "Who would have thought the old man to have so much blood in him?" (Act V, Sc 1, l 34). Fear of retribution—a primitive impetus for guilt—affects them differently. Eventually for Macbeth it is only death that can be envisioned as an escape. For "not all the waters in the rough rude sea" are going to rid him of his mind—that cruel repository of thoughts, actions, dreams. Here is Macbeth tormented by life's "fitful fever" envying Duncan's death:

> In the affliction of these terrible dreams
> That shake us nightly: better be with the dead,
> Whom we, to gain our peace, have sent to peace,
> Than on the torture of the mind to lie
> In restless ecstasy. Duncan is in his grave;
> After life's fitful fever he sleeps well; … (Act III, Sc 2, ll 18–23)

He is unable to sleep for "restless ecstasy." With casual genius Shakespeare brings together states of restlessness with ecstasy. Lady Macbeth tries to put forward an absence of meaning to the act. She suggests it can be washed off with water, like any other stain. While Lady Macbeth urges Macbeth to shake off his torment, he is unable to look forward to his future as king. Eventually he is unable—or they are unable to get past their conscience.

Unlike Macbeth who is single-minded in his ambition, Dr. Faustus's greed is undifferentiated. He wants everything:

> Shall I make spirits fetch me what I please? Resolve me of all ambiguities? Perform what desperate enterprise I will? I'll have them fly to India for gold, Ransack the ocean for orient pearl, And search all corners of the new-found world … And chase the Prince of Parma from our land And reign sole king of all the provinces! (Act I, Sc 1, ll 79–84)

Faustus's desire corresponds to Lacan's idea that desire is the underside of the demand, the unspeakable residue that demand tries to voice (Lacan, 1958–1959). Faustus is dimly aware of the dangers of plenitude: will it end desire itself? What happens to the unspeakable residues, once demands are fulfilled?

Revolution

In popular imagination, it is the French Revolution that is often considered as the harbinger of modernity and change. As it gave birth to Romanticism, the idea of revolution captured European imagination and changed the associations forever, making it synonymous with liberty, fraternity, and equality.

Interestingly, the German equivalent (*Sturm und Drang*, translated as storm and stress) captures the turbulence that the English equivalent simply does not. Romantic restlessness is closer to "restive" (from *resister*) and signals what is desirable and good. This marks a shift from the Middle Ages when the humoral theory of Hippocrates (suggesting the body and the temper were determined by the balance between the four humors) leaned towards equanimity and stillness.

The Romantic hero (Satan, Prometheus, Adonais, etc.) is restless and here, unlike with Doctor Faustus, energy is magnificence. A good case in point is the Romantic rereading (or mis-reading) of Milton's Satan. Romantics erase the obvious Christian context within which Milton writes of it, as a "justification of God's ways to man." The lines that apparently demonstrate the wickedness of Satan are read by the Romantic poets as a heroic rebellion against despotic authoritarianism:

> The mind is its own place, and in itself can make a heaven of hell, a hell of heaven. (Book I, ll 254–255)

and/or

> All is not lost, the unconquerable will, and study of revenge, immortal hate, and the courage never to submit or yield. (Book I, ll 106–108)

Here, for instance, is the arch Romantic, Shelley eloquently defending Satan:

> Nothing can exceed the energy and magnificence of the character of Satan as expressed in Paradise Lost. It is a mistake to suppose that he could ever have been intended for the popular personification of evil … Milton's Devil as a moral being is as far superior to his God as … (Shelley, 1821, p. 27)

Is "restive" the condition under which the "symptom" is born? By "symptom" Freud does not mean undesirable detritus, but a rather wondrous manifestation of compromise. In the symptom, he saw the psychic strategy of pleasing two warring parts of our self and thereby the basis of psychic survival. This understanding brings the symptom and thereby illness itself in proximity to Romanticism. To put it simply, the neurotic (or "hysteric") was understood as someone tyrannized by their superego (usually God—Jehovah or Jove) but is unable to get rid of the dissidence (id).

Following this analogy, the ego itself can be read as a Romantic text. Dora and Ratman in particular might be quotidian versions of Prometheus and Satan. And Freud is asking repeatedly that we respect the symptom, however outrageous they may appear—as, for instance, about rats eating their way into the anus. He will listen to the rogue side of his Ratman (1909d) who cannot help wishing his father dead: "… the idea had come to him that she would be kind to him if some misfortune were to befall him; … his father's death had forced itself upon his mind …" (p. 178). This is then followed by "If my father dies, I shall kill myself upon his grave" (p. 179); Freud will eventually arrange it into a meaningful manifestation of human desire.

Leaving home

The nineteenth century, which was the great age of Romanticism, was also the age of expansion. The late eighteenth and nineteenth centuries were storm and stress but these ages were also simultaneously the ages of imperialism, of colonial expansion. We hear of early travelers setting out to explore the wealth of the Orient, often never to return home. What kind of restlessness is it that makes someone leave home in search of some Holy Grail, some elusive gold? While restless figures have stitched together the greatest epics (Ulysses, Aeneas, Oedipus), the eighteenth and nineteenth centuries had explorers and missionaries, traders and rulers setting out on long adventures into unknown places. The centuries of colonialism that followed may be seen as an expansion of ancient restlessness.

The Victorian poet Tennyson reimagines Homer's Ulysses after his return to Ithaca. Casting him as an early colonizer prototype, he has an interesting take on the insatiable colonizing appetite when he imagines Ulysses as an angry old man, unable to adapt to the stillness of his life at home. Instead, he urges his fellow travelers to "sail beyond the sunset" until they die. This poem written during the age of expansion brings in the aggressive restlessness of imperialism intimately, and it is hard to read this without irony. Is the irony ours as postcolonial subjects, or is Tennyson himself a bit hum-ho about it? These lines swing me in the direction of the latter:

> It little profits that an idle king,
> By this still hearth, among these barren crags,
> Match'd with an aged wife, I mete and dole
> Unequal laws unto a savage race,
> We are not now that strength which in old days
> Moved earth and heaven, that which we are, we are;
> One equal temper of heroic hearts,
> Made weak by time and fate, but strong in will
> To strive, to seek, to find, and not to yield. ("Ulysses," ll 1–9)

Unlike the colonizer who seeks to possess by force, the immigrant feels the inadequacy of his home (container) and searches for a better home. He makes the choice of leaving home. If this is experienced as a choice (and not an exile), this is closer to the depressive position, rather than the paranoid-schizoid (war and persecution). This entails mourning, perhaps a lifelong one. While some might argue that the immigrant is a lonely figure restless for a home, Salman Rushdie (1992) writing about the movie *The Wizard of Oz* (1939) gave a pertinent counterpoint: "In its most potent emotional moment, this is inarguably ... about the joys of going away, of leaving the grayness and entering the color, of making a new life in the 'place' where you won't get into any trouble." He wrote, "'Over the Rainbow' is, or ought to be, the anthem of all the world's migrants, all those who go in search of the place where 'the dreams that you dare to dream' really do come true. It is a celebration of Escape, a grand paean to the Uprooted Self, a hymn—the hymn—to Elsewhere" This way of looking at restlessness and we might say Rushdie's little ode to movement, adds another note to the oedipal narrative of leaving home.

Rushdie's ode to restlessness is of a piece with postmodern thinking. We can see it as coterminous with the centrality of separation as fundamental to individuation, in the West. It can be recast as being essential to developing our own apparatus for thinking and this being the *sine qua non* of modernity itself.

Furthermore, contemporary postmodern thinking places restlessness alongside indeterminacy and hybridity as requisite conditions for thinking (Bhabha, 1994). This inflects much contemporary psychoanalytic thinking as well, by several versions of relationality from interpersonal to intersubjective and field models.

Freud as Oedipus

Psychoanalysis has been cast by thinkers such as Herbert Marcuse (1955) as the Romantic hero who can liberate us from enslaving symptoms. Freud inaugurated a respect for the symptom, which he cast as a compromise struck by a conflicted psyche.

He also noted that disturbing this striving for equilibrium would have painful consequences. In his paper on female homosexuality (1920a), Freud mentions how the lifting of neurotic inhibitions would often be followed by separation. Somewhat acerbically, he concludes that the sole condition under which the marriage could be maintained was neurosis (p. 150). Here he is invoking the role of the superego in the perpetration of neurosis, in order to maintain the psychic economy.

Psychoanalysis has been understood as the usher of psychic change. This makes it restless. Based largely on the idea of psychic conflict, the mind is conceived as a cauldron with unstable, often combustible substances that may combine in all kinds of unpredictable ways. Restlessness appears as a symptom which beckons psychoanalytic thinking but can signify very varied states of mind.

If we go back to the originary myth of psychoanalysis—as inevitably we must—Oedipus is marked by restlessness. He chooses to leave a known and familiar universe with his royal parents in Corinth, leaving behind a kingdom to inherit. While on his way, a dispute erupts over the right of way, during which he infamously kills a man—on the crossroads to Thebes. In order to continue his journey, he must now solve the riddle of the Sphinx. In doing so, he also saves Thebes from the slaughtering monster. Accordingly, he becomes the king and marries the queen.

After years of ruling Thebes with his queen and children, despite spectacular discouragement, he decides to excavate the pollution that has overtaken his land. Why? His tone is peremptory, his reason is justice. But what truly resonates is that Oedipus is restless for truth.

This seems to add to what drew Freud to this doomed figure. The contrast with Jocasta highlights the difference between them. Feeling himself getting closer to the truth of parricide and incest, he pursues it more fiercely. He reports such a dream to Jocasta. She tells him to disregard such dreams saying, all sons have dreamt it at some point. Oedipus will not be deterred. The plague in Thebes may be read as a consequence of the destruction of truth and this must be undone. The parricide and incest cannot be reversed. The Chorus, that represents most of humanity, concerns itself very little with the truth and is fickle.

If Oedipus is the hero—rather than any other character—it could well suggest he is restless in a pervasive environment of untruth (let us recall that his parents in Corinth never told him about his parentage). With Oedipus as a prototypical adopted child who needs to find out the truth of his parentage, we could read the Theban crossroads as a restless junction between truth seeking and truth hating parts of our minds.

This restlessness can be reflected in the structure of writing too. In the tightly contrapuntal structure of his writings, Freud often maintained the tension between thesis and antithesis, without any resolution except for very momentary ones. It is as though the taut structure of his writing, more than the content, bears witness to the restlessness inherent in striving for truth. In *The Interpretation of Dreams* (1900a), he interprets all kinds of unpleasant and painful dreams as illuminating the centrality of the pleasure principle, while in *Beyond the Pleasure Principle* (1920g) he admits he can no longer stretch that paradigm to fit traumatic, repetitive dreams which are clearly unpleasurable.

The economic model of the mind that Freud posits, appears to correspond with the aim of maintaining an equilibrium; as the psychic economy seeks to maintain homeostasis. This is not as much a hedonistic expression of desire, as a discharge of unpleasurable stimuli (DeRose, 2022). The binaries (pleasure vs. reality) set up are thus quickly undone by Freud. This makes for a restless structure in his writing. Oedipus-like, Freud too is always casting his gaze into the darkness, searching for the truth of the present. Not resting on the truth of the past writing. Not absolute and unchanging (Oedipus saved Thebes once) but restless, contingent, fleeting (that savior moment has passed). What remains consistent is his allegiance to truth. In our understanding of the Freudian model of the mind, truth is mostly (though not solely) the repressed truth. But as we move towards Bion and Meltzer, we move from the idea of the repressed unconscious to the absence or unformulated "unconsciousizing" function. Attention shifts to a primitive unconscious that is unable to utilize the thinking apparatus to organize psychic experience, or simply give meaning to experiences.

Protoemotional experiences

We often use the expression "to be moved by something." This is the root word for emotion (Latin *ex movere*) as well. The etymological connection between movement and emotion is in this instance, intuitive. Freud recognized that that old bulwark "resistance" gets in the way of any new thought; or to begin with, it causes motion. With great violence, we fend off any motion inside us, for restfulness is always accompanied by fragility.

Walter Benjamin (1940) observed that "The greater the share of the shock factor in particular impressions, the more we have to screen against stimuli. Efficiency here means screening the impressions from entering experience" (p. 319). The fragility of the mind intensifies the assaults of life and a walling it up protects the mind from crumbling. This also severs contact with one's own experiences. These impressions piling up may be regurgitated.

I wondered about what might constitute the antonyms of restlessness: restful, easy, peaceful, quiet, relaxing, calm? I suggest the capacity for emotional experiences is an antidote to restlessness. In fact, we may say an emotional experience in the way Meltzer (1986) defines it is one where the turbulence has been lived out. Meltzer identifies it as:

> An emotional experience is an encounter with the beauty and mystery of the world which arouses conflict between L, H and K, and minus L, H and K. While the immediate meaning is experienced as emotion, maybe as diverse as the objects of immediate arousal, its significance is always ultimately concerned with intimate human relationships. (p. 26)

Meltzer is here expanding on Bion's idea that most of our lives are spent mindlessly. Most areas of interaction are either too casual to involve emotion, or so contractual as to preclude "spontaneous emotional response." He reserves the "term 'intimate' human relationships, on the other hand ... for the emotional experiences that set thought in motion" (p. 27).

In the purview of emotional experience, I might consider adding religious experiences like conversion. Such experiences, perhaps in the Augustinian tradition, recognize the catastrophic impact of certain powerful emotional encounters. Modernism challenges the epiphanic, by taking away the finality of any singular encounter, and opens the door to the ongoing nature of such encounters. The epiphanic gives way to the episodic, the molecule to particles, the heroic to the quotidian.

For these microunits of experience, art and psychoanalysis continue to search for language. Restlessness seeks language that it can be communicated. Language contains the restlessness of unnameable experiences. But if language is a container, it is also an inadequate one, for the ineffable (Bion) or the enigmatic (Lacan) are by definition unknowable. And yet we are restlessly in search of ways of communicating with our objects—imaginary and real, external and internal. But these encounters may have a spectral (Lacan) or hallucinatory (Bion) quality, as the experiences have not been metabolized. To return to chemical reactions, there are also combustion reactions that produce smoke, heat, and water. This is somewhat akin to protoemotional encounters.

If we turn to D. H. Lawrence's *Sons and Lovers* (1913a), we see a very poignant instance of an attempt to forge a language for protoemotional encounters.

It is true of course that Lawrence never acknowledged Freud, and yet psychoanalysis was clearly reverberating through his writing; not least in his work called *Fantasia of the Unconscious* (1922). Obviously I do not just mean it in the narrow sense of libidinal love between sons and mothers. Lawrence fashions a narrator who is not omniscient in the conventional sense, but has access to unconscious knowledge. Right at the start, the narrator observes the little boy, William, coming home a bit late. By now the unhappy failure of his parents' marriage is established. The mother hands her son a cup of tea: "He was miserable, though he did not know it, because he had let her go alone" (p. 8).

This is a highly unusual sentence, as it draws attention to William's state that is unknown to him. Lawrence is distinguishing here between conscious and unconscious suffering. Furthermore, the little boy William does not know "it," but the narrator does. We are made privy to what is unknown to the characters—this is conventional. But the narrator's omniscience acquires a different dimension with his presumed access to the unconscious: "Nevertheless, there was a state of peace ... Neither knew that she was more tolerant because she loved him less" (p. 55).

At other moments, Lawrence names it as such: "The latter was unconsciously jealous of his brother, and William was jealous of him" (p. 84).

Storytellers often direct us with adverbs: he said it gingerly, she added softly, they looked sheepishly. What Lawrence achieves is an unconscious inflection to this kind of adverbial signposting.

We see this in the awkward syntax, the tense and clumsy adverbial comments: "Her still face, with the mouth closed tight from suffering, and disillusion and self-denial, and her nose the smallest bit on one side, and her blue eyes so young, quick, and warm, made his heart contract with love" (p. 81).

It is a clumsy, heavy sentence with too many weighty words as the mouth is closed tight from "suffering, and disillusion and self-denial ..." The external does not correspond to an internal state, but the unconscious experience shapes physiognomy. Lawrence is forging a language for protoemotions; perhaps not always elegantly. But the intensity forms the musical score of this story.

The death of William follows his inability to break up with his girlfriend, Lily. Inarticulate but intense, William brokenly tries to form his response: "She is not like you, Mater." Feeling his own ambivalence and sensing mother's disappointment, he says: "I cannot leave her, Mother." He returns to London—the heaviness of the mood foretells his tragic death. Unable to bear the turmoil of the emotional experience, he dies of an unexplained illness.

The experience is an unbearable one of his disappointment, heavy with his mother's sense of betrayal, and the fear of not being able to love Lily. This preoccupation with the unbearability of emotion is constant. After William's death, slowly and somewhat effortfully, Mrs. Morel returns to life, and Paul takes William's place. There is a moment where she looks at Paul:

> She had never expected him to live. And yet he had a great vitality in his young body. Perhaps it would have been a relief

to her if he had died. She always felt a mixture of anguish in her love for him. (p. 81)

This short fragment captures the intensity of emotion that the mother feels for this boy with his delicate frame. To read this as murderous wishes would be a profound misreading, rather the language strives to convey the unbearability of love that is inevitably accompanied by an anguish and a dread of vulnerability. If she cannot protect him from life, it were better he died than suffer seeing how vulnerable he is. It is not a death wish as much as it is a passionate, unbearable, even primitive love.

Eventually she will die because of an overdose he will give her. To love, is to suffer. If the characters are wrestling with the weight of their intensities, Lawrence is struggling to tell the story in a way that captures the shifting, restless dynamic of intimate relationships. The fidgetiness of feelings gives the book a strange restlessness. Paul lugs around the bulk of it—as protagonist, but nobody is spared the quicksilver (Old English, from *cwicu* alive + *seolfer* silver) of feelings. It seems here that feelings are synonymous with constant movement. I suggest that restlessness might then be born at the point of contact with feelings which are yet protoemotions, which threaten to either engulf or disperse the subject. Here I would like to quote:

> Upon each slash, the proto-emotions—a term that is of course not susceptible to unambiguous definition and denotes a range of states … they are the bearers of an excess. Emotions inform the mind about the state of its relations with the object (with the world) … However, if untransformed, they are scattered in an immense mental space, so that the subject may in effect bleed to death in his own tissues on account of a surgical shock. (Bion, 1970, p. 12 in Civitarese, 2013)

These unbearable encounters like undigested emotions leave behind the "ghosts of departed quantities" (Bion, 1965), uncanny residues that will not let the mind rest, but will rock us back and forth from the truth—mostly led by our shifting capacity to bear pain.

In the case material discussed, I would like to think of restlessness in at least two ways. The material is loosely based on a combination of patients, who all seem to have addictive traits. The object they are addicted to is changeable, but not their relationship to the object. Mina is a placeholder for them. Interestingly she kept getting drawn to people who turned out to be addicts: gambling, sex, pornography, and drugs. It is as though she needs the proximity of addicts to feel intense excitement, which she restlessly searches for. I will try next to trace the psychoanalytic story of restlessness through my work with Mina.

Restlessness of drive and object

Winnicott (1958) observes that the "so-called normal child" is able to play and get excited, "without feeling threatened by a physical orgasm of local excitement" (p. 35). This is not so for other children, such as those marked by "manic-defence restlessness." Such children are unable to tolerate their excitement. Winnicott understands "orgasm" here as a necessary discharge of excitement which enables a return to a zero state. But if the child is unable to reach a climax, the restlessness becomes manic. This insight is delivered in a characteristically off the cuff manner. An orgasm is a way of signaling fullness: "A physical climax is needed, and every parent knows the moment when nothing brings an exciting game to an end except a smack—which provides a false climax, but a very useful one" (p. 35). Here is the secular, psychoanalytic version of much Christian writing discussed in the religious poems above.

However, while Winnicott is writing about the antisocial child, I think the eluded orgasm, or the inability to feel a climax might be crucial to understanding addiction in general. Too many patients tell us about not being able to sleep and of nocturnal activities mostly done in great privacy if not secrecy that may include efforts both to cancel the arousal by white noise or stimulate it by creating yet more excitement: pornography, junk food. Sometimes it can be alternating uppers with downers, anecdotally, as the poet Auden did, perhaps to get a grip on the vagaries of moods. The day with all its sunshine and dazzling brightness colludes with us in putting on a smiling public face. The restless figure somewhat uncannily tears off our veil from us and sometimes we scramble to patch it up again, and at other times we are face to face with it, walking the moors, the streets, loitering, overeating, stalking. Stealthily engaged in keeping away experiences.

A clinical vignette

Forty-year-old Mina came with the question of whether or not to leave a husband who was addicted to sex (mostly online). She said he had left his phone around and she went over everything and she hadn't been able to stop. She would recite over and over again these exchanges which she had learned verbatim. If what I said sounded like men do cheat, she would berate me obliquely by saying she hated women like her mother who "ate shit." If what I said sounded to her like the husband was "a jerk," she would talk about falling apart without him. The analysis quickly became a concrete extension of her inner world, and I the placeholder for the rude interlocutor.

Mina was marked by a restlessness that had a life of its own. "I can't sit at home, I have to go to a café, I have to go out, I have to swim, I have to travel." She would feel a lot of relief from physical activities, as though she were masturbating. Her husband's sexual addiction (like Winnicott's antisocial child) meant he could not have an orgasm and so he could not stop.

She went on to fall in love with a series of men after him, and each time it would be turbulent, leading to great bouts of restlessness. She would curl up on the couch shivering with sexual longing and trying to shake it off: "Sometimes I put on music—and dance—it's very sexual …" She needs to constantly have sex or listen to trance music, or dance. If she can have the three together (she often goes to carnivals), she is able to obliterate consciousness. After these carnivals, she returns animated, but in the next session, she is like a collapsed balloon. The dip that inevitably follows the climax is violently disabled. The contrast with the pre-orgasmic trembling makes all other moments seem lifeless. She has never known satiety, but only ever the depression of emptiness. I begin to see when she spoke of her partner's inability to have an orgasm, she was talking about herself. She needs to go from one ecstatic state to another and avoid all the troughs and valleys.

To suffer pain, Bion writes repeatedly, one has to have respect for pain. But Mina equates pain with frustration. "I need to discharge this feeling." Her self-flagellation has been her version of "suffering." I would like to suggest this is not so much either an "evasion" of suffering or *prima facie* a manifestation of masochism, but more that masochism is for her a concrete way of experiencing pain. She does things to the pain to relieve herself of it—makes it concrete (masochistic self-beating), binge eats it, regurgitates it, sexualizes it (I haven't had a release).

Clinical vignette continued
> I would bring her attention to something she was trying to get away from: the slights by her newly recognized boyfriend, the spiteful comment by her boss. Perhaps I felt sadistic: "How much more do you want it to hurt?" This is how she experienced it. Feeling my impatience, she would start burping, and it felt like an intolerance of the session—as I was bringing back to her mouth/head what should have been expelled and was disgusting to her now. The terms she uses like discharge, release, and energy all seem to suggest the absent (but therefore extremely present) objects in the mind. But as I began to see it in the nowness of the session, it occurred to me that each time she picks up my frustration with her million antennae, it overwhelms her and she gets terrified I am going to eject her from the session. This state of perennial and intense vulnerability is what she restlessly tries to get rid of. What appears as disregard of my presence, is actually a carefully devised strategy of concealing her dependency.

Restlessness may here be thought of as pleas made to the imaginary object. Lacan (1958–1959) writes: "Every time that you have to deal with something which is properly speaking a phantasy, you will see that it can be articulated in these terms of reference of the subject as speaking to the imaginary other. This is what defines the phantasy, every phantasy is articulated in terms of the subject speaking to the imaginary other" (p. 12).

Back to the clinical vignette
> When she talks about leaving her husband, she is also talking about how terrified she is of her dependence on me. If she keeps her eyes closed, she can momentarily obliterate this truth. A lot of mental energy seems to be expended in getting rid of my awareness—particulate remains of objects—which are experienced as unwanted. Her vocabulary is akin to early hydraulic models of the mind, before

the object was recognized as the giver of meaning. Psychoanalysis too seemed to have evolved from a mechanistic self to a vibrant internal world crowded with objects. There is a dread of seeing her vulnerability which makes her unseeing, of "sleepwalking" through life. So much so, that she does not see she has been having an affair for three years with a close friend who is married, until I feel compelled to name it. After this, she is seized by desire for this man which makes her tremble. All such sensations feel unbearable to her and she speaks as though she were a battery powered object. "I need to charge, release, discharge energies."

This is one kind of restlessness—where the mind meets the truth it expelled and tries to shake it off. In such moments, she cannot see (literally keeps her eyes screwed tightly, to let in only a little light) what she is doing. With Mina the superego had taken on a resemblance to what Bion calls the cruel, murderous superego:

> It is a super-ego that has hardly any of the characteristics of the super-ego as understood in psycho-analysis: it is "super" ego. It is an envious assertion of moral superiority without any morals. … The most important characteristic is its hatred of any new development in the personality as if the new development were a rival to be destroyed. The emergence therefore of any tendency to search for the truth, to establish contact with reality … is met by destructive attacks on the tendency and the reassertion of the "moral" superiority. (Bion, 1962a, pp. 97–98)

A brief digression into *Hamlet*

Let me digress here to Hamlet who wanders around at night as though he dare not sleep "for in that sleep of death, what dreams may come." He is unable to mourn his father, for that would also mean accepting his death. His superego demands action; passivity is acceptance of injustice. Revenge is based on a rejection of something that has happened. He tells himself he needs to be sure that his uncle and his mother were responsible and/or complicit. He invents a lie detector of his own. *The Mousetrap* is the play within the play (about the murder of an old duke) staged by

Hamlet where he means to trap his father's murderer/s by him watching the expressions of the suspects in the audience.

One way of thinking about this tormented figure is to see how the superego has split. Unlike *Macbeth* where the conflict is closer to id vs. superego (or ambition vs. conscience), here we have the superego split into murderous splinters. Hamlet wants to do the right thing, but no voice emerges as that of supreme ethical imperative. So "conscience doth make traitors of us all," may well mean that conscience itself is waylaid by traitorous dissent. No sooner does a voice emerge, than there is another voice challenging it:

Claudius is a liar and a murderer. He must be punished: "Now might I do it pat … And so I am revenged" (Act III, Sc 3, ll 77–78).

Gertrude could be a conspirator. Or she could have been lied to. After feeling moved by the performance of one of the actors, Hamlet wonders aloud, how to know if someone is telling the truth or not, for actors are so convincing:

> What's Hecuba to him, or he to her,
> That he should weep for her? (Act II, Sc 2, ll 586–587)

But at the same time, he is unsure of his suspicions: "I'll have grounds more relative than this" (Act II, Sc 2, ll 632–633).

The ghost could have lied to him:

> The spirit that I have seen
> May be the devil: and the devil hath power
> To assume a pleasing shape; … (Act II, Sc 2, ll 627–628)

But also: "It is an honest ghost" (Act I, Sc 5, l 154).

But he should take revenge for the murder of his father. But revenge is not his to take: "… suffer outrageous fortune or take arms against a sea of troubles" (Act III, Sc 1, ll 65–67).

It is just such a splintered superego that causes Mina torment. Her husband wronged her. So she must leave him. But she collapses without him. Staying with him was weakness. To be weak is contemptible. She would never do to another what he did to her. So now when she is doing that, she cannot open her eyes (her eyes are only a slit open).

She must also prove she can do what her husband did. Yet she would never do something as wicked as him.

Such splitting is not between repressed desires and a conscientious superego, but a battlefield where shards of superego battle each other murderously. The session often resembles this battlefield, leaving a debris of the thinking apparatus and not a cohesive unit with two warring sides. One might say the restlessness was born of an inability to bear protoemotions:

> … they are not thoughts, but souls of thoughts waiting to be actually dreamt; hence they are proto-concepts or pre-conceptions, like the bed of a river as opposed to the water that flows over it (but which could also not flow). (Civitarese, 2013, p. 103)

A few more words about the clinical vignette

It was not just her but also my inability to bear her protoemotions.

When she told me her story first, we could not get past her concrete reality (husband's sex addiction). The shock, humiliation (of having to tell it to me) and excitement caused a turmoil that made it difficult to digest. The external concrete reality kept a compelling presence and she would burp continually in response to anything outside what she called the "yo-yo" movement. As though she were pleading with me to let her expel the nasty truth and not ingest it.

Years later, and somewhat imperceptibly, we came upon her craving for excitement and sex, to the exclusion of almost anything else. Her husband was no longer of interest (she did not need to restlessly locate it in him), as her own sexual appetite took us by storm.

The restlessness found its home in sexual voraciousness. Bringing me to the same question: did her sexual appetite fuel her restlessness, or was the restlessness in search of a stage?

Now I could feel how much she needed me but grew impatient to be acknowledged. Otherwise, I was being used as an addiction. More sessions, more words. "Words, words, words" (Act II, Sc 2, l 210).

I grew restless with being used as an opiate. I hear her repeating "sexual needs," "loneliness," "need space." In the scatter of these words, I say something about how she wants it all, and how incompatible much of it sounds. This was obviously a red rag. I realized that I was provoked at being just another bedfellow and wanted her to be "monogamous" (to see ours as a meaningful relationship, and not just another casual encounter). And perhaps I wanted that she would always be lonely till she could bear how vulnerable this made her feel. The uncertainty this brings in its wake quells some of the old restlessness.

Conclusion

As psychoanalysis continues to search for its own *raison d'être*, we often have to be content with the moments of contact and expansion in the sessions itself. In doing so, we hope to strengthen the muscularity of the thinking apparatus.

Seen from different vertices (romantic love, religious poetry, migration, colonialism) restlessness is both a dread of, and a longing for change. It often signals pain, urging both modification and evasion. It takes us both towards thinking, and away from it. In different analytic moments, we respond to it differently: with patience and impatience, by colluding and by standing apart. The question that recurs, like a refrain, is whether restlessness is a symptom of a psychic conflict (as often suggested by the repressive model) or whether it is "primary," born of the chaos of disorganized psychic experience and seeking a stage where it can find expression.

I have used some fragments from Lawrence's visceral *Sons and Lovers* to illustrate the restless writing that seems to capture the quicksilver of the unconscious whose movements may be likened to the subatomic particles' interactions. This leads into a clinical vignette that illuminates the hydra headed experience of restlessness—a communication of an experience that is seeking a thinker.

CHAPTER EIGHT

Cowardliness

Salman Akhtar

Cowardliness or cowardice is a topic that attracts guilty fascination with gingerly dollops of pity and disgust. Given the revulsive dysphoria induced by its mere mention, it is hardly surprising that little literature exists on the characterological trait. Even the two great pieces of fiction involving cowardice, *Lord Jim* (Conrad, 1900) and *The Four Feathers* (Mason, 1902), fail to grapple with the pertinent intricacies of cowardliness by treating it as a single hemorrhage of courage and by devoting the rest of the text to the protagonist undoing the actual and ethical damage done by that dastardly act. Both books thus end up being about courage, not cowardice. Even Philip Reiff, the well-known North-American sociologist, who set out to write a book about cowardice, succumbed to a similar slippery slope and did not include "cowardliness" or "cowardice" in that book's title; he named it *The Triumph of the Therapeutic* (Reiff, 1966) and emphasized the potential of psychoanalysis to release man from the prison of his fears.

The topic of cowardice has received somewhat greater attention from poets. T. S. Eliot (1963) maps the wide terrain of cowardice by juxtaposing "Do I dare / Disturb the Universe?" with "Shall I part my hair behind / Do I dare to eat a peach." Robert Service (1907) impishly brings up the nearly unmentionable link between cowardice and virginity: "And many a maid remains a maid / because she is afraid." Langston Hughes's poem "Dreams" (1951) warns about the life-depleting quality of cowardly inaction and D. H. Lawrence's poem "Snake" (1913b) underscores the regret that follows cowardly behavior: "And I have something to expiate: / A pettiness."

Moving on from sociologists, novelists, and poets to psychoanalysts, one encounters a gaping hole in contributions to the understanding of this curious, if unattractive, character trait. And it is this void that I aim to fill with my modest contribution. In it, I will explicate the descriptive features of cowardliness, its ontogenetic origins, and its psychosocial consequences. I will also offer a few clinical illustrations to shed light upon the phenomenology and psychodynamics of cowardliness as well as upon the potential therapeutic interventions aimed at its amelioration. The discourse will conclude with brief comments upon the existence of cowardice in professional circles of psychoanalysis and upon the silent but important role it plays in society at large.

Etymology, definition, and descriptive features

The current English word "coward" is derived from the Old French *coart* (Modern French *couard*), which, in turn, is traceable to *cauda*, the Latin word for tail. Thus, *coart* meant "the one with a tail" and was aimed at conjuring up the image of an animal turning away from attack and displaying its tail in a flight of fear. It also brings the image of a dog putting its tail between its legs when retreating from danger ("*dum daba ke bhaga*" in Urdu).

The three other most widely spoken languages, namely, Spanish, Chinese, and Arabic, bring further nuances to this nosological realm. Spanish *cobardía*, for instance, is emphatically feminine. Chinese *qiendo* and Arabic *juban* lack gender specificity but the Arabic application of it to women has a clearly diminutive form. Together with English, all these languages depict cowardice as something "less than manly," "feminine" (in a derogatory way), and even "subhuman." Such derisive dehumanization is evident in the English colloquialism "chicken-hearted" or simply "chicken" (verb: "chickened out"), German *Feigheit* (meaning "a soft egg"), Persian *buzdil* (meaning "with the heart of a goat"), and

Turkish *ödlek* (with its slang association to *ödlek* inferring *ördek* and meaning "a duck").

While interesting, especially in their substantial overlaps, these diverse etymologies reveal more about societal attitudes about cowardice than about the components of the trait itself which, based upon the knowledge I have gained from clinical and social experience, seems multilayered and quite complex. Moreover, many diverse realms (e.g., physical, intellectual, moral) can become the psychic locale of cowardice. *Physical cowardice* involves an inordinate fear of injury, and the resulting restriction of exploratory and playful motor activity; one avoids athletics, amusement, park rides, and any possibility of physical altercation. *Intellectual cowardice* results in inhibition of mental activity; one cannot think "outside the box" and gets scared if new insights do pop off in the mind. *Moral cowardice* manifests as the inability to uphold ethical standards and speak the truth under difficult circumstances; one lies, suddenly seems to lack words, and adopts the "silence of the complicit" (Akhtar, 2013). Regardless of the psychosocial realm inhabited by cowardliness, a careful look reveals the attribute to be a combination of four meta-features.

- *Lack of courage:* Here it is important to recognize that courage does not imply absence of fear. A courageous person is not the "danger-defying type" (Glover, 1940). He knows that his stance and actions can have adverse consequences (as financial loss, physical injury, personal ridicule) and yet he pursues what his core convictions tell him to do (Akhtar, 2013). The coward, in contrast, is terrified of danger, averse to confrontation, and lacking in conviction over his own beliefs. Fascinatingly, a tendency of such sort can also be discerned in the formation of dreams. Generally speaking, dreams do not depict a full-blown actualization of the prohibited wish in question. Termed "dream cowardice" by Garma (1966), this mechanism assures, for instance, that the desire to make love with an incestuous object is manifested as merely rubbing against them.
- *Subjective sense of weakness:* Cowardliness represents a "crippling of the will" (Menaker, 1979, p. 93). The coward readily succumbs to fear and withdraws from conflicted situations. There is a subjective lack of psychic fortitude and of perceived bodily strength. One feels weak, child-like, and helpless.

- *Retreat into rationalization:* Cowardliness seeks justification. This is found in "logical" explanations of why confrontation (cleverly substituted for assertiveness) is hardly laudable and might complicate matters further. Generalizations and platitudes involving patience and forgiveness are deployed to mask one's inability (and unwillingness) to swim against the stream when needed. Recognition of such timidity fills the coward's heart with shame and self-disgust; these are often drowned in drink or covered over by the narcissistic fantasy of having deliberately engineered the defeat. The spineless combatant of yesterday thus transforms himself into the lofty bestower of victory to others.
- *Pseudo-equanimity:* Cowardliness is frequently accompanied by a defensive attitude of not caring and remaining unperturbed by oppression, injustice, and abuse. Such "stoicism" serves as a shield against the shame over one's incapacity to be bold. Akin to Deutsch's (1942) "as if" characters, the coward displays "an air of mild amiability and negative goodness" (p. 307).

Together these four features (lack of courage, subjective sense of weakness, retreat into rationalization, and pseudo-equanimity) complete the phenomenological portrait of cowardliness. And, as can be anticipated, these meta-traits have deep rooted and complex origins as well as multilayered and varied consequences.

Origins and consequences

There is sadness on both ends of cowardice. Its origin is mired in ego-weakening breeches in early attachments during childhood. Its consequences are often regret-inducing, tragic, and at times, fatal. A thorough consideration of both the origins and consequences of cowardliness is therefore essential to fully understand the phenomenon and to evolve therapeutic strategies for its diminution.

Origins

At the core of cowardliness lies fear. Now, since fear is ubiquitous and "hard-wired," it is not the mere existence of fear that leads to cowardice. It is the lack of the restraint over instinctive, amygdala-based fear by experientially acquired cortical input that results in the exaggerated fear associated with cowardice. The former type of fear is modulated by a shorter, rapid, and subcortical route and the latter much diminished and rational apprehension by a complex hippocampal and cortical route (Damasio, 1999; Pally, 2000). When the latter correction is lacking, fear grows and pervades the character. Translated into psychoanalytic terms, this means a child's instinctive fears are diminished by maternal demonstrations of fortitude and her "containment" of the child's anxieties. Internalization of such maternal attitudes imparts courage to the child's interactional and exploratory capacities; Freud's (1923b) dictum that "the character of the ego is a precipitate of abandoned object cathexes" (p. 26) lends support to my proposal here. The child who turns out to be brave gives testimony to ample internalizations of maternal fortitude. The child who turns out to be cowardly lacks such internal foundation.

A related, if developmentally earlier, notion is that of the mother providing a psychic skin that "holds" and "contains" the vacillating and scattered internal experiences of the infant (Bick, 1968); internalization of such maternal coverage, in turn, lays yet another layer to the foundation of a solid core to the psychic self of the child. Yet another factor pertinent in the genesis of courage vs. cowardice is the extent to which a healthy, non-conflicted identification with the same-sex parent has taken place in the course of development. Exceptions notwithstanding, a cis-gender child takes in the era-specific and culture-specific roles (and, their attendant interpersonal actions) played by his or her same-sex parent in order to consolidate a societally useful identity. If such identifications are deficient (e.g., due to an actually absent or emotionally disengaged parent), weakness in certain sectors of ego can result and add to cowardly tendencies.

The most important etiological factor in cowardice, however, is a condensation of body mutilation anxieties (including, of course, "castration anxiety") and a dreading of separation and aloneness. An "ocnophil" (Balint, 1968) *par excellence*, the coward clings to his objects and is willing to sacrifice personal dignity at the altar of social relatedness. Cowardice, at its bottom, reflects the fear of being disliked and being alone. Meltzer (1973) notes:

> Where dependence on good internal objects is rendered infeasible by damaging masturbatory attacks and where dependence on a good external object is unavailable or not acknowledged, and

addictive relationship to a bad part of the self—the submission to tyranny takes place. An illusion of safety is promulgated by the omniscience of the bad part ... Where a dread of loss of an addictive relation to a tyrant is found in psychic structure, the problem of terror will be found at its core, as the force behind the dread and the submission. (p. 78)

Thus, a combination of ego-weakness, thin-skinned nature, and conflict-avoidance (due to the dread of bodily combat and injury as well as loss of love objects) undergirds the psychosocial surface of cowardice.

Consequences

The saga on the "distal" end of cowardliness is no less bleak. It is true that occasionally an action (or inaction) born out of cowardice jolts the individual into reparative efforts, atonement, and even boldness (e.g., the protagonists in *Lord Jim* and *The Four Feathers*). However, more often one comes across the dark shadow of private shame and regret as consequences of cowardly action or inaction.

Shame is an inevitable, though secret, companion of cowardice. This is because the coward knows that he is a coward. He does not lack ideas, beliefs, opinions, and convictions. He lacks the fortitude to hold on to them in the face of opposition and does not have the courage to express them openly. Aware of his hapless stance, the coward is chronically ashamed of himself. Unable to receive "narcissistic confirmation from one's peers to diminish the margins between the ego and the ego ideal" (Chasseguet-Smirgel, 1985, p. 161), the coward constantly feels blemished and defective. This results in an ongoing rupture in self-continuity; the coward acts one way while wistfully realizing that he would like to act in another way. Defensively, he withdraws from vigorous interactions while, at times, privately indulging in contempt for others and narcissistic self-inflation.

A more devastating consequence of cowardliness is regret. Having done something cowardly or not having acted boldly when that was required leaves the coward filled with regret; the distress arising from acts of omission is far more painful than that from acts of commission (Kahneman & Tversky, 1982). Though myriad illustrations of either exist, those more common clinically encountered include agreeing to an arranged marriage in the face of parental pressure, succumbing to the gaslighting by an abusive parent or sibling, and signing on an unjust property settlement during divorce proceedings (cowardly acts of commission), and not approaching a young woman or man one has a huge crush upon, being too conflicted to attend a nephew's wedding or an uncle's funeral (cowardly acts of omission).

Chronic regret over such decisions involves intricate disturbances of ego and superego functioning. The impaired ego functions are evident via loss of flexibility in considering matters of the inner world and external reality, in disturbances of the subjective experience of time which seems to have stopped, and in the masochistic submission to a life in bondage. Cognition is flooded with "contrafactual thought, or imaging states contrary to the fact: especially what might have been" (Landman, 1993, p. 37). The superego disturbances include hypercriticism of past actions or inactions and their (real or imaginary) consequences, lack of self-forgiveness, mockingly triumphant attitude toward the hapless sectors of the ego, and an unfortunate jettisoning of current pleasures at the altar of an even-unachievable renewal of the past. At times a well-systematized "if only" fantasy (Akhtar, 1996) comes to dominate the mind and keeps one trapped in an existence of nostalgic wistfulness. Joseph Heller's (1974) *Something Happened* and Louis Begley's (1993) *The Man Who Was Late* are exemplary novels that capture devastating regret that haunts the protagonists after their cowardly failure to capture love when it appeared in their lives. Clearly, cowardliness begets shame and regret. Protecting one from interpersonal skirmishes, it leaves one internally tormented often for the rest of one's life.

Clinical illustrations

Since the clinical situation involves two parties—both human, both fallible—it seems only fair to address the existence and manifestations or cowardice in both of them.

Patient's cowardliness

The "fundamental rule" (Freud 1900a) of psychoanalysis—emanating from the principle of psychic determinism, connections of all things in the system Ucs, and instinctual drives seeking their fulfillment through preconscious and conscious derivatives—impels the patient to speak without censorship and expose all his mental contents for the analyst's inspection. Not accustomed to such openness, the patient feels scared. This fear is more marked when it comes to revealing personal fantasies. Freud (1908e) distinguishes between the child who does not conceal his fantasies and can openly put them into action in the form of play ("Mom! Look, I am Superman!") and the adult who

> is ashamed of his phantasies and hides them from other people. He cherishes his phantasies as his most intimate possessions, and as a rule would rather confess his misdeeds than tell anyone his phantasies. (p. 145)

Clinical experience provides ample evidence of the hesitation and fear patients experience in talking about their death wishes towards their children, prohibited erotic strivings, and grandiose self-images and ambitions. The suffocating smog of cowardice that might descend upon the patient at such times has to be resolved by the analyst's patience, non-judgmental attitude, and gentle encouragements to proceed. However, it is the patient himself who must overcome such resistance and put ordinary social reserve and momentary cowardice aside.

Clinical vignette: 1

> Jack Rheuban, a middle-aged lawyer, sought help for depression, increased drinking, and loss of interest in his marital life. As our discourse unfolded, it became clear that Jack was a secretive man who had kept many parts of his life hidden from his wife. With time, the existence of this tendency during his childhood came to the surface. The secrets of that era included his drawing elaborate diagrams of his plans to kill his forever critical and mocking father once he grew up. Another secret, which he had more difficulty revealing, involved touching his older sister's genitalia while she was asleep. He claimed that he never understood why he did that except that doing something "weird" made him feel strangely special and powerful.
>
> About this time, Jack found himself badly stuck in a session. With great difficulty, he revealed that he needed to tell me something but was afraid to do so; he feared that I would shame him, find

him disgusting, and stop seeing him. I responded by saying that we needed to observe two things here: *one*, that he was already trusting me enough to consider telling me whatever was troubling him so much and *two*, that by imagining me laughing at him, he was transposing the image of his father upon me.

Jack relaxed somewhat after this intervention and then asked if he could turn his chair around so that he would not be facing me. I agreed. Then too he needed a long pause before telling me that he often picks his nose and eats the snot gathered on his fingertip. I responded by saying something along these lines: "I think you are relieved that you told this to me because now you are not alone with this secret. I also understand that you would fear being shamed by me since this is something that under ordinary social circumstances would be found disgusting and be mocked. However, for the work you and I have undertaken, the question is hardly of shame and ridicule. The question is one of understanding. In other words, how do we understand this behavior? Frankly, it is too early for me to say anything about it, but I have a vague sense that it might be akin to one of the often "weird" things you have done in the past to keep yourself feeling vital, alive, and even special. What do you think?"

The point here is not what I said but the fact that my patient, Jack, was able to overcome his trepidation and not give in to cowardliness. Now this incident demonstrates only a momentary block of assertiveness and self-assured dignity; some might even question whether such fleeting fears qualify to be called "cowardice". The objection of such colleagues would certainly be tempered by the following clinical vignette where a lifelong pattern of timidity and conflict-avoidance dominated the clinical picture.

Clinical vignette: 2

Bobby Schwartz, a forty-four-year-old fledging writer, sought help for solving a particular dilemma in his life. He hated his father, wished him dead on a daily basis, but could not express even the slightest aggression towards the old man. The origin of his hatred had to do with the fact that he was born with a congenital anomaly that resulted not only in his being bullied by neighborhood kids and school mates but also by his father. Beginning from his early childhood to his current age of forty-four, Bobby encountered constant mocking and denigration by his father for this defect. Bobby hated his father but since he was financially compromised and his father—old and wealthy—was a potential source of significant inheritance, he felt afraid to express anger toward him. This led Bobby to loathe himself for being such a coward.

The matter was compounded by the fact Bobby's father insisted upon their meeting once a month for lunch. This took place in an expensive restaurant which Bobby could not afford to visit on his own. Besides tolerating the envy of his father's affluence during such encounters, Bobby also had to put up with the father making frequent and derisive references to his congenital defect. Fuming with rage, he sat there feeling helpless—a pawn in his father's diabolical chess game. All Bobby wanted was for his father to die and to inherit his nearly 10–15 million dollars' worth of property. Bobby said that he had heard of me, seen my publications on Amazon, and was impressed by me. He had therefore come to see me to seek the answer of just one question. Should he stand up to his father, tell him to go fuck himself, and lose the money that might come to him? Or should he continue to act like a sissy, a coward in front of his father in the hope that the old man will die and leave him enormous wealth? Bobby added that he had seen many therapists to no avail. Some told him to stop meeting his father altogether and choose dignity over money. Others advised to the contrary. Neither helped. Bobby was frozen. Righteously enraged on the one side and intimidated and cowardly on the other. "What should I do, please tell me?" he said.

I responded by saying something like this: "Look, you cannot get rid of your father and your rage towards him even if you run away to a far-off land or express your anger directly at him; it has become a deep part of your psyche. So, running away or raging at him hardly makes any sense. On the other hand, those who minimize how 10–15 million dollars can alter your life are also out of their minds. Frankly, I do not think you can either give up your father or renounce the hope of a grand inheritance." Bobby looked relieved and excited by my answer. Quickly, he said, "So what should I do?" I responded by saying: "Frankly I do not know but whatever you have to do is not simple.

It would take a lot of time and thought. I do, however, know the first step of this process and if you want, I can tell it to you." He said, "Please!" I said, "Cry."

This clinical interaction shows the complexities of cowardice—in so far as Bobby's inability to confront his father was both a sign of characterological weakness but also of worldly savvy. Moreover, the situation presented not as a "convergent conflict" (where compromise is possible) but as a "divergent conflict" (where mourning is required) to use A. Kris's (1988) terminology. My recommendation ("Cry!") was an interpretation directed to mobilize the mourning process.

While Bobby entered and completed analytic treatment with me, Gina, the patient reported upon below, bolted from her ongoing analysis. Cowardice got in her way and precluded her continuing treatment once she came upon some searingly painful internal and external realities.

Clinical vignette: 3

Gina Destefano suffered from intense jealousy and was pressed to seek treatment by her exasperated boyfriend. With unmistakable evidence of mental pain, Gina talked about how she got scared of losing her boyfriend each time he paid attention to another woman; this ranged from his laughing at a witty remark by her sister to his short, if jovial, banter with a waitress. Over the course of Gina's treatment, the history of a philandering father got fleshed out. His adultery became quite public at two crucial developmental junctures in Gina's life: when she was five and when she was sixteen. The oedipal "betrayal" thus got traumatically actualized and led to lifelong dread of being left in favor of another woman. The pain was worsened by the fact that Gina had grown up as "Daddy's girl" up to age five.

Underlying this dramatic scenario lay a subtler, far more painful relational scenario. Gina was born as an "accident" some eight years after her brother. Her mother was a prominent lawyer and within a few months of giving birth, gave her baby over to a live-in nanny and went back to her busy practice. This much Gina knew. She nonetheless insisted that her mother was very loving and devoted to her care. As a "proof" of this, Gina recalled that whenever she wanted a toy (e.g., a Barbie doll, a toy pony), the mother would immediately get on her computer and order it. As our work progressed, new information began to surface. It turned out that it was not months but weeks after which Gina's mother had gone back to full-time work. More devastating was Gina's "accidental" discovery of numerous unopened packages containing children's toys in her family's garage. The postage marks on them confirmed that while Gina's mother did order them, she hardly ever opened them and hid them away in the garage; she obviously didn't have the time or desire to play with Gina using those toys. This "discovery" shook Gina up. She became increasingly restless in the treatment and decided to break it off. "This will change my view of my mother and I just cannot bear that," she said. No amount of empathic validation, affirmative intervention, and resistance interpretation helped. Gina just did not possess the fortitude to tolerate the affects consequent upon the rupture of her "personal myth" (E. Kris, 1956). She dropped out of treatment.

Unlike these cases where it was patients themselves who were trapped in a courage—cowardice dilemma, there are times that the clinician encounters the tragic effects of a parent's cowardice upon the offspring.

Clinical vignette: 4

Steve Abramson, a PhD student in his early thirties, recalled the following incident with great shame and pain. His highly creative but shy and awkward father was visiting the town where Steve attended a prestigious university. His father was a Hollywood "script-doctor" (fixing glitches in the screenplays of stalled-off movies) and also a permanent ghostwriter for a famous and wealthy film personality who had lost his zest for work but was clinging onto his fame. Steve was excited upon meeting his father in the city's most opulent hotel and invited him to come and see his dorm room and the little office in his department where he spent his days hammering out his PhD dissertation. The response of his father was devastating; he could not accept his son's invitation because the rich and powerful man (for which he was ghostwriting and who paid his travel and lodging expenses) would not approve of it. Steve's shame over his father's cowardice was limitless and extended to himself. "I am his son. How can I be any good with a father like that?"

In such circumstances empathic interventions in accordance with Kohut's (1977) assertion that a growing child needs an idealizable parent (and draws ego-strength from such filiation) are indicated. The narcissistic deflation consequent on a child encountering parental cowardice is best exemplified by the following incidence in the life of a young Sigmund Freud.

> One day, to show how radically life had improved for Austria's Jews, Jacob Freud told his son this story: "When I was a young fellow, one Saturday I went for a walk in the streets of your birthplace, beautifully decked out, and with a new fur cap on my head. Along comes a Christian, knocks off my cap into the muck with one blow and shouts: 'Jew, off the sidewalk!'" Interested, Freud asked his father "And what did you do?" His father's submissive response, Freud recalled soberly, perhaps a little ungenerously, "did not seem heroic to me"; was his father not a "big strong man"? Stung by the spectacle of a cowardly Jew groveling to a gentile, Freud develops fantasies of revenge. He identified himself with the splendid, intrepid Semite Hannibal, who had sworn to avenge Carthage no matter how mighty the Romans, and elevated him into a symbol of the contrast between the tenacity of Jewry and the organization of the Catholic Church. They would never find him, Freud, picking up his cap from the filthy gutter.
> (Gay, 1988, pp. 11–12)

The working analyst encounters both the succumbing and rebelling responses to his patients' encounters with parental cowardice and has to respond by a judicious blend of empathic responses and interpretive unmasking of defensive strategies implicit in both reactions. Not easy by any means, this task is rendered more complex by the need on the analyst's part to struggle with his or her own tendency towards cowardice.

Analyst's cowardliness

Two caveats must be entered as one approaches this matter. *One*, like the great pieces of fiction mentioned at the outset of this chapter, the illustrations of the analyst's cowardice (Akhtar, 2013) frequently involve his overcoming that cowardice; they thus become illustrations of the analyst's courage. This needs to be avoided here. *Two*, there are many attributes of the analyst's attitude that can be mistaken for cowardice; these need explicit reflection before a meaningful discussion of his cowardice can take place. The four things the analyst's cowardice is *not* include: (a) his usual non-judgmental and non-retaliatory stance (e.g., if an angry patient calls me an "Indian asshole" and I do not respond in kind, it is not because of cowardice; it is because I am interested in understanding—and helping him understand—what about me made him so angry and why, all of a sudden, an ethnic reference has popped up in our dialogue); (b) his active use of patience as a specific technical measure (see Akhtar, 2015b for an elaboration of this idea); (c) his deliberate restraint of the "compulsion to interpret" (Epstein, 1979; see Akhtar, 2014, pp. 61–62 for a clinical illustration of this dynamic); and (d) his genuine fear that the patient might turn violent and cause bodily harm to the analyst.

Ruling these four circumstances out and by not indulging in how this or that particular analyst (including myself) overcame his cowardice permits us to take a serious look at his craven stance. This, I believe, is most apparent in situations where the analyst knows what is the right thing to say but cannot muster courage to say it. A block of such sort might arise from the analyst's rigid adherence to "neutrality," from the unanalyzed sectors of his personality, from the delicate nature of issues brought forth by the patient, and from specific transference–countertransference impasses in their relationship. One example of each follow though certainly more can be given.

Clinical vignette: 5

Mary McKinley, a deeply religious businesswoman who already has three latency-age daughters from a previous marriage, becomes pregnant after an impulsive one-night stand with her boss during an out-of-town business meeting. She found herself profoundly conflicted since her religious upbringing prohibited her from seeking an abortion while her pragmatic self tells her to immediately discontinue the pregnancy. Mary was torn and pleaded to her analyst for help: "Please, for just this one time, put your reserve aside and tell me what should I do?" The analyst "knew" in the depth of his being that Mary "should" get an abortion: carrying this pregnancy to term and giving birth to a baby would complicate her life in a most severe way. But the analyst could not tell this to his patient and clung to "neutrality." He continued to "analyze" while the clock kept ticking and the patient became more desperate for guidance. The analyst found his stance to be both admirable and shameful at the same time. In fact he was stuck with his cowardice.

Clinical vignette: 6

A female supervisee of mine was told by her unhappily married patient that he frequents "gentlemen's clubs." She noted this but did not follow-up on it; she made no inquiry as to what he did there. When I encouraged her to look into these inhibitions, she appeared uneasy. Later she explained her hesitation on the grounds that he "stays there only for a short time" and "he just gets some tapes from there." Still the supervisee failed to ask what these tapes depict. Still later, the patient told her that he often visits the website named www.fuckingmachines.com. As I, by now, had come to expect, the supervisee did not ask any questions about what this website depicted. She was stuck with her cowardice.

Clinical vignette: 7

A middle-aged successful and well sought-after psychologist saw his divorced male patient get involved with a woman who was clearly inappropriate for him. She was far less educated than the patient, was culturally different, and had serious physical ailments. The analyst interpreted his patient's "rescue fantasy" (Akhtar, 2009) to no avail. The patient relentlessly pursued the relationship and proposed to this woman; soon the couple were close to getting married. The analyst who was trapped in a very unhappy marriage of more than two decades found himself suddenly paralyzed. His authentic self wished to loudly and explicitly tell his patient not to marry this woman. His awareness of this being a countertransference response (to a considerable extent) prevented him from saying anything to this effect. He thought an interpretive approach is the way to go. The patient got married and within a few months was miserable and regretful. "Why did you not stop me? Did you not see that it was wrong for me to marry her?" the patient said. The analyst was dumbfounded, and found himself standing naked with his cowardice.

What these three examples have in common is this: while understanding, contemplation, patience, neutrality, and a non-judgmental stance on the analyst's part are clinical virtues, these benevolent and wise attitudes can also be enlisted by the analyst's timidity and clinical cowardice. I assert that it is possible, if not necessary, to put neutrality aside and take definitive actions. Situations demanding such departure are not restricted to anticipated bodily harm to the analyst, patient, or a helpless third party (e.g., a child) as Hoffer (1985) declares, but extend to more subtle interventional choices as exemplified by these three vignettes listed above. The issue is not to conduct an analysis for its own sake but to help the patient. Perhaps medically trained psychoanalysts (and I am one of them) feel this need more intensely and perhaps some "lay" colleagues consider such helpfulness as being weak-kneed in the face of potential negative transference. Both viewpoints have their merit. However, I believe that "technical" virtuosity of the analyst can at times serve as rationalization of his cowardice and have a deleterious impact on the patient's life.

Under fortunate circumstances, the psychoanalyst does not deny this possibility and becomes aware that maybe, just maybe, it is his cowardice that is impeding the progress of his work with a patient. When this happens, the analyst might greatly benefit by (i) seeking consultation, (ii) consider alternate modalities of treatment, (iii) referring the patient to someone else, and most importantly (iv) modifying and/or mourning his theory of technique. These recommendations made by Goldberg (2012) in connection with failed analyses seem equally pertinent to the analyst's discovery of treatment-impeding cowardice within himself.

Concluding remarks

In this contribution, I have explicated the descriptive features of cowardliness and traced their ontogenetic origins. These go back to a condensation of (i) early breeches of the mother–child bond, leading to thin-skinnedness and weakness of the core self, (ii) deficient identification with the same sex parent resulting in the fragility of role-related interpersonal and executive actions, (iii) excessive bodily mutilation anxieties manifesting as fear of confrontation and combat, and (iv) a pervasive intolerance of separation and separateness causing difficulty in disagreeing with others and openly expressing one's opinions and preferences. A similarly complex tapestry of affects and ego attributes underlies cowardliness on its distal end. Its consequences thus include an ongoing, if private, sense of shame and a profound vulnerability to regret (owing to missed opportunities and risks not taken). Moving on to the clinical situation, I have emphasized that dilemmas of courage and cowardice are faced by both the patient and analyst. I have provided illustrations of such difficulties and also delineated some therapeutic strategies to deal with them.

Now as I approach the end of my discourse, I wish to touch upon two potentially thorny matters. The first pertains to the social ambience of the psychoanalytic profession and the second involves the society at large. Let me first address the former. While the clinical and organizational discourses in psychoanalysis have recently become more open, tabooed topics still exist. As a result, many analysts fear speaking openly in professional settings and remain cautious in their academic expression. Feelings ranging from queasy apprehension to outright terror seep up in the hearts of many analysts when it comes to declaring their stance on issues such as the Christian–Jewish divergence in psychoanalytic theory and practice (Akhtar, 2022b), the use of puberty-blocking medications for transgender children, the existence of racial and religious anti-Black, anti-Arab, and anti-Muslim prejudice in organized psychoanalysis. One can talk about the profound suffering that has been endured by Jews over centuries and one can talk about the rising anti-Semitism in today's world, but one cannot talk about the Israeli atrocities toward Palestinians in the occupied territories. Dread of being maligned and ostracized propels such analysts to secrecy. Such institutionally inculcated cowardice is harmful for the growth and advancement of the field even though superficially it sustains calm, cordiality, and cohesion.

This brings me to my final point. A quick glance at society at large reveals that for the courageous, it erects statues, establishes monuments, and names roadways, and for the cowardly, it spins jokes and invents slurs. However, a deeper look reveals that while publicly celebrating courage, the society quietly rewards cowardliness. This is because cowardliness involves renunciations of authenticity and ascribes to group cohesion at all costs; these attributes find acceptance and support by the society. Freud's (1930a) *Civilization and Its Discontents* goes even further and proposes that cultural institutions that enforce repression of man's instinctual (sexual and aggressive) freedom might themselves be the creation of such renunciation. So, perhaps cowardliness is not so bad after all and, rather than attempting to "cure" it, we analysts should leave it alone. Yes?

References

Abend, S. M. (1982). Some observations on reality testing as a clinical concept. *Psychoanalytic Quarterly*, 51: 218–237.

Abraham, K. (1921). Contributions to the theory of the anal character. In: *Selected Papers on Psychoanalysis* (pp. 370–392). New York: Brunner/Mazel.

Abraham, K. (1923). Contributions to the theory of the anal character. *International Journal of Psychoanalysis*, 4: 400–418.

Abraham, K. (1924). The influence of oral eroticism on character formation. In: *Selected Papers of Karl Abraham, M.D.* (pp. 393–406). New York: Brunner/Mazel.

Ainsworth, M. D. S., & Bell, S. M. (1970). Attachment, exploration, and separation: Illustrated by the behavior of one-year-olds in a strange situation. *Child Development*, 41(1): 49–67.

Aisenstein, M. (2009). The death of the dead father? In: L. Kalinich & S. Taylor (Eds.), *The Dead Father: A Psychoanalytic Inquiry* (pp. 65–74). London: Routledge.

Akhtar, S. (1992). *Broken Structures: Severe Personality Disorders and Their Treatment*. Northville, NJ: Jason Aronson.

Akhtar, S. (1994). Object constancy and adult psychopathology. *International Journal of Psychoanalysis, 75*: 441–455.

Akhtar, S. (1995). Review of "Losing and Fusing: Borderline Transitional Object and Self Relations", by R. A. Lewin, MD & C. G. Schulz. *Psychoanalytic Quarterly, 64*: 583–588.

Akhtar, S. (1996). "Some day …" and "if only …" fantasies: Pathological optimism and inordinate nostalgia as related forms of idealization. *Journal of the American Psychoanalytic Association, 44*: 725–753.

Akhtar, S. (1999). Review of "Diversity and Direction in Psychoanalytic Technique" by F. Pine. *International Journal of Psychoanalysis, 80*: 1025–1028.

Akhtar, S. (2002). Forgiveness: origins, dynamics, psychopathology, and clinical relevance. *Psychoanalytic Quarterly, 71*: 175–212.

Akhtar, S. (2009). *Comprehensive Dictionary of Psychoanalysis*. London: Karnac.

Akhtar, S. (2012). Normal and pathological generosity. *Psychoanalytic Review, 99*: 645–676.

Akhtar, S. (2013). *Good Stuff: Courage, Generosity, Resilience, Gratitude, Forgiveness, and Sacrifice*. Lanham, MD: Jason Aronson.

Akhtar, S. (2014). Psychoanalytic treatment of trauma and the analyst's personality. *Psychoanalytic Inquiry, 34*: 204–213.

Akhtar, S. (2016). *Shame: Developmental, Cultural, and Clinical Realms*. London: Karnac, pp. 93–114.

Akhtar, S. (2022a). *In Leaps and Bounds: Psychic Development and Its Facilitation in Treatment*. Bicester, UK: Phoenix.

Akhtar, S. (2022b). Review of "Credo?: Psychoanalysis and Religion" by Patrick Casement. *Journal of the American Psychoanalytic Association, 70*: 421–426.

Anzieu, D. (1987). Some alterations of the ego which make analyses interminable. *International Journal of Psychoanalysis, 68*: 9–19.

Anzieu, D. (1995). *The Skin-Ego*. N. Segal (Trans.). London: Routledge.

Arango, A. C. (1989). *Dirty Words: The Expressive Power of Taboo*. New York: Jason Aronson.

Aristotle (1984). *The Complete Works of Aristotle*, Vols I and II. J. Barnes (Ed.). Princeton, NJ: Princeton University Press.

Arlow, J. A. (1979). The genesis of interpretation. *Journal of the American Psychoanalytic Association, 27*: 193–206.

Azzerad, M. (1994). *Come as You Are: The Story of Nirvana*. New York: Doubleday.
Balint, M. (1968). *The Basic Fault: Therapeutic Aspects of Regression*. London: Tavistock.
Barahona, R. (2018). Review of "Psychoanalytic Technique: Contributions from Ego Psychology" by C. Paniagua. *Psychoanalytic Quarterly, 87*: 369–379.
Barkley-Levenson, E. E., & Fox, C. R. (2016). The surprising relationship between indecisiveness and impulsivity. *Personality and Individual Differences, 90*: 1–6.
Becker, E. (1975). *Escape from Evil*. New York: The Free Press.
Beebe, B. (2022). Video accompaniment for the mother-infant interaction picture book: Origins of attachment. https://www.youtube.com/watch?v=TifkQl3iOdc (accessed February 2023).
Begley, L. (1993). *The Man Who Was Late*. New York: Alfred A. Knopf.
Benau, K. (2017). Shame, attachment, and psychotherapy: Phenomenology, neurophysiology, relational trauma, and harbingers of healing. *Attachment: New Directions in Relational Psychoanalysis and Psychotherapy, 11*: 1–27.
Benjamin, W. (1940). "On Some Motifs in Baudelaire." https://warwick.ac.uk/fac/arts/english/currentstudents/undergraduate/modules/fulllist/first/en122/lecturelist2019-20/benjamin_motifs_in_baudelaire.pdf (last accessed on December 17, 2022).
Berger, A. A. (1993). *An Anatomy of Humor*. New Brunswick, NJ: Transaction.
Bergler, E. (1936). Obscene words. *Psychoanalytic Quarterly, 5*: 226–248.
Berman, N. C., Wheaton, M. G., Fabricant, L. E, & Abramowitz, J. S. (2012). Predictors of mental pollution: The contribution of religion, parenting strategies, and childhood trauma. *Journal of Obsessive-Compulsive and Related Disorders, 1*: 153–158.
Berry, J. M., & Sobieraj, S. (2016). *The Outrage Industry: Political Opinion Media and the New Incivility*. New York: Oxford University Press.
Bhabha, H. (1994). *The Location of Culture*. London: Routledge.
Bick, E. (1968). The experience of skin in early object relations. *International Journal of Psychoanalysis, 49*: 484–486.
Billow, R. M. (2013). Outrageousness and outrage. *International Journal of Group Psychotherapy, 63*: 316–345.
Bion, W. R. (1961). *Experiences in Groups and Other Papers*. London: Tavistock.

Bion, W. R. (1962a). *Learning from Experience*. London: Tavistock.
Bion, W. R. (1962b). A theory of thinking. *International Journal of Psychoanalysis, 43*: 306–310.
Bion, W. R. (1965). *Transformations*. London: William Heinemann.
Bion, W. R. (1970). *Attention and Interpretation*. London: Tavistock.
Blackman, J. (2004). *101 Defenses: How the Mind Shields Itself*. New York: Brunner-Routledge.
Blackman, J. (2010). *Get the Diagnosis Right: Assessment and Treatment Selection for Mental Disorders*. New York: Routledge.
Blackman, J. (2013a). *The Therapist's Answer Book: Solutions to 101 Tricky Problems in Psychotherapy*. New York: Routledge.
Blackman, J. (2013b). Object clarification in lonely heterosexual men. In: A. K. Richards, L. Spira, & A. Lynch (Eds.), *Encounters with Loneliness: Only the Lonely*. New York: IP Books.
Blackman, J. (2016). Combined book review of "Diagnostic and Statistical Manual of Mental Disorders, 5th Edition", "Clinical Handbook of Psychological Disorders: A Step-by-Step Treatment Manual" (D. Barlow, Ed.), and "Essentials of Psychiatric Diagnosis: Responding to the Challenges of DSM-V", by A. Frances. *Psychoanalytic Psychology, 33*: 651–663.
Blackman, J. (2017). Pick up the baby! (Or dire consequences will ensue). *International Forum of Psychoanalysis, 26*: 33–37.
Blackman, J. (2018). Defensive arrogance in adult philanderers. In: S. Akhtar & A. Smolen (Eds.), *Arrogance: Developmental, Cultural, and Clinical Realms* (pp. 58–74). London: Routledge.
Blackman, J., & Dring, K. (2023). *Developmental Evaluation of Children & Adolescents: A Psychodynamic Guide*. London: Routledge.
Blechner, M. J. (2007). Approaches to panic attacks. *Neuropsychoanalysis, 9*: 91–100.
Blos, P. (1966). *On Adolescence*. New York: International Universities Press.
Blum, H. P. (1991). Dyadic psychopathology and infantile eating disorder psychoanalytic study and inferences. In: S. Akhtar & H. Parens (Eds.), *Beyond the Symbiotic Orbit Advances in Separation-Individuation Theory* (pp. 285–298). Hillsdale, N.J: Analytic Press.
Boris, H. N. (1986). The "other" breast—greed, envy, spite, and revenge. *Contemporary Psychoanalysis, 22*: 45–59.
Bowen, C. (2018). *Why Do Babies' Heads Smell So Good? Here's How Your Brain Reacts to the Unique Scent*. New York: Romper.

Bowlby, J. (1965). *Attachment*. New York: Basic Books.
Bowlby, J. (1983). *Attachment: Attachment and Loss: Volume I*. New York: Basic Books.
Bratman, S. (1997). Health food junkie. *Yoga Journal*, 3: 42–50.
Bratman, S. (personal communication July 2015).
Brenner, C. (1982). *The Mind in Conflict*. New York: International Universities Press.
Brenner, I. (2021). Disinformation, disease, and Donald Trump. *International Journal of Applied Psychoanalytic Studies*, 18(2): 232–241.
Bretherton, I. (1992). The origins of attachment theory: John Bowlby and Mary Ainsworth. *Developmental Psychology*, 28(5): 759–775.
Brown, G. (2015). Psychotherapy with people who smell. *Psychoanalysis Culture and Society*, 20: 29–48.
Burket, J., & Deutsch, S. (2019). Metabotropic functions of the NMDA receptor and an evolving rationale for exploring NR2A-selective positive allosteric modulators for the treatment of autism spectrum disorder. *Progress in Neuro-Psychopharmacology and Biological Psychiatry*, 92: 142–160.
Casement, P. (1985). *Learning from the Patient*. New York: Guilford.
Charan, R. (2006). Conquering a culture of indecision. *Harvard Business Review*, 84: 75–82.
Chasseguet-Smirgel, J. (1985). *Creativity and Perversion*. New York: W. W. Norton.
Chess, S., & Thomas, A. (1995). *Temperament in Clinical Practice*. New York: Guilford.
Civin, M. (1990). The preconscious and potential space. *Psychoanalytic Review*, 77: 573–585.
Civin, M. (2000). *Male Female Email*. New York: Other Press.
Civin, M. (2022). "No body talk, nobody talk". Presented at the 9th Delphi Psychoanalytic Symposium: Delphi, Greece, August 25–28.
Civin, M. (2023). "… whatever …" In: V. Tsolas & C. Anzieu-Premmereur (Eds.), *A Psychoanalytic Exploration of the Contemporary Search for Pleasure: The Turning of the Screw* (pp. 197–206). London: Routledge.
Civitarese, G. (2013). The grid and the truth drive. *Italian Psychoanalytic Annual*, 7: 91–114.
Cohen, J. R., & Ferrari, J. R. (2010). Take some time to think this over: The relation between rumination, indecision and creativity. *Creativity Research Journal*, 22: 68–73.

Conrad, J. (1900). *Lord Jim*. London: Oxford University Press, 2008.

Cooperman, M. (1983). Some observations regarding psychoanalytic psychotherapy in a hospital setting. *The Psychiatric Hospital, 14*: 21–28.

Cozolino, L. (2014). *The Neuroscience of Human Relationships: Attachment and the Developing Brain*. New York: W. W. Norton.

Dague-Greene, A., & August, J. (2020). *General English–Spanish Dictionary*. Princeton, NJ: Princeton University Press.

Damasio, A. (1999). *The Feeling of What Happens*. London: Heinemann.

DeFalco, A. (2016). In praise of idleness: Aging and the morality of inactivity. *Cultural Critique, 92*: 84–113.

Denby, D. (2005, August 22). Dirty business. *The New Yorker*.

DeRose, T. (2022). On "Beyond the Pleasure Principle". https://freud.org.uk/2021/02/02/freud-in-focus-podcast/ (accessed on 17 December 2022).

Desai, A. (2024). Afterword. In: V. Tsolas & C. Anzieu-Premmereur (Eds.), *A Psychoanalytic Exploration of the Contemporary Search for Pleasure: The Turning of the Screw* (pp. 207–209). London: Routledge.

Deutsch, H. (1942). Some forms of emotional disturbance and their relationship to schizophrenia. *Psychiatric Quarterly, 11*: 301–321.

Diagnostic and Statistical Manual of Mental Disorders-5-TR (2022). Washington, DC: American Psychiatric Press.

Dirty Harry (1971). Motion picture. Directed by D. Siegel. Burbank, CA: Warner Brothers.

Dodd, N. (1994). *The Sociology of Money*. New York: Continuum.

Donald Trump, dismissed by some early on as perhaps even a joke, but he has charged to the top of the polls with his outrageousness. (2015). www.CNN.Transcripts.com (last accessed on April 28, 2023).

Donne, J., & Gardener, H. (1957). Holy sonnet. *The Metaphysical Poets*. London: Penguin.

Dorpat, T. (1976). Structural conflict and object relations conflict. *Journal of the American Psychoanalytic Association, 24*: 855–874.

Dorsey, E. (1992). Review of "Anne Sexton: A Biography" by D. W. Middlebrook. *Modern Psychoanalysis, 17*: 105–108.

Dougherty, B. (2010). *The Friar's Club 2069 Rather Naughty Jokes*. New York: Black Dog & Leventhal.

Einstein, A. (1905). Annus mirabilis. In: *The Collected Papers of Albert Einstein*, Vol. II. J. Stachel (Ed.). Princeton, NJ: Princeton University Press, 1990.

Eliot, T. S. (1963). *Collected Poems: 1909–1962*. New York: Harcourt, Brace & World.

Epstein, L. (1979). Countertransference with borderline patients. In: L. Epstein & A. H. Feiner (Eds.), *Countertransference* (pp. 375–406). New York: Jason Aronson.

Erikson, E. H. (1950). *Childhood and Society*. New York: Basic Books.

Euclid (c. 300 BC). *Euclid's Elements*. T. Heath (Trans.). Santa Fe, NM: Green Lion, 2017.

Fairbairn, W. R. D. (1952). *An Object Relations Theory of Psychoanalysis*. New York: Basic Books.

Fairbrother, N., & Rachman, S. (2004). Feelings of mental pollution subsequent to sexual assault. *Behavior Research and Therapy, 40*: 173–189.

Feldman, M. J. (1955). The use of obscene words in the therapeutic relationship. *American Journal of Psychoanalysis, 15*: 45–48.

Fenichel, O. (1945). *The Psychoanalytic Theory of Neurosis*. New York: W. W. Norton.

Ferenczi, S. (1911). On obscene words. In: *First Contributions to Psycho-Analysis* (pp. 132–153). New York: Brunner/Mazel, 1980.

Ferenczi, S. (1914). The ontogenesis of the interest in money. In: *First Contributions to Psycho-Analysis* (pp. 319–331). New York: Brunner/Mazel, 1980.

Ferro, A. (2004). *The Waking Dream and Narrations: Seeds of Illness, Seeds of Recovery*. London: Routledge.

Flanagan, S. (2001). Lexicographic and syntactic explorations of doubt in twelfth-century Latin texts, *Journal of Medieval History, 27*: 219–240.

Freud, A. (1936). *The Ego and Mechanisms of Defence*. New York: International Universities Press, 1966.

Freud, A. (1965a). *Normality and Pathology in Childhood*. New York: International Universities Press.

Freud, A. (1965b). Diagnostic skills and their growth in psychoanalysis. *International Journal of Psychoanalysis, 46*: 31–38.

Freud, S., with Breuer, J. (1895d). *Studies on Hysteria*. *S. E., 2*: 1–323. London: Hogarth.

Freud, S. (1900a). *The Interpretations of Dreams*. *S. E., 4–5*: 1–626. London: Hogarth.

Freud, S. (1901b). *The Psychopathology of Everyday Life*. *S. E., 6*: 1–296. London: Hogarth.

Freud, S. (1905c). *Jokes and Their Relation to the Unconscious. S. E.*, 8: 1–247. London: Hogarth.

Freud, S. (1905e). Fragment of an analysis of a case of hysteria. *S. E.*, 7: 1–122. London: Hogarth.

Freud, S. (1908b). Character and anal erotism. *S. E.*, 9: 167–176. London: Hogarth.

Freud, S. (1908e). Creative writers and day-dreaming. *S. E.*, 9: 141–154. London: Hogarth.

Freud, S. (1909d). Notes upon a case of obsessional neurosis. *S. E.*, 10: 155–318. London: Hogarth.

Freud, S. (1914c). On narcissism: an introduction. *S. E.*, 14: 69–102. London: Hogarth.

Freud, S. (1915b). Thoughts for the times on war and death. *S. E.*, 14: 273–300. London: Hogarth.

Freud, S. (1915e). The unconscious. *S. E.*, 14: 159–216. London: Hogarth.

Freud, S. (1916d). Some character-types met with in psycho-analytic work. *S. E.*, 14: 310–333. London: Hogarth.

Freud, S. (1918b). From the history of an infantile neurosis. *S. E.*, 17: 1–124. London: Hogarth.

Freud, S. (1919h). The "uncanny". *S. E.*, 17: 217–252. London: Hogarth.

Freud, S. (1920a). The psychogenesis of a case of female homosexuality. *S. E.*, 18: 145–174. London: Hogarth.

Freud, S. (1920g). *Beyond the Pleasure Principle. S. E.*, 18: 7–64. London: Hogarth.

Freud, S. (1923b). *The Ego and the Id. S. E.*, 19: 1–66. London: Hogarth.

Freud, S. (1925h). Negation. *S. E.*, 19: 235–239. London: Hogarth.

Freud, S. (1926d). *Inhibitions, Symptoms and Anxiety. S. E.*, 20. London: Hogarth.

Freud, S. (1930a). *Civilization and Its Discontents. S. E.*, 21: 64–145. London: Hogarth.

Freud, S. (1933a). *New Introductory Lectures on Psycho-Analysis. S. E.*, 22: 7–182. London: Hogarth.

Freud, S. (1937d). Constructions in analysis. *S. E.*, 23: 257–269. London: Hogarth.

Galatzer-Levy, R. (2017). Science and psychoanalysis: An interview with Robert Emde. *American Psychoanalyst, 51*: 5–6.

Garma, A. (1966). *The Psychoanalysis of Dreams*. New York: Jason Aronson.

Gay, P. (1988). *Freud: A Life of Our Time*. New York: W. W. Norton.

Gilligan, C. (2009). *In a Different Voice: Psychological Theory and Women's Development*. Cambridge, MA: Harvard University Press.

Glover, E. (1940). *The Psychology of Fear and Courage*. London: Penguin.

Goldberg, A. (2012). *The Analysis of Failure*. London: Routledge.

Goldman, D. (2003). The outrageous prince: Winnicott's "uncure" of Masud Khan. *British Journal of Psychotherapy*, 19: 486–501.

Gorender, M. E. (2005). Bad breath: The perversion of breath. *International Forum of Psychoanalysis*, 14: 201–205.

Gray, P. (1982). "Developmental lag" in the evolution of technique for psychoanalysis of neurotic conflict. *Journal of the American Psychoanalytic Association*, 30: 621–655.

Greene, A. (1974). Surface analysis, deep analysis. *International Journal of Psychoanalysis*, 55: 415–423.

Guarton, G. B. (1999). Transgression and reconciliation: A psychoanalytic reading of Masud Khan. *Contemporary Psychoanalysis*, 35: 301–310.

Guntrip, H. (1969). *Schizoid Phenomena, Object Relations and the Self*. New York: International Universities Press.

Haberman, M. (2022). *Confidence Man: The Making of Donald Trump and the Breaking of America*. New York: Penguin.

Haight, D. F. (1977). Is money a four-letter word? *Psychoanalytic Review*, 64: 621–629.

Hartmann, H. (1939). *The Ego and the Problem of Adaptation*. New York: International Universities Press.

Heller, J. (1974). *Something Happened*. New York: Alfred A. Knopf.

Herbenick, D., Rosenberg, M., Golzarri-Arroyo, L., Fortenberry, J. D., & Fu, T. (2022). Changes in penile-vaginal intercourse frequency and sexual repertoire from 2009 to 2018: Findings from the National Survey of Sexual Health and Behavior. *Archives of Sexual Behavior*, 51: 1419–1433.

Herbert, G., & Gardener, H. (1957). The collar. *The Metaphysical Poets*. London: Penguin.

Hilty, R. (2020). Unpleasant bodily odour in a psychoanalytic treatment: Bridge or drawbridge to a troubled past? *British Journal of Psychotherapy*, 36: 200–215.

Hoffer, A. (1985). Toward a definition of psychoanalytic neutrality. *Journal of the American Psychoanalytic Association*, 33(4): 771–795.

Holmes, O. (2022, October 25). "World's dirtiest man" dies in Iran at 94 a few months after first wash. *The Guardian*.

Hopkins, G. M., & Smith, K. E. (1976). Carrion comfort. *Gerard Manley Hopkins: Poetry and Prose*. Exeter, UK: Wheaton.

Hopkins, L. B. (1998). D. W. Winnicott's analysis of Masud Khan. *Contemporary Psychoanalysis*, 34: 5–47.

Horn, S. (2021, May 4). Does it have to be so lonely at the top? *CEO World Magazine*.

Household Air Pollution (2022). https://who.int/en/news-room/fact-sheets/detail/household-air-pollution-and-health (accessed on November 28, 2022).

Hughes, L. (1951). Dreams. In: *The Collected Poems of Langston Hughes* (p. 142). New York: Vintage.Ishikawa, R. (2015). *Psychological Trauma and Feelings of Dirtiness* (UK edn.). London: Nova Science.

Jelliffe, S. E. (1915). Technique of psychoanalysis. *Psychoanalytic Review*, 2: 191–199.

Jewkes, R. K., & Wood, K. (1999). Problematizing pollution: Dirty wombs, ritual pollution, and pathological processes. *Medical Anthropology*, 18: 163–186.

Johnson, A., & Szurek, S. (1952). The genesis of antisocial acting out in children and adolescents. *Psychoanalytic Quarterly*, 21: 323–343.

Johnson, D. R. (1984). Representation of the internal world in catatonic schizophrenia. *Psychiatry*, 47: 299–314.

Jones, E. (1913). The God complex. In: *Essays in Applied Psychoanalysis*, Volume II (pp. 244–265). New York: International Universities Press, 1973.

Kahneman, D. (2019). Memories of a summer with David Rapaport in 1960, and possible sequelae. Rapaport-Klein Study Group, Austen Riggs Center, Stockbridge, MA. www.psychomedia.it/rapaport-klein 57th Annual Meeting: June 7–9 (last accessed November 11, 2022).

Kahneman, D., & Tversky, A. (1982). Variants of uncertainty. *Cognition*, 11: 143–157.

Kahneman, D., Lovallo, D., & Sibony, O. (2013). On making smart decisions. *HBR's 10 Must Reads*. Brighton, MA: Harvard Business Review Press.

Kalinich, L., & Taylor, S. (Eds.) (2009). *The Dead Father: A Psychoanalytic Inquiry*. New York: Routledge.

Kanwal, G. S. (2016). Perspectives on decision-making: Implications for understanding psychopathology in psychiatric and psychoanalytic practice. *Neuropsychoanalysis*, 18: 31–43.

Karpman, B. (1948). Coprophilia: A collective review. *Psychoanalytic Review*, 35: 253–272.

Karpman, B. (1949). A modern Gulliver: A study in coprophilia. *Psychoanalytic Review*, 36: 260–282.

Kayatekin, M. S. (2016). *Psychoanalytic Conversations. From the Psychotherapeutic Hospital to the Couch*. Lanham, MD: Rowman & Littlefield.

Kayatekin, M. S., Bombel, G., & Lan-Czelusta, K. (2024). Evaluation of professionals. In: R. Boland & M. L. Verduin (Eds.), *Kaplan and Sadock's Synopsis of Psychiatry* (pp. 4599–4606). Baltimore, MD: Lippincott Williams & Wilkins, in press.

Kernberg, O. F. (1967). Borderline personality organization. *Journal of the American Psychoanalytic Association*, 15: 641–685.

Kernberg, O. F. (1970). A psychoanalytic classification of character pathology. *Journal of the American Psychoanalytic Association*, 18: 800–822.

Kernberg, O. F. (1975). *Borderline Conditions and Pathological Narcissism*. New York: Jason Aronson.

Kernberg, O. F. (1984). *Severe Personality Disorders: Psychotherapeutic Strategies*. New Haven, CT: Yale University Press.

Kernberg, O. F. (2007). The almost untreatable narcissistic patient. *Journal of the American Psychoanalytic Association*, 55: 503–539.

Kernberg, O. F., & Caligor, E. (2005). A Psychoanalytic Theory of Personality Disorders. In: *Major Theories of Personality Disorder*. New York: Guilford.

Khan, M. M. R. (1974). *The Privacy of the Self*. New York: International Universities Press.

Khan, M. M. R. (1986). Outrageousness, compliance and authenticity. *Contemporary Psychoanalysis*, 22: 629–650.

Klein, M. (1945). The Oedipus complex in the light of early anxieties. *International Journal of Psychoanalysis*, 26: 11–33.

Klein, M. (1950). On the criteria for a successful termination of psychoanalysis. In: *Envy and Gratitude and Other Works 1946–1963* (pp. 43–47). New York: Free Press, 1975.

Klein, M. (1952). The mutual influences in the development of ego and the id. In: *Envy and Gratitude and Other Works 1946–1963* (pp. 57–60). New York: Free Press, 1975.

Klein, M. (1957). Envy and gratitude. In: *Envy and Gratitude & Other Works 1946–1963* (pp. 176–235). New York: Free Press, 1975.

Knotts, D. (1960s). The nervous man on the street. The neurosurgeon who is trying to beat the heat. *The Steve Allen Show.* https://youtu.be/54wdCLdrfVk (last accessed January 31, 2023).

Kohut, H. (1977). *Restoration of the Self.* New York: International Universities Press.

Kramer, S. (1983). Object-coercive doubting: a pathological defensive response to maternal incest. *Journal of the American Psychoanalytic Association, 31*: 325–351.

Kris, E. (1956). The personal myth: A problem in psychoanalytic technique. *Journal of the American Psychoanalytic Association, 4*(4): 653–681.

Kris, A. (1988). Some clinical applications of the distinction between divergent and convergent conflicts. *International Journal of Psychoanalysis, 69*: 431–441.

Lacan, J. (1958–1959). Desire and its interpretation. http://lacaninireland.com/web/wp-content/uploads/2010/06/Book-06-Desire-and-its-interpretation.pdf (last accessed October 29, 2022).

Lacan, J. (1962). *The Seminar of Jacques Lacan: Book X: Anxiety.* Paris: Seuil.

Lacan, J. (1982). *Ecrits: A Selection*: New York: W. W. Norton.

LaMothe, R. (2003). Poor Ebenezer: Avarice as corruption of the erotic and search for a transformative object. *Psychoanalytic Review, 90*: 23–43.

Landman, J. (1993). *Regret.* New York: Oxford University Press.

Larkin, P. (2013). *Poems.* M. Amis (Ed.). London: Faber and Faber.

Larkin, P. (2015). Poetry of departures. *The Less Deceived.* London: Faber and Faber.

Lawrence, D. H. (1913a). *Sons and Lovers.* H. Baron & C. Baron (Eds.). Cambridge: Cambridge University Press, 2002.

Lawrence, D. H. (1913b): *D. H. Lawrence: The Complete Poems.* V. S. Pinto & W. Roberts (Eds.). New York: Penguin, p. 349.

Lawrence, D. H. (1922). *Fantasia of the Unconscious & Psychoanalysis and the Unconscious.* London: Heinemann, 1971.

Legman, G. (1968). *Rationale of the Dirty Joke: An Analysis of Sexual Humor.* New York: Castle.

Lehmiller, J. J. (2020). *Tell Me What You Want: The Science of Sexual Desire and How It Can Help You Improve Your Sex Life.* New York: Adfo.

Lemma, A. (2014). Off the couch, into the toilet: exploring the psychic uses of the analyst's toilet. *Journal of the American Psychoanalytic Association, 62*: 35–56.

Levin, S. (1969a). A common type of marital incompatibility. *Journal of the American Psychoanalytic Association, 17*: 421–436.

Levin, S. (1969b). Further comments on a common type of marital incompatibility. *Journal of the American Psychoanalytic Association, 17*: 1097–1113.

Levy, D. M. (1950). The strange hen. *American Journal of Orthopsychiatry, 20*: 355–362.

Lewis, H. B. (1971). Shame and guilt in neurosis. *Psychoanalytic Review, 58*: 419–438.

Lim, V. (2019). "To be or not to be": Hamlet's humanistic question. *Review of English Studies, 70*: 640–658.

Loewald, H. W. (1960). On the therapeutic action of psychoanalysis. *International Journal of Psychoanalysis, 41*: 16–33.

Lorenz, E. (1993). *The Essence of Chaos*. Seattle, WA: University of Washington Press.

Luepnitz, D. A. (2009). Thinking in the space between Winnicott and Lacan. *International Journal of Psychoanalysis, 90*: 957–981.

Lynch, A. A., & Richards, A. D. (2010). Leo Rangell: The journey of a developed Freudian. *Psychoanalytic Review, 97*: 361–391.

MacLean, P. (1990). *The Triune Brain in Evolution: Role in Paleocerebral Functions*. New York: Springer.

Mahler, M., Pine, F., & Bergman, A. (1975). *The Psychological Birth of the Human Infant*. New York: Basic Books.

Mann, A. (2012). What organizational consultants do and what it takes to become one: Commentary on papers by Kenneth Eisold and Marc Jacobs. *Psychoanalytic Dialogue, 22*: 547–554.

Marcovitz, E. (1970). Dignity. In: M. S. Temeles (Ed.), *Bemoaning the Lost Dream: Collected Papers of Eli Marcovitz, MD* (pp. 120–130). Philadelphia, PA: Philadelphia Association for Psychoanalysis.

Marcuse, H. (1955). *Eros and Civilization: A Philosophical Inquiry into Freud*. Boston, MA: Beacon.

Marty, P., & de M'Uzan, M. (1963). La pénsee opératoire. *Revue Française de Psychanalyse, 27*: 345–356.

Mason, A. E. W. (1902). *The Four Feathers*. Boston, MA: Little, Brown, 1988.

Masterson, J. (1981). *The Narcissistic and Borderline Disorders: An Integrated Developmental Approach*. New York: Brunner-Mazel.

Matsunaga, H., Kiriike, N., Matsui, T., Iwasaki, Y., & Stein, D. J. (2001). Taijin kyofusho: A form of social anxiety disorder that responds to serotonin reuptake inhibitors? *International Journal of Neuropsychopharmacology*, 4: 231–237.

Matte-Blanco, I. (1975). *The Unconscious as Infinite Sets: An Essay in Bi-logic*. London: Gerald Duckworth and Company.

McDougall, J. (1989). The dead father: On early psychic trauma and its relation to disturbance in sexual identity and in creative activity. *International Journal of Psychoanalysis*, 70: 205–219.

McDougall, J. (2000). Sexuality and the neosexual. *Modern Psychoanalysis*, 25: 155–166.

Meers, D. R. (1970). Contributions of a ghetto culture to symptom formation—psychoanalytic studies of ego anomalies in childhood. *Psychoanalytic Study of the Child*, 25: 209–230.

Meissner, W. W. (2009). Volition and will in psychoanalysis. *Journal of the American Psychoanalytic Association*, 57: 1123–1156.

Meltzer, D. (1964). The differentiation of somatic delusions from hypochondria. *International Journal of Psychoanalysis*, 45: 246–250.

Meltzer, D. (1973). *Sexual States of Mind*. London: Karnac.

Meltzer, D. (1986). What is an emotional experience? *Studies in Extended Metapsychology*, 43: 21–33.

Menaker, E. (1979). Masochism and the emergent ego. In: L. Lerner (Ed.), *Selected Papers of Esther Menaker* (pp. 72–101). New York: Human Sciences.

Menninger, K. (1938). *Man Against Himself*. New York: Harcourt Brace & Co.

Merriam-Webster's Collegiate Dictionary (1993). Tenth edition. Springfield, MA: Merriam-Webster.

Military Decision-making Process (MDMP) (2015). Fort Leavenworth, KS: Center for Army Lessons Learned (CALL) handbook no. 15-06.

Miller, S. B. (1985). *The Shame Experience*. Hillsdale, NJ: Analytic Press.

Miller, S. B. (1986). Disgust: Conceptualization, development and dynamics. *International Review of Psycho-Analysis*, 13: 295–307.

Miller, S. B. (1993). Disgust reactions—their determinants and manifestations in treatment. *Contemporary Psychoanalysis*, 29: 711–734.

Milton, J. (1667). *Paradise Lost*. London: Penguin, 2000.

Morin, E. (2008). *On Complexity*. New York: Hampton.

Nelson, R. (1963). Fools rush in where angels fear to tread. https://youtube.com/watch?v=kyU2pGWA6Jc (last accessed on January 30, 2023).

Newark, D. A. (2014). Indecision, and construction of self. *Organizational Behavior and Human Decision Processes*, 125: 162–174.

Ng, A. H., & Hynie, M. (2014). Cultural differences in indecisiveness: The role of naïve dialecticism. *Personality and Individual Differences, 70*: 45–50.

Nikelly, A. (2006). The pathogenesis of greed: causes and consequences. *International Journal of Applied Psychoanalytic Studies, 1*: 65–78.

Orcutt, C. (2019). Masud Khan. *Psychoanalytic Review, 106*: 489–508.

Orwell, G. (1949). *Nineteen Eighty-Four*. London: Secker & Warburg.

Oxford English Dictionary (2023). Version 15.4.301, MobiSystems, Inc. Oxford: Oxford University Press.

Pally, R. (2000). *The Mind Brain Relationship*. London: Karnac.

Papiasvili, E. (2020). The dawn of the subject: On the verge of destruction and creativity. *Revue pro Psychoanalytickou Psychoterapii a Psychoanalyzu, 22*: 100–114.

Papiasvili, E., & Mayers, L. (2013). The ascent of psychiatry and psychology in 1800–1945: Multiple dimensions of mental conditions emerge. In: T. Plante (Ed.), *Abnormal Psychology across the Ages: History & Conceptualizations* (pp. 31–57). Denver, CO: Clio.

Parens, H. (1973). Aggression: a reconsideration. *Journal of the American Psychoanalytic Association, 21*: 34–60.

Phillips, A. (2014). *Missing Out: In Praise of the Unlived Life*. New York: Picador.

Plato (c. 360 BC). *Timaeus*. In: Z. Donald & B. Sattler (Eds.), *Stanford Encyclopedia of Philosophy* (pp. 112–114). Stanford, CA: Stanford University Press, 2005.

Poland, W. S. (1975). Tact as a psychoanalytic function. *International Journal of Psychoanalysis, 56*: 155–161.

Pope, A. (1709). An essay on criticism. https://phrases.org.uk/meanings/fools-rush-in-where-angels-fear-to-tread.html (last accessed on March 21, 2023).

Prince, R. (2022). Creating alternative reality: A case study. *American Journal of Psychoanalysis, 82*: 364–373.

Rachman, S. (1993). Pollution of the mind. *Behaviour Research and Therapy, 32*: 311–314.

Racker, H. (1968). *Transference and Countertransference*. Madison, CT: International Universities Press.

Rangell, L. (1963b). On friendship. *Journal of the American Psychoanalytic Association, 11*: 3–54.

Rangell, L. (1969a). The intrapsychic process and its analysis—a recent line of thought and its current implications. *International Journal of Psychoanalysis, 50*: 65–77.

Rangell, L. (1969b). Choice-conflict and the decision-making function of the ego: A psychoanalytic contribution to decision theory. *International Journal of Psychoanalysis, 50*: 599–602.

Rangell, L. (1971). The decision-making process—a contribution from psychoanalysis. *Psychoanalytic Study of the Child, 26*: 425–452.

Rangell, L. (1980). *The Mind of Watergate. An Exploration of the Compromise of Integrity.* New York: W. W. Norton.

Rangell, L. (1986). The executive functions of the ego: An extension of the concept of ego autonomy. *Psychoanalytic Study of the Child, 41*: 1–37.

Rangell, L. (1987). A core process in psychoanalytic treatment. *Psychoanalytic Quarterly, 66*: 222–249.

Rangell, L. (2009). The role of unconscious volition in psychoanalysis: Commentary on Meissner, W. *Journal of the American Psychoanalytic Association, 57*: 1157–1165.

Reich, W. (1933). *Character Analysis.* V. R. Carfagno (Trans.). New York: Farrar, Straus and Giroux, 1972.

Reiff, P. (1966). *The Triumph of the Therapeutic.* New York: Harper & Row.

Renik, O. (1993). Analytic interaction: Conceptualizing technique in light of the analyst's irreducible subjectivity. *Psychoanalytic Quarterly, 62*: 553–571.

Rizzuto, A. (1991). Shame in psychoanalysis: The function of unconscious fantasies. *International Journal of Psychoanalysis, 72*: 297–312.

Robertiello, R. C. (1974). Physical techniques with schizoid patients. *Journal of the American Academy of Psychoanalysis, 2*: 361–367.

Roberts, R., & Itten, T. (2006). Laing and Szasz: Anti-psychiatry, capitalism, and therapy. *Psychoanalytic Review, 93*: 781–799.

Rozentsvit, I. (2023). Neurological correlates of behavior and thought in men and women. Paper presented at the Psychohistory Forum, January 14, 2023 (unpublished).

Rushdie, S. (1992). Out of Kansas. Revisiting "The Wizard of Oz." https://newyorker.com/magazine/1992/05/11/out-of-kansas (last accessed January 11, 2023).

Salzman, P. C. (2001). *Understanding Culture: An Introduction to Anthropological Theory.* Prospect Heights, IL: Waveland.

Savelle-Rocklin, N. (2016). *Food for Thought: Perspectives on Eating Disorders.* Lanham, MD: Rowman & Littlefield.

Schore, A. N. (2000). The self-organization of the right brain and the neurobiology of emotional development. In: M. Lewis & I. Granic (Eds.),

Schore, A. N. (2002). Dysregulation of the right brain: A fundamental mechanism of traumatic attachment and the psychopathogenesis of posttraumatic stress disorder. *Australian and New Zealand Journal of Psychiatry*, 36: 9–30.

Schore, A. N. (2010). Attachment and regulation of the right brain. *Attachment and Human Development*, 2: 23–47.

Schwartz, D. P. (1986). Loving action and the shape of the object. In: D. B. Feinsilver (Ed.), *Towards a Comprehensive Model for Schizophrenic Disorders* (pp. 323–344). Hillsdale, NJ: Analytic Press.

Searles, H. (1960). *The Non-Human Environment*. Madison, CT: International Universities Press.

Service, R. (1907). *Songs of a Sourdough*. Toronto, ON: William Briggs.

Shakespeare, W. (1595). *A Midsummer Night's Dream*. London: Arden, 2009.

Shakespeare, W. (c. 1600). *Hamlet*. London: Arden, 2017.

Shakespeare, W. (1606). *Macbeth*. London: Arden, 1988.

Shelley, P. B. (1840). A defence of poetry. *English Essays: Sidney to Macaulay*. The Harvard Classics. 1909–1914. https://resources.saylor.org/wwwresources/archived/site/wp-content/uploads/2011/01/A-Defense-of-Poetry.pdf (accessed on November 10, 2022).

Sidoli, M. (1996). Farting as a defence against unspeakable dread. *Journal of Analytical Psychology*, 41: 165–178.

Silvan, M. Z. (2005). Do we do what we think we do? Implicit theories in the analyst's mind. *Journal of the American Psychoanalytic Association*, 53: 945–956.

Slavson, S. R. (1964). *A Textbook in Analytic Group Psychotherapy*. New York: International Universities Press.

Smolen, A. G. (2015). The development of greed in childhood. In: S. Akhtar (Ed.), *Greed: Developmental, Cultural and Clinical Realms* (pp. 3–20). London: Karnac.

Soldt, P. (2006). The dialectics of affective and conceptual thought: Some general remarks on primary and secondary process functioning. *Scandinavian Psychoanalytic Review*, 29: 33–42.

Solms, M. (2021). Revision of drive theory. *Journal of the American Psychoanalytic Association*, 69: 1033–1091.

Spitz, R., & Wolf, K. (1946). Anaclitic depression—an inquiry into the genesis of psychiatric conditions in early childhood, II. *Psychoanalytic Study of the Child, 2*: 313–342.

Stapleton, K., Beers Fägersten, K., Stephens, R., & Loveday, C. (2022). The power of swearing: What we know and what we don't. *Lingua, 277*: 103406.

Stone, L. (1954). On the principal obscene word of the English language—(an inquiry, with hypothesis, regarding its origin and persistence). *International Journal of Psychoanalysis, 35*: 30–56.

Stubbs, M. (2008). Cultural perceptions and practices around menarche and adolescent menstruation in the United States. *Annals of the New York Academy of Science, 1135*: 58–66.

Summer Interlude (1951). Motion picture, directed by I. Bergman. Svensk Filmindistri.

Taylor, F. (2015). *The Downfall of Money: Germany's Hyperinflation and the Destruction of the Middle Class*. New York: Bloomsbury.

Tennyson, A. (1947). *Poems of Tennyson*. London: Oxford University Press.

The Aristocrats (2005). [Video]. IMDb. https://imdb.com/title/tt0436078/ (last accessed March 5, 2023).

The Wizard of Oz (1939). K. Vidor & V. Fleming, directors. Beverly Hills, CA: Metro-Goldwyn-Mayer (MGM).

Thiel, A., Thiel, J., Oddo, S., Langnickel, R., Brand, M., Markowitsch, H. J., & Stirn, A. (2014). Obsessive-compulsive disorder patients with washing symptoms show a specific brain network when confronted with aggressive, sexual, and disgusting stimuli. *Neuropsychoanalysis, 16*: 83–96.

Thomas, E., Voges, J., Chiliza, B., Stein, D. J., & Lochner, C. (2017). Sniffing out olfactory reference syndrome. *South African Journal of Psychiatry, 23*: 10–16.

Thuketana, N. S., & Westhof, L. (2018). Group work during visual art activities to reduce inductiveness. *South African Journal of Childhood Education, 8*: 447–461.

Ticho, E. (1972). The development of superego autonomy. *Psychoanalytic Review, 59*: 217–233.

Tsolas, V., & Anzieu-Premmereur, C. (2023). *A Psychoanalytic Exploration of the Contemporary Search for Pleasure: The Turning of the Screw*. New York: Routledge.

Ünsal, E., & Kayatekin, M. S. (2022). Decision making in organizations. Lecture delivered at Department of Business Administration, Koç University, Istanbul, Turkey, December 20.

Vance, P., & Pockriss, L. (1960). Itsy Bitsy Teenie Weenie Yellow Polkadot Bikini. Popular song released by Fontana.

Waelder, R. (1936). The principle of multiple function. *Psychoanalytic Quarterly, 5*: 45–62.

Washington Post (2017, May 24). Dirty Words from Lenny Bruce and George Carlin to Stephen Colbert. https://washingtonpost.com/news/morning-mix/wp/2017/05/24/dirty-words-from-lenny-bruce-and-george-carlin-to-stephen-colbert/ (last accessed August 23, 2023).

Welner, M., DeLisi, M., Saxena, A., Tramontin, M., & Burgess, A. (2022). Distinguishing everyday evil: Towards a clinical inventory of extreme and outrageous behaviors, actions and attitudes. *Journal of Psychiatric Research, 154*: 181–189.

White, R. (2022). The dirtiest cities in the world. *Everyday Tourist.* https://everydaytourist.ca/globe-trekking-international-travel/the-dirtiest-cities-in-the-world (accessed on January 28, 2022).

Winnicott, D. W. (1949). Mind and its relation to the psyche-soma. *British Journal of Medical Psychology, 27*: 201–209.

Winnicott, D. W. (1956). The antisocial tendency. In: *Collected Papers: Through Paediatrics to Psycho-analysis* (pp. 306–315). London, Tavistock, 1958.

Winnicott, D. W. (1958). Hate in the countertransference. In: *Through Paediatrics to Psycho-analysis: Collected Papers* (pp. 194–203). New York: Brunner/Mazel, 1992.

Winnicott, D. W. (1960). The theory of parent-infant relationship. In: *The Maturational Processes and the Facilitating Environment* (pp. 37–55). New York: International Universities Press. 1965.

Winnicott, D. W. (1971). Transitional objects and transitional phenomena. In: *Playing and Reality.* London: Penguin.

Winnicott, D. W. (1986). *Home Is Where We Start From. Essays by a Psychoanalyst.* New York: W. W. Norton.

Wolf Man (1958). How I came into analysis with Freud. *Journal of the American Psychoanalytic Association, 6*: 348–352.

Wray, J. (2004). Interview with Haruki Murakami. *Paris Review, 170*: 4.

Yates, J., & Oliveira, S. (2016). Culture and decision making. *Organizational Behavior, and Human Decision Processes, 136*: 106–118.

Yeats, W. B. (1956). *Collected Poems of W. B. Yeats.* London: Macmillan.

Index

Abend, S. M., 48
Abraham, K., xix
Abramowitz, J. S., 15
addictive disorder, 41
"affect-regulation", 55
affect-tolerance, 55
aggression, 7, 28, 49, 59, 72, 81, 90, 101
    drive, 25–26
    identification with aggressor, 44
    jokes and, 21–22
    oral, 20
Ainsworth, M. D. S., 14
Aisenstein, M., 102
Aitia, 89
Akhtar, S., xix, 6, 13, 27, 28, 37, 40, 44, 50, 57, 58, 69, 93, 101, 126, 128, 131, 153, 157, 163, 164, 165, 167
aloofness, 50–51 *see also* shyness
ambivalence, 124 *see also* indecisiveness
'American flirtation', 86, 87, 101
anal stage, 6
analyst's cowardliness, 163–166 *see also* cowardliness
Anatomy of Humor, The, 22

antisocial, 56 *see also* outrageousness tendency, 69, 70–71, 81
anxiety, 13, 55, 59
    castration, 103, 155
    existential anxiety, 105–106
    olfactory-based, 10–11
    relational, 10–11
    self–object fusion, 50
    signal, 111
    social, 10, 56
Anzieu, D., 8
Arango, A. C., 20
Aristocrats joke, 3, 21–22 *see also* dirtiness
Aristotle, 89
Arlow, J. A., 48
"asymmetry", 91
August, J., 48
Azzerad, M., 102

Balint, M., 57, 155
Barahona, R., 113
Barkley-Levenson, E. E., 106
Becker, E., 27

Beebe, B., 53
Beers Fägersten, K., 19
Begley, L., 157
Bell, S. M., 14
Benau, K., 13
Benjamin, W., 140
Berger, A. A., 22
Bergler, E., 20
Bergman, A., 32
Bergman, I., 88, 90–91
Berman, N. C., 15
Berry, J. M., 66
Bhabha, H., 138
Bick, E., 155
Billow, R. M., 66
Bion, W. R., xxii, 93, 140, 141, 143, 145
    "constant conjunction", 133
    pain, 145
    proto-mental system, 99
    super-ego, 147
Blackman, J., 49, 51, 52, 54, 55, 57, 58
Blechner, M. J., 58
Blos, P., 61
Blum, H. P., 40, 41
bodily smells, 8 *see also* dirtiness
Bombel, G., 124
Boris, H. N., 26
Bowen, C., 11
Bowlby, J., 14, 56
Brand, M., 7
Bratman, S., 7
Brenner, C., 48
Brenner, I., 69
Bretherton, I., 55
Breuer, J., 78
Brown, G., 8
Bruce, L., 21–22
Burgess, A., 66
Burket, J., 57

Caligor, E., 126
camera shyness, 59–60 *see also* shyness
Carlin, G., 21–22
Casement, P., 71–72, 79
castration anxiety, 103
cause and effect, 88–89
Charan, R., 109

Chasseguet-Smirgel, J., 156
Chess, S., 49
Chiliza, B., 10
chronic elusiveness, 52 *see also* shyness
"civilized outrageousness", 81 *see also* outrageousness
Civin, M., 89, 97, 98
Civitarese, G., 143, 149
"clean eating", 7
Cohen, J. R., 107
complementary identifications, 94
Conrad, J., 151
conscious, 91
    memory, 91
    and preconscious mind, 91–92
    self-consciousness, 52
    unconscious and, 89, 91, 93
consciousness, 92–93
"constant conjunction", 133
contemporary disaffection, 101–104
Cooperman, M., 124
coprophilia, 4, 18 *see also* dirtiness
counter-forces, 13
cowardice *see* cowardliness
cowardliness, xxii, 151, 166–168
    analyst's, 163–166
    clinical illustrations, 157–166
    consequences, 156–157
    descriptive features, 153–154, 166
    dream cowardice, 153
    etiological factor in, 155
    etymology, 152–153
    factors shaping courage and, 155
    impaired ego functions, 157
    institutional cowardice in psychoanalysis, 167
    intellectual cowardice, 153
    in literature, 151–152
    moral cowardice, 153
    origins, 154–156
    paradox of cowardice, 167–168
    impact of parental cowardice, 163
    patient's, 157–163
    physical cowardice, 153
    regret, 156–157
    shame, 156

societal rewards and psychoanalytic perspectives, 167–168
superego disturbances, 157
Cozolino, L., 14
"cutaneous re-introjection", 6

Dague-Greene, A., 48
Damasio, A., 155
death drive, 101–104
decision making, 58, 105 *see also* indecisiveness
    intuitive, 108
    rational, 108–109
    unconscious, 108
decisiveness, 107 *see also* indecisiveness
"deep", 86
DeFalco, A., 107
DeLisi, M., 66
de M'Uzan, M., 87, 98
Denby, D., 21
DeRose, T., 139
Desai, A., 102
Deutsch, H., 154
Deutsch, S., 57
developmental conflicts, 72
"dialogue", 109 *see also* indecisiveness
dirtiness, xx, 3, 24
    anal stage, 6
    Aristocrats joke, 21–22
    bodily smells, 8
    of body, 5–9
    "clean eating", 7
    clinical vignette, 15–16
    contact with the disgusting, 15–16
    coprophilia, 4, 18
    cultural icons to taboo subjects, 3–4
    "cutaneous re-introjection", 6
    "Dirty Harry", 3–4
    dirty jokes, 21–22
    "dirty mind", 17
    dirty money, 22–23
    "dirty movie", 4
    dirty sexual fantasies, 17–18
    of environment, 4–5
    evolution of profanity in comedy, 21–22
    fear of, 10–12
    filth, sexuality, and guilt, 7
    Great Stink, The, 4
    Gulliver's Travels as therapeutic intervention, 18
    inner dirtiness, 14
    jiko-shu-kyofu, 10
    from Lady Macbeth's guilt to inner shame, 12–15
    of language, 18–20
    from Lenny Bruce to George Carlin, 21–22
    mental contamination, 14
    of mind, 12–18
    multifaceted nature of dirtiness, 12–15
    obscene words, 20
    olfactory-based anxieties, 10–11
    "orthorexia", 7
    physical filth to psychological significance, 5–9
    profanity, 21
    psychological landscape of dirty words, 19–20
    psychological link between wealth and dirtiness, 22–23
    "share regret", 16
    from taboos to teenage slang, 20
    taijin kyofusho, 10
    "tendentious jokes", 22
    urinary eroticism, 17
    urolagnia, 17
    "word vomit", 16–17
disaffection, contemporary, 101–102
dissolution of "third", 102–104
distrustfulness, 56–57 *see also* shyness
Dodd, N., 27
Donne, J., 130
Dorpat, T., 117
Dorsey, E., 69
doublethinking, 97–98
Dougherty, B., 21
dream cowardice, 153 *see also* cowardliness
Dring, K., 52
"dry humping", 54

ego, xxi, 110–111, 116–117, 126, 136, 157
see also indecisiveness
Einstein, A., 88, 89
Eliot, T. S., 151
elusiveness, 51–52 see also shyness
emotion(al), 140
  distancing, 50, 51
  experiences, 132, 140–144
  and obscene words, 19
  proto-, 141, 142, 143, 149
Epstein, L., 164
Erikson, E. H., 56
Euclid, 87–88
Euclidean, 87–91 see also shallowness
existential anxiety, 105–106 see also indecisiveness

Fabricant, L. E, 15
faint-heartedness, 49–50 see also shyness
Fairbairn, W. R. D., xix
Fairbrother, N., 15
FCC see Federal Communications Commission
FDS see feminine deodorant spray
Federal Communications Commission (FCC), 21
Feldman, M. J., 19
feminine deodorant spray (FDS), 61
feminine modesty, 60–61 see also shyness
Fenichel, O., 13, 17
Ferenczi, S., 19, 23
Ferrari, J. R., 107
Ferro, A., 133
Flanagan, S., 105
fleeting engagement, 57–58 see also shyness
Fortenberry, J. D., 101
fourth dimension, 88
Fox, C. R., 106
French Revolution, 134
Freud, A., 13, 26, 44, 58, 111, 117
Freud, S., xix, xxi, 5, 6, 8, 13, 24, 78, 86, 87, 97, 102, 113, 116, 132, 155, 158
  'American flirtation', 86, 87, 101
  Beyond the Pleasure Principle, 139
  Civilization and Its Discontents, 168
  connection between feces and money, 22–23
  difference and thinking, 98
  ego, 8
  "fundamental rule" of psychoanalysis, 157
  humor in dirty language, 21
  inhibition of speech, 55
  Interpretation of Dreams, The, 89, 139
  masochistic outrageousness, 69–70
  as Oedipus, 138–140
  impact of parental cowardice on narcissistic deflation, 163
  perspectives on unconscious, 92–93
  symptom, 135–136
  "tendentious jokes", 22
  toilet training, 6
  topographical model and unconscious mind, 89–90, 101
  unconscious and conscious, 91
  "Unconscious, The", 92
  about words, 18
Fu, T., 101

Gardener, H., 130
Garma, A., 153
Gay, P., 163
Gilligan, C., 55
Glover, E., 153
Goldberg, A., 166
Goldman, D., 69
Golzarri-Arroyo, L., 101
Gorender, M. E., 9
Gray, P., 112, 113
Great Stink, The, 4 see also dirtiness
greed, 25, 26
  to avarice, 25–28
  and generosity, 25–28
  greediness, 27
Greene, A., 89
Guarton, G. B., 69
Gulliver's Travels, 18
Guntrip, H., xix

Haberman, M., 12
Haight, D. F., 23
Hamlet, 147–150
Hartmann, H., 49
Harvard Online Library Information System (HOLLIS), 66
healthy shyness, 58–59 *see also* shyness
Heller, J., 157
Herbenick, D., 101
Herbert, G., 130
Hilty, R., 8
Hoffer, A., 166
"holding environment", 38, 70–71, 79
Holmes, O., 3
Hopkins, G. M., 69, 130
Horn, S., 109
Hughes, L., 152
human mental functioning, 108 *see also* indecisiveness
    intuitive decision making, 108
    rational decision making, 108–109
Hynie, M., 106

Icarus, myth of, 132
identifications, complementary, 94
idleness, 107 *see also* indecisiveness
"imagination compact", 131
indecisiveness, xxi–xxii, 105, 126
    ambivalence, 124
    analysis of decision-making process, 111
    clinical vignettes, 114–116, 117–121, 122–123, 124
    "close process monitoring", 113
    decisions in psychoanalytic technique, 113
    and decisiveness, 107
    developmental patterns and regression, 123
    "dialogue", 109
    discussion, 125–126
    doubt and existential anxiety, 105–106
    idleness, 107
    illustrations from clinical practice, 114–125
    intrapsychic and interpersonal roots, 121–122
    intuitive decision making, 108
    "object relations conflicts", 117
    observations from related fields, 106–110
    obsessive-hypomanic personality organizations, 122
    "partially internalized conflicts", 117
    phases of intrapsychic conflict, 111–112
    productive decision-making to paralyzing ambivalence, 124–125
    psychoanalytic cure, 112
    psychoanalytic evolution, 112–113
    psychoanalytic understanding of roots of, 110–113
    rational decision making, 108–109
    reflective rumination, 106
    role of ego in, 110–111, 116–117, 126
    role of others in decision-making, 117
    "structural conflict", 117
    from symbiotic dependence to co-decision-making, 125
    systems of human mental functioning, 108
    "unconscious decision making", 108
inhibition, 50, 55
inner dirtiness, 14 *see also* dirtiness
institutional cowardice, 167 *see also* cowardliness
insula, 14
intellectual cowardice, 153 *see also* cowardliness
Interpretation of Dreams, The, 89
intrapsychic conflict, 111–112 *see also* indecisiveness
intuitive decision making, 108 *see also* indecisiveness
Ishikawa, R., 14
Itten, T., 107
Iwasaki, Y., 10

Jelliffe, S. E., 17
Jewkes, R. K., 19
jiko-shu-kyofu, 10 see also dirtiness
Johnson, A., 58
Johnson, D. R., 125
jokes, 22
    dirty, 21
Jones, E., xix
judgment, 58

Kahlbaum, K. L., 47
Kahneman, D., 108, 109, 156
Kanwal, G. S., 110
Karpman, B., 7, 18
Kayatekin, M. S., 108, 117, 124
Kernberg, O. F., xix, 69, 70, 72, 114, 117, 126
Khan, M. M. R., xix, 68
Kiriike, N., 10
Klein, M., 25, 28, 99, 100
Knotts, D., 55
Kohut, H., 163
Kramer, S., 58
Kris, A., 161
Kris, E., 162

Lacan, J., 102, 103, 134, 146
    language, 141
LaMothe, R., 27
Lan-Czelusta, K., 124
Landman, J., 157
Langnickel, R., 7
Larkin, P., 128
Lawrence, D. H., 141–143, 152
Legman, G., 21
Lehmiller, J. J., 17
Lemma, A., 11–12
Levin, S., 54
Levy, D. M., 62
Lewis, H. B., 13
Lochner, C., 10
Loewald, H. W., 113
Lorenz, E., 92
Lovallo, D., 109
Loveday, C., 19
Luepnitz, D. A., 69
Lynch, A. A., 111

Macbeth, 12–15, 132–134, 148
Mahler, M., 32, 53
manic defenses, 99–100
Mann, A., 108
Marcovitz, E., xix
Marcuse, H., 138
Markowitsch, H. J., 7
Marty, P., 87, 98
masochistic outrageousness, 69–70
    see also outrageousness
Mason, A. E. W., 151
Masterson, J., 57
Matsui, T., 10
Matsunaga, H., 10
Matte-Blanco, I., 89, 91
Mayers, L., 47
McDougall, J., 8, 17
Meers, D. R., 57
Meissner, W. W., 112
Meltzer, D., 10, 140, 155
Menaker, E., 153
Menninger, K., xix
mental contamination, 14 see also dirtiness
Miller, S. B., 13, 15
Milton, J., 135
miserliness, xx, 25, 44–45
    case of miserly adult, 42–44
    case of miserly child, 28
    developmental roots and cultural influences, 25–28
    greed, 26
    greed and generosity, 25–28
    greediness, 27
    from greed to avarice, 25–28
    innate aggressive drive, 25–26
Missing Out, 128
mistrust, 57
modernity, 128–129, 134, 141
moral cowardice, 153 see also cowardliness
Morin, E., 48
Murakami, H., 107–108

nervousness, 55–56 see also shyness
Ng, A. H., 106
Nikelly, A., 27

INDEX

object relations, 8, 11, 41, 44, 50, 53, 63, 113, 116, 117, 125
obscene words, 20 *see also* dirtiness
obsessive compulsive disorder (OCD), 7
obsessive-hypomanic personality organizations, 122 *see also* indecisiveness
OCD *see* obsessive compulsive disorder
Oddo, S., 7
oedipal
    betrayal, 161
    phallic-oedipal psychic phase, 17
    pre-, 39, 80
    roots, 80
    triangle, 102
    unconscious guilt, 70
    years, 39
Oedipus, 138–139
olfactory-based anxieties, 10–11 *see also* dirtiness
olfactory reference syndrome, 10
Oliveira, S., 106
optimistic outrageousness, 70–72 *see also* outrageousness
Orcutt, C., 69
orgasm, 144
orthorexia, 7
Orwell, G., 97
oscillatory shyness, 57–58 *see also* shyness
outrageousness, xx, 65
    aims, 69
    antisocial tendencies, 69, 70–71, 81
    "civilized outrageousness", 81
    clinical illustration, 67, 73–80
    descriptive characteristics, 65–68
    developmental challenges, 73–80
    developmental conflicts, 72
    "holding environment", 79
    manifestations and impacts, 67–68
    masochistic outrageousness, 69–70
    optimistic outrageousness, 70–72
    path to understanding, growth, and creativity, 80–82
    perspectives from clinical literature, 66
    power of outrage, 66
    psychoanalytic understanding, 78
    sadistic outrageousness, 72–73
    therapeutic role-responsiveness and projective identification, 72
    three psychodynamic configurations, 68–73
    "unconscious hope", 71–72, 81
overreaching, 132–134

Pally, R., 155
Papiasvili, E., 47, 48
Parens, H., 49
parental cowardice, 163 *see also* cowardliness
PEP-Web *see* Psychoanalytic Electronic Publishing Web
phantasy, 146
Phillips, A., 128
"philobats", 57
physical cowardice, 153 *see also* cowardliness
Pine, F., 32
Plato, 88, 89
Pockriss, L., 49
Poland, W. S., xix
Pope, A., 59
postmodern thinking, 137–138 *see also* restlessness
preconscious, 91–92
Prince, R., 69
profanity, 21 *see also* dirtiness
prophaseis, 89
protoemotional experiences, 140 *see also* emotion(al); restlessness
    emotion, 140
    emotional experience, 140–141
    fragility of mind, 140
    language of, 141–143
    proto-emotions, 143
    Sons and Lovers, 141–143, 150
    unconscious, 141–142
psyche, 90
    Freudian and oedipal perspectives of, 139–140
    skin-ego, 8
psychoanalysis, 24, 138, 151, 157, 167
    on indecisiveness, 110
    individuality, 117

language, 141
on thinking, 93
and words, 18
Psychoanalytic Electronic Publishing
    Web (PEP-Web), 68, 69

Rachman, S., 14, 15
Racker, H., 94
Rangell, L., xix, 110, 111–112, 125–126
Rapaport, D., 108
rational decision making, 108–109
    see also indecisiveness
reflective rumination, 106 *see also*
    indecisiveness
regret, 156–157
    remorse vs., 58
    share, 16
Reich, W., xix
Reiff, P., 151
Renik, O., 48
restlessness, xxi–xxii, 127, 131, 150
    and addiction, 144
    and ambition, 132–133
    choice and regret, 127–128
    clinical vignette, 145–147, 149–150
    colonialism, 136–137
    "constant conjunction", 133
    doubt and belief, 129–131
    of drive and object, 144–147
    ego, 136
    Freud as Oedipus, 138–140
    Freudian and oedipal perspectives
        of psyche, 139–140
    Freudian symptomatology,
        135–136
    in *Hamlet* and psychoanalysis,
        147–150
    historical and linguistic
        exploration, 128–129
    imaginary other, 146
    imagination, absence, and
        attribution, 131–132
    "imagination compact", 131
    immigration, 136–137
    leaving home, 136–138
    lunatic, lover, poet, 131–132
    Macbeth, 132–134

"manic-defence restlessness", 144
Missing Out, 128
myth of Icarus, 132
Oedipus, 138–139
overreaching, 132–134
poetic struggles of faith, 129–131
postmodern thinking, 137–138
protoemotional experiences,
    140–144
religious poetry, 129–131
"restive", 129
"restless" etymology, 129
restless ages, 128
restless minds, 131–132
revolution, 134–136
romantic hero, 135
romantic restlessness, 135
Rushdie's ode to restlessness, 137
"so-called normal child", 144
splintered superego, 147–149
superego, 147
"symptom", 135
understanding pain, 145–146
unlived life, 127–128
Winnicott's insights and
    perspectives, 144
revenge, 147–148, 163
revolution, 134–136
Richards, A. D., 111
Rizzuto, A., 11
Robertiello, R. C., 11
Roberts, R., 107
romantic hero, 135
romantic restlessness, 135 *see also*
    restlessness
Rosenberg, M., 101
Rozentsvit, I., 57
Rushdie, S., 137

sadistic outrageousness, 72–73 *see also*
    outrageousness
Salzman, P. C., 27
Savelle-Rocklin, N., 7
Saxena, A., 66
Schore, A. N., 14
Schwartz, D. P., 126
Searles, H., 98

self-consciousness, 52–53
self-preservation, 49
Service, R., 151
sexual fantasies, 17–18
Shakespeare, W., 3, 134
    Hamlet, 106
    Macbeth, xxii, 12–13, 132–134, 148
    Midsummer Night's Dream, A, 131
"shallow", 86
shallowness, xxi, 85
    Bergman's narrative complexity, 90–91
    castration anxiety, 103
    cause and effect, 88–89
    clinical vignettes, 94–97, 99
    complementary identifications, 94
    complexities of, 87
    conscious and preconscious mind, 91–92
    conscious and unconscious mind communication, 91–92
    contemporary disaffection, 101–102
    contemporary disaffection and death drive, 102–104
    deeper realities in psychoanalytic practice, 100–101
    depth in human psyche, 92–93
    depths of consciousness, 92–93
    difference and thinking, 98–102
    dimensions of thinking, 97–98
    dissolution of "third", 102–104
    from doublethinking to representation, 97–98
    Einstein's fourth dimension, 88
    Euclidean and topographic, 87
    first topography and "shallow", 89–92
    Freudian and Winnicottian perspectives on unconscious, 92–93
    Freud's topographical model and unconscious mind, 89–90
    implications for psychoanalytic technique, 102–104
    manic defenses and, 99–100
    as opposed to superficial, 94–102
    post-Euclidean, 88–93
    preconscious, 91
    psychoanalytic reflections, 85–87
    beyond superficiality, 100–101
    superficiality and death drive, 101–102
    time, 88
    unconscious and conscious, 89, 91, 93
shame, 13, 156 *see also* dirtiness
    burden of self-perceived dirtiness, 13–14
    components, 13
    experience of self-shame, 14
    inner stain, 13–14
    origins of, 14
shameful inhibition, 50 *see also* shyness
Shelley, P. B., 135
shyness, xx, 47, 63
    "affect-regulation", 55
    affect-tolerance, 55
    aggression and self-preservation, 49
    aloofness, 50–51
    camera, 59–60
    chronic elusiveness, 52
    coping with past experiences, 60
    elusiveness, 51–52
    faint-heartedness, 49–50
    feminine modesty, 60–61
    fleeting engagement, 57–58
    healthy, 58–59
    inhibition, 50
    inhibition of ego function, 55
    inhibition of speech, 55
    multifaceted origins of, 48
    nervousness, 55–56
    in new groups, 62–63
    object-coercive doubting, 58
    oscillatory, 57–58
    as response to trauma, 60
    role of judgment and risk assessment, 58–59
    self-consciousness, 52–53
    beyond sexual exhibitionism, 49
    socially appropriate restraint, 61–62
    solitariness, 53
    standoffishness, 53–54

tentativeness, 59
those who back out, 57–58
those who get scared off, 58–59
timidity, 49
unassertiveness, 54
unconscious desires and shameful inhibition, 50
unfriendliness, 50
unsociability, 56
wariness and distrustfulness, 56–57
withdrawnness, 55
Sibony, O., 109
Sidoli, M., 8
Silvan, M. Z., 113
Slavson, S. R., 62
Smith, K. E., 130
Smolen, A. G., 28
Sobieraj, S., 66
Soldt, P., 109
solitariness, 53 *see also* shyness
Solms, M., 48
Sons and Lovers, 141–143, 150
SPEBSQSA, 54
Spitz, R., 53
splintered superego, 147–149
standoffishness, 53–54 *see also* shyness
Stapleton, K., 19
Stein, D. J., 10
Stephens, R., 19
Stirn, A., 7
Stone, L., 20
Stubbs, M., 61
superego, 26, 55, 57–58, 94, 111, 117, 138, 147
disturbances, 157
self-consciousness, 52
splintered, 147–149
"superficial", 86
"symmetry", 91
symptom, 135–136, 138
Szurek, S., 58

taijin kyofusho, 10 *see also* dirtiness
Tennyson, A., 136, 137
tentativeness, 59 *see also* shyness
Theseus, 131
Thiel, A., 7

Thiel, J., 7
thinking, 93
difference and, 98–102
dimensions of, 97–98
from doublethinking to representation, 97–98
unconscious decision making, 108
Thomas, A., 49
Thomas, E., 10
Thomas Dubitus, 105
Thuketana, N. S., 121
Ticho, E., 58
timidity, 49 *see also* shyness
Tramontin, M., 66
transitional object, 98
Triune Brain, 57
Tversky, A., 156

Ulysses, 136–137
unassertiveness, 54 *see also* shyness
unconscious, 89, 90, 92
communication, 8–9
and conscious, 89, 91–92, 93
decision making, 108
desires, 50
element of feminine modesty, 61
Freudian and Winnicottian perspectives on, 92–93
Freud's topographical model and unconscious mind, 89–90
guilt, 70, 80
"hope", 71–72, 81
Unconscious as Infinite Sets, The, 89
unfriendliness, 50 *see also* shyness
Ünsal, E., 108
unsociability, 56 *see also* shyness
urinary eroticism, 17 *see also* dirtiness
urolagnia, 17 *see also* dirtiness

Vance, P., 49
Voges, J., 10

Waelder, R., 78
wariness, 56–57 *see also* shyness
wealth and dirtiness, 22–23 *see also* dirtiness
Welner, M., 66

Westhof, L., 121
Wheaton, M. G., 15
White, R., 5
Winnicott, D. W., xix, xx, 8, 26, 37, 40, 69, 70, 71, 79
    antisocial tendency, 81
perspectives on unconscious, 92–93
    "so-called normal child", 144
    transitional object, 98

withdrawnness, 55 *see also* shyness
Wolf, K., 53
Wolf Man, 24
Wood, K., 19
words, 18
Wray, J., 108

Yates, J., 106
Yeats, W. B., 127